Home Cooking

CONTENTS

FOR COOKS WHO CARE

America's Best Homemade Recipes!

OVER 600 FAMILY-PROVEN RECIPES!

WOMEN'S CIRCLE
Home Cooking

EDITOR
JUDI MERKEL

ART DIRECTOR
VICKI MACY

GRAPHIC ART
RONDA BOLLENBACHER
CAROL DAILEY

PHOTOGRAPHY
RHONDA DAVIS
NANCY SHARP
MARY JOYNT

Published by
The House of White Birches, Inc.
306 East Parr Road
Berne, Indiana 46711

PUBLISHERS
CARL H. MUSELMAN
ARTHUR K. MUSELMAN

CHIEF EXECUTIVE OFFICER
JOHN ROBINSON

MARKETING DIRECTOR
SCOTT MOSS

CREATIVE DIRECTOR / MAGAZINES
DAN KRANER

CIRCULATION MANAGER
CAROLE BUTLER

PRODUCTION
SANDRA RIDGWAY

ADVERTISING DIRECTOR
JANET PRICE-GLICK

DISPLAY ADVERTISING
LAUREL SMITH

CLASSIFIED ADVERTISING
SHARYL BERRY

(219) 589-8741
Fax: (219) 589-8093

Women's Circle Home Cooking cookbook is a collection of recipes obtained from *Women's Circle Home Cooking* magazine which is published by The House of White Birches, 306 East Parr Road, Berne, Indiana 46711.

RETAILERS: If you are not presently being provided House of White Birches magazine copies by your area newsstand wholesaler, contact the House of White Birches (219) 589-8741 in Berne to set up a direct account.

CONTRIBUTORS: We welcome your articles with or without photos–please send manuscript and editorial materials to *Home Cooking*, 306 East Parr Road, Berne, IN 46711. Every effort is made to return submissions if accompanied by return postage. Publisher not responsible for loss or damage, so please keep a copy for your files.

Printed in U.S.A.

Exclusively distributed by:

P.S.I. & Associates, Inc.
13322 S.W. 128th St.
Miami, Florida 33186
(305) 255-7959

Beverages
TO DRINK

FRESH PEACH BRACER
Makes 3-1/4 cups

1 cup sliced fresh or thawed
  peaches
1 cup plain yogurt
1 cup skim milk
1 tablespoon honey

Combine all ingredients in container of electric blender. Process until smooth.

Mrs. Bruce Fowler, Woodruff, S.C.

ORANGE JULIUS

1/2 cup frozen orange–juice concentrate
1/2 cup milk
1/2 cup cold water
1/4 cup sugar
1/2 teaspoon vanilla
5-6 ice cubes

Blend all ingredients on highest speed of blender for 50 seconds. A very special warm–weather treat. Serve in long–stemmed glasses!

Susan J. Defendorf, Holley, N.Y.

LEMON BISHOP

8 whole lemons, unpeeled
Whole cloves
2 tablespoons brown sugar, packed
3 cups bottled grape juice, heated
1 pint hot water
Cinnamon

Stud lemons thickly with whole cloves; place in shallow baking pan and bake at 325 degrees for 1 hour, or until lemons begin to juice. Prick lemons with a fork. Dust lightly with brown sugar, and place in a punch bowl. Add grape juice and hot water. Dust surface of punch with a few shakes of cinnamon. Serve hot in cups.

Barbara Burt, Amarillo, Texas

APPLE JULEP
7-1/4 cups

1 quart unsweetened apple juice
2 cups unsweetened pineapple juice
1 cup unsweetened orange juice
1/4 cup lemon juice
Mint sprigs (optional)

Combine fruit juices, stirring well. Chill. Before serving, garnish with mint sprigs, if desired. About 120 calories per cup.

Mrs. Bruce Fowler, Woodruff, S.C.

CHERRY BERRY SLUSH
Serves 6

1 (12-ounce) package frozen red raspberries or 1-1/2 cups fresh raspberries
1/2 of a 16-ounce package frozen unsweetened pitted dark sweet cherries or 2 cups fresh pitted dark sweet cherries
1 (6-ounce) can frozen apple juice concentrate, thawed

1 (24-ounce) bottle 7-Up, chilled

Thaw frozen fruit, do not drain. Put raspberries into blender and blend until smooth. Strain out seeds. Place berries into mixing bowl. Place cherries in blender with apple juice concentrate. Cover and blend until smooth. Combine with berries in mixing bowl. Cover and freeze overnight or up to 2 months.

For each serving, scrape spoon across frozen slush mixture and spoon about 3/4 cup into 10-ounce glass. Slowly pour in about 1/2 cup of 7-Up. Stir gently to mix.

Candace Croteau, Lawrence, MA

CHOCOLATE COFFEE
(for dessert)
Serves 6

2 tablespoons instant coffee
1/4 cup sugar
Dash salt
2 (1-ounce) squares unsweetened chocolate
1 cup water
3 cups milk
Whipped cream

In saucepan, combine coffee, sugar, salt, chocolate, and water. Stir constantly over low heat until chocolate melts. Simmer for four minutes. Then slowly add milk, stirring constantly, until heated and thoroughly mixed. When piping hot, remove from heat and beat with rotary beater until frothy. Pour into cups and top with whipped cream.

ZESTY FRUIT REFRESHER

1 cup cranberry cocktail juice
1 cup prune juice (Welch's)
2 cups apple juice

Mix all the above juices and place in refrigerator. When ready to serve, place 1/2 cup fruit juice mixture into glass tumbler and fill rest of glass with ginger ale.

M. Powell Hamilton, Ontario, Canada

FRUIT LOW-BALL

Serves 6

1 (10-ounce) package frozen peaches
1/4 cup firmly-packed light brown sugar
1/4 teaspoon cinnamon
1 quart buttermilk
1 medium orange

Thaw peaches. Combine peaches, sugar, and cinnamon in blender. Whirl at medium speed until smooth. Add buttermilk; whirl again.

To serve, pour into six 8-ounce glasses. Slice orange very thin; garnish each glass edge with an orange wheel. Top with dash of cinnamon. Very zesty and refreshing with the buttermilk!

Judie Betz, Lomita, CA

ORANGE-TOMATO COCKTAIL

Serves 6

1-1/2 cups chilled tomato juice
1 cup chilled orange juice
1 tablespoon lemon juice
1/2 teaspoon salt
1 slice onion

Blend all ingredients in blender about 30 seconds or until thoroughly mixed. Add 4 ice cubes, one at a time, and blend until mixed.

Agnes Ward, Erie, PA

PINEAPPLE SLUSH

Makes 3 cups

1 (5-1/4 ounce) can pineapple tidbits, undrained
1 medium banana, chilled
1/4 cup milk
2 cups pineapple sherbet

Combine all ingredients in container of electric blender; process until smooth.

Edna Askins, Greenville, Texas

MOCHA

Serves 8-10

2/3 cup instant cocoa mix
1/2 cup instant coffee
8 cups boiling water
Sweetened whipped cream or Cool Whip

Mix cocoa and coffee in pot or pitcher. Pour in boiling water and stir. Serve hot and topped with Cool Whip or whipped cream.

Betty Klopfenstein, Waterman, Ill.

CHOCOLATE-PEANUT-BUTTER MILK SHAKE

Makes 2 cups

2 tablespoons powdered chocolate drink mix
3 tablespoons crunchy peanut butter
1 cup milk, chilled
1 teaspoon honey
Dash cinnamon
Dash nutmeg
8 ice cubes

Place all ingredients in blender. Cover and process until frothy. Pour into vacuum containers.

Annie Emchil, New Castle, Ind.

MELON SHAKE

1 serving

1/2 cup watermelon, cantaloupe or honeydew melon balls
2 large scoops vanilla ice cream (about 1 cup)
1/4 cup milk

Place melon balls in blender. Add ice cream and milk. Cover and blend until smooth. Serve immediately.

Phyllis Beaty, Rossville, Ga.

LO-CALORIE BANANA MILK SHAKE

6 ounces skimmed milk
1/2 teaspoon vanilla
1 banana, sliced frozen
1/2 teaspoon Sprinkle Sweet or sweetener

Put milk in blender. Add vanilla and frozen banana, a little at a time. If a thicker shake is desired, add ice cubes until desired thickness.

Betty Klopfenstein, Waterman, IL

SPICY MILK TEA

Serves 4

6 whole cloves
4 thin slices fresh ginger or 1/2 teaspoon ground ginger
2 cinnamon sticks
4 cups water
4 teaspoons jasmine tea
1 cup milk or half-and-half
Honey
Cardamom, optional
Mint sprigs for garnish

Bring water to boil. Add cinnamon, cloves, and ginger. Cover; simmer 10 minutes. Add tea and steep for a few minutes. Add milk. Bring to boil again. Remove from heat. Strain into a teapot. Serve with a sprinkle of cardamom and a bit of honey. Garnish with mint.

For 1 serving:
Boil 1 cup water. Add 1/2 cinnamon stick, 3 cloves, 2 slices fresh ginger, and 1 teaspoon tea.

Arlene Ranney, Eureka, Calif.

EASY PARTY PUNCH

3-ounce package raspberry gelatin
3-ounce package cherry gelatin
3 cups boiling water
5 cups cold water
3 cups pineapple juice
12 ounces frozen orange juice
2 pints pineapple or lemon sherbet

Dissolve gelatins in boiling water; add next 3 ingredients. Stir in one tray ice cubes until melted. Spoon in sherbet. Serve immediately or let stand at room temperature.

Barbara Brittain, San Diego, CA

GOOD LUCK PUNCH
Makes 1 gallon

1 quart fresh rhubarb
Water to cover
3 cups sugar
2 cups water
Juice of 6 lemons
1 cup pineapple juice
1 quart gingerale

Cut rhubarb into 1-inch pieces; cover with water and cook until soft, about 12-15 minutes. Drain through cheesecloth. Should be about 3 quarts of juice. Dissolve sugar in the 2 cups water and cook 10 minutes to make a syrup.

Combine all juices, except ginger ale, pouring over chunk of ice in punch bowl. Just before serving, add ginger ale.

PARTY PINK PUNCH

1 (46-ounce) can pineapple juice
1 large bottle lemon lime pop
1 small can pink lemonade, frozen
1 can water
2 large bottles strawberry pop
Sugar, if desired
Raspberry sherbet

Mix first six ingredients. Drop spoonfuls of sherbet on top before serving. Delicious!

Barbara Brittain, San Diego, Calif.

AUTUMN PUNCH
Makes 7-1/2 quarts

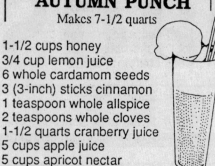

1-1/2 cups honey
3/4 cup lemon juice
6 whole cardamom seeds
3 (3-inch) sticks cinnamon
1 teaspoon whole allspice
2 teaspoons whole cloves
1-1/2 quarts cranberry juice
5 cups apple juice
5 cups apricot nectar
3 quarts ginger ale
Crushed ice

Combine first 6 ingredients in a saucepan; bring to a boil; reduce heat; simmer 10 minutes. Strain and discard spices. Chill. Combine chilled mixture with remaining juices and ginger ale. Serve over ice.

Mrs. Bruce Fowler, Woodruff, S.C.

RHUBARB PUNCH

1 quart diced rhubarb
1 quart water
3/4 - 1 cup sugar
1/4 cup lemon juice

Cook rhubarb in water until very tender. Let drain through cloth-lined colander or strainer. Add sugar; stir to dissolve. Add lemon juice. Chill to serve.

This recipe makes a delicious soft pink punch.

May Ann Kooker, Bluffton, OH

SHERBERT PUNCH

3 (2-liter) bottles 7-Up, chilled
1/2 gallon orange or raspberry sherbet

Soften sherbet. Add by large scoops to punch bowl. Pour chilled 7-Up over the sherbet and serve.

Sue Thomas, Casa Grande, Ariz.

SPICY CALIFORNIA PUNCH

4 cups unsweetened grapefruit juice
4 cups orange juice
2 cups honey
1/4 cup lime juice
1 teaspoon allspice
1 teaspoon nutmeg

In a 3-quart container, combine 4 cups each of both grapefruit juice and orange juice, then add honey, lime juice, and spices. Let stand at room temperature for 1 hour to allow flavors to blend. Chill. To serve, pour over ice in a punch bowl or several pitchers.

Agnes Ward, Erie, Pa.

TROPICAL FRUIT SMOOTHIE
Makes 5 cups

1 (15-ounce) can cream of coconut
1 medium banana
1 (8-ounce) can juice packed crushed pineapple
1 cup orange– juice
1 tablespoon bottled lemon juice
2 cups ice cubes

In blender, combine all ingredients, except ice; blend well. Gradually add ice; blend until smooth. Serve immediately; refrigerate leftovers.

Peggy Fowler Revels, Woodruff, S.C.

COFFEE COOLER

4 quarts strong coffee, cold
1 cup sugar
2 quarts vanilla ice cream
1 tablespoon vanilla
1 quart whole milk

Combine coffee, milk, and vanilla. Add sugar and stir until dissolved. Chill thoroughly and pour over ice cream that has been spooned into a punch bowl. Serves about 50 small punch cups.

Sue Thomas, Casa Grande, Ariz.

Breads TO MAKE

ELEPHANT EARS

1 package dry yeast
1 cup warm water
2 eggs, beaten
4 cups flour
6 tablespoons sugar
Sugar and cinnamon mix; set aside

Soften yeast in warm water. Combine all ingredients except cinnamon and sugar; mix well. Divide dough into 12 pieces. Let sit 10 minutes. Roll out on a lightly floured board. Using hands, stretch each piece cirinto cular shape. Heat vegetable oil in 10-inch skillet (cast iron is the best). Place each circle of dough in the hot grease. Turn once; the surface will bubble and blister and should be lightly browned. Turn with spatula and broad knife. Place on absorbent paper toweling; sprinkle immediately with mix of sugar and cinnamon. If you tear a hole in the circle as it is being stretched that will not matter.
Note: This will be a favorite for all ages. The recipe has been around a long time but each time we make them someone has never heard of individuals making them. They are becoming more popular at public events.

Phyllis M. Peters, Kendallville, Ind.

COLBY BUNS
Makes 1 dozen

2 eggs, beaten well
1 cup instant-blending flour
1/2 teaspoon dill weed
1/2 teaspoon salt
1 cup whole milk

1/3 cup shredded colby cheese

Preheat oven to 450 degrees and grease muffin tin. Do not use paper baking cups. Combine all ingredients and beat until batter is smooth. Fill muffin cups one-third full; bake for 20 minutes. Decrease heat to 350 degrees, but do not open oven door. After 25 more minutes, remove pan from oven and, with a fork, poke holes in each bun. Return to oven for 5 minutes to let buns dry out. Serve hot, with honey.

Linda Hutton, Hayden, Iowa

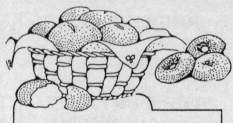

BACON CHEESE NUT BREAD

12 slices bacon, cooked crisp and
   crumbled
1 egg
3 cups biscuit mix
3/4 cup shredded sharp cheese
1 cup milk
2 tablespoons minced onion
Dash Tabasco sauce
3/4 cup coarsely chopped walnuts

Beat egg lightly. Stir in biscuit mix and shredded cheese. add milk, onion and Tabasco sauce. Mix well.The dough will be stiff. Stir in bacon and walnuts.Turn into greased 9x5x3" pan. Bake in 350–degree oven for 50 minutes or until loaf tests done. Let stand 5 minutes; then turn out onto cake rack to cool. It's great!

Barbara Nowakowski, No. Tonawanda, Ny.

PEPPER AND ONION CORN STICKS
Makes 14

1 cup sifted flour
1 cup cornmeal
2 tablespoons sugar
2-1/2 teaspoons baking powder
1 teaspoon salt
1/4 cup chopped green pepper
2 teaspoons instant minced onion
1 cup milk
1 egg, beaten
1/4 cup oil

Sift together flour, cornmeal, sugar, baking powder, and salt. Stir in green pepper and onion. Add remaining ingredients and mix until just combined. (Do not overmix.) Pour into hot, well-greased corn-stick pans. Bake in 425-degree oven 12-15 minutes or until browned.

Margaret Hamfeldt, Louisville, Ky.

FRIED BREAD
Makes 3 dozen

2 cups sifted flour
1 teaspoon baking soda
1 teaspoon salt
1 tablespoon shortening
3/4 cup water
Oil for deep frying

Mix dry ingredients; work shortening in and add water; mix well. Shape into 6 balls of equal size. Roll one ball at a time to 1/8-inch thickness; cut each into 6 wedges. Fry in hot oil at 375 degrees until puffy and brown.

SWEDISH RYE BREAD
Makes 2 loaves

3 cups milk, scalded
1 package dry yeast
1/2 cup granulated sugar
3 tablespoons brown sugar
3/4 cup dark corn syrup
2 cups rye flour
3-1/2 cups all-purpose flour, or enough to make a stiff dough

Dissolve yeast in 1/4 cup milk. Add yeast, brown and white sugars, corn syrup, and rye flour to the scalded milk; beat well. Add white flour; mix well; cover, and let rise overnight.

Shape into 2 loaves and place on a buttered cookie sheet. Cover with towel; let rise until double in bulk. Preheat oven to 350 degrees and bake bread 1 hour, or until loaf sounds hollow when tapped with finger.

Agnes Ward, Erie, PA

HEALTH BREAD

3 packages dry yeast
2 cups warm water
1/2 cup sugar

Dissolve yeast in warm water; add sugar and set aside.

Mix together:
2 cups hot water
1 cup shortening
1 cup molasses
2 cups All Bran
2 cups oatmeal
2 cups rye or cracked wheat flour
2-1/2 teaspoons salt
1/2 cup wheat germ

When cool, add yeast mixture and stir well. Add enough white flour to handle dough easily. Knead; let double in bulk. Put into bread pans; let rise again. Bake at 350 degrees for 1 hour.

VITAMIN-RICH BREAD
Makes 1 loaf

1 cup seedless raisins
1/2 cup white raisins
2 teaspoons baking soda
1 tablespoon melted butter or margarine
1-1/2 cups orange juice or apple juice (heated)
2 eggs
1 cup sugar
1-1/4 cups sifted flour
1/4 teaspoon salt
2 cups bran flakes

Combine raisins, white raisins, baking soda, butter, and heated orange or apple juice in a bowl. Let stand for 10 minutes. Beat eggs and sugar together well. Stir in flour and salt. Combine with raisin mixture and bran flakes; beat only until well-blended. Turn into greased 9-inch loaf pan and bake at 350 degrees for about 1 hour. Cool 5 minutes in pan before turning out onto rack. Store 24 hours for easier slicing.

Agnes Ward, Erie, Pa.

THRIFTY THREE-GRAIN BREAD
Serves 12

1 cup cornmeal, yellow or white
1 cup rye flour
1 cup graham flour
2 teaspoons baking soda
1 teaspoon salt
1/4 teaspoon allspice
1/8 teaspoon ginger
3/4 cup molasses
1-3/4 cups sour milk
1/4 cup light cream

Place dry ingredients in a large mixing bowl; mix well. In separate bowl stir together molasses, sour milk, and cream. Pour liquid into dry mixture; stir only until well moistened. Pour batter into greased 9-inch loaf pan; bake at 350 degrees for 1 hour and 15 minutes. Cool thoroughly before slicing.

Gwen Campbell, Sterling, Va.

IRISH SODA BREAD

4 cups flour
1 teaspoon salt
1 teaspoon baking soda
4 tablespoons caraway seeds
2 cups buttermilk
2 cups raisins

Mix dry ingredients and seeds; add liquid and stir to blend, just until all ingredients are moistened. Add more buttermilk, if needed. Mix in raisins. Place dough in greased 9 x 5 x 3 inch loaf pan. Bake at 425 degrees for approximately 45 minutes, until toothpick inserted in center comes out clean. If loaf is browning too fast, place sheet of aluminum foil on top. Remove from pan and cool on a wire rack.

Note: This bread has a hard crust, but a moist interior.

Carme Venella, Laurel Springs, Nj.

PEANUT BUTTER BREAD

3/4 cup sugar
1/2 cup peanut butter
1 teaspoon vanilla
1-3/4 cups milk
2-1/4 cups flour
4 teaspoons baking powder
1/2 teaspoon salt

Cream together sugar, peanut butter, and vanilla. Add milk and mix well. Combine flour, baking powder, and salt. Add to creamed mixture and beat well. Place in a greased loaf pan and bake at 350 degrees for 45-50 minutes, or until golden brown. Allow to cool for 10 minutes before removing from pan. This is a very moist loaf with a rich peanut taste.

Lillian Smith, Quebec, Canada

CRANBERRY NUT BREAD

Makes 1 loaf

2 cups all-purpose flour
1 cup sugar
1-1/2 teaspoons baking powder
1 teaspoon salt
1/2 teaspoon baking soda
3/4 cup orange juice
1 tablespoon grated orange peel
2 tablespoons shortening
1 egg, well beaten
1-1/2 cups Ocean Spray fresh or
    frozen cranberries, coarsely
    chopped
1/2 cup chopped nuts

Preheat oven to 350 degrees. In a bowl, mix together flour, sugar, baking powder, salt, and baking soda. Stir in orange juice, orange peel, shortening, and egg. Mix until well-blended. Stir in cranberries and nuts. Turn into a 9x5-inch loaf pan, greased on bottom only. Bake for 55 minutes or until toothpick inserted in center comes out clean. Cool on a rack 15 minutes; remove from pan.

VERY LEMON BREAD

1/3 cup butter, melted
1 cup sugar
3 tablespoons lemon extract
2 eggs
1-1/2 cups sifted flour
1 teaspoon baking powder
1 teaspoon salt
1/2 cup milk
1-1/2 tablespoons grated lemon rind
1/2 cup chopped pecans

In a large bowl, mix butter, sugar, and lemon extract. Beat eggs into butter mixture. Sift together flour, baking powder and salt. Add flour mixture, alternately, with milk to the butter mixture, beating just enough to blend. Add lemon rind and nuts. Pour into greased and floured 9x5x3-inch loaf pan and bake at 350 degrees for 1 hour. Remove from pan and while warm, drizzle a mixture of 1/4 cup lemon juice and 1/2 cup sugar over

top and in cracks that form while baking. Store in foil for 24 hours before slicing.

Really excellent!

Agnes Ward, Erie, Pa

PINEAPPLE MACADAMIA NUT BREAD

2 cups all-purpose flour
1-1/2 tablespoons double-acting
    baking powder
1/2 teaspoon salt
1/4 teaspoon freshly grated nutmeg
1/2 stick (1/4 cup) unsalted butter,
    softened
3/4 cup plus 1 tablespoon sugar
2 large eggs at room temperature
2/3 cup milk
1 teaspoon vanilla
3/4 cup drained and chopped
    canned pineapple
3/4 cup chopped Macadamia nuts

In a bowl sift together flour, baking powder, salt, and nutmeg. In another bowl with an electric mixer, cream together butter and 3/4 cup of the sugar; beat in eggs one at a time. Stir in flour mixture, alternately with milk, and stir in vanilla. Fold in pineapple and nuts; turn batter into a well-buttered and floured 7-cup loaf pan, 9-1/2x5x2-3/4-inches. Sprinkle remaining 1 tablespoon sugar over batter and bake bread in a preheated 350 degree oven for 45-55 minutes, or until a tester comes out clean. Let the bread cool in the pan on a rack for 10 minutes; turn out onto rack, and let it cool completely.

Marcella Swigert, Monroe City, Mo.

BANANA COCONUT BREAD

2 cups flour
2 teaspoons baking soda
1/2 teaspoon salt
3 eggs
1/2 teaspoon lemon extract or
    lemon juice
1/4 cup sour cream

1 cup sugar
1 cup finely chopped nuts
1-1/2 cups sliced bananas
1/2 cup shredded coconut

Preheat oven to 325 degrees. Into a large bowl, sift together flour, baking soda and salt; set aside. Put eggs, butter, lemon extract, sour cream, and sugar in blender and mix. Pour egg mixture into flour mixture, stirring thoroughly. Fold in nuts, bananas, and coconut. Pour batter into 2 lightly buttered 9 x 5 x 3 inch loaf pans. Bake 45-50 minutes.

Agnes Ward, Erie, Pa.

CANTALOUPE NUT BREAD

1-3/4 cups all-purpose flour
1/4 teaspoon baking soda
2/3 cup sugar
1 egg
1/2 cup chopped walnuts or pecans
2 teaspoons baking powder
1/4 teaspoon salt
1/3 cup shortening
1 cup mashed cantaloupe pulp

In large mixing bowl, mix flour, baking powder, soda, and salt, sifting 3 times. Add nuts to the flour mixture, distributing thoroughly. In a separate bowl, cream sugar and shortening until light and fluffy. Add egg and mix well. Then add mashed cantaloupe pulp and mix thoroughly. Add flour and nut mixture, 1/2 cup at a time, beating well after each addition. Turn batter into a well-greased and floured loaf pan (8x4x2-inch) and bake at 350 degrees for 50 minutes or until bread tests done. Cool. Recipe yields 1 loaf—10 to 12 slices. Nuts may be omitted, if desired. This bread is very good plain, served with slices of cantaloupe or served with whipped cream. The finished loaf may look deceiving, just like any other plain bread, but the taste sets it apart from any ordinary loaf. Really delicious.

Shirley Ann Crist, Marion, Ind.

PUMPKIN SWIRL BREAD

Makes 1 loaf

1 (8-ounce) package cream cheese, softened
1/4 cup sugar
1 egg, beaten
1-3/4 cups flour
1-1/2 cups sugar
1 teaspoon baking soda
1 teaspoon cinnamon
1/2 teaspoon salt
1/4 teaspoon ground nutmeg
1 cup canned pumpkin
1/2 cup margarine, melted
1 egg, beaten
1/3 cup water

Combine cream cheese, sugar, and 1 beaten egg, mixing until well-blended. Set aside. Combine dry ingredients. Add combined pumpkin, margarine, egg, and water, mixing just until moistened. Reserve 2 cups pumpkin batter; pour remaining batter into greased and floured 9x5-inch loaf pan. Pour cream cheese mixture over pumpkin batter; top with reserved pumpkin batter. Cut through batters with knife several times for swirl effect.

Bake at 350 degrees for 1 hour and 10 minutes, or until wooden pick inserted in center comes out clean. Cool 5 minutes; remove from pan.

Marcella Swigert, Monroe City, Mo.

CINNAMON BREAD

Sweet Dough recipe
1 teaspoon cinnamon
1/3 cup sugar
1/4 cup melted margarine

Using the Sweet Dough recipe, roll dough on a well-floured board. Spread with margarine, reserving 1 tablespoonful. Sprinkle cinnamon/sugar mixture over dough, reserving some for top. Roll into a loaf, sealing edges. Place in greased bread pan, brushing top with 1 tablespoon melted margarine. Let rise about 1-1/2 hours. Then sprinkle with remaining cinnamon mixture on top. Bake at 375 degrees for 40 minutes.

CHOCOLATE ALMOND ZUCCHINI BREAD

3 eggs
2 cups sugar
1 cup vegetable oil

1 teaspoon vanilla
2 cups grated zucchini
2 squares baking chocolate, melted
3 cups flour
1 teaspoon salt
1 teaspoon cinnamon
1/4 teaspoon baking powder
1 teaspoon baking soda
1 cup chopped almonds

Beat eggs until lemon colored. Beat in sugar and oil. In large bowl, add egg mixture, vanilla, and zucchini to chocolate. Sift together dry ingredients and stir into zucchini mixture. and floured loaf pans (9x5x3 inch) and bake in 350 degree oven for 1 hour and 20 minutes or until tested done. Cool 15-20 minutes, then turn onto rack and cool thoroughly.

Agnes Ward, Erie, Pa.

ZUCCHINI NUT BREAD

Makes 2 loaves

1-1/4 cups wheat germ
3-1/4 cups flour
3-1/4 teaspoons baking powder
1 teaspoon salt
2 teaspoons cinnamon
1 cup chopped nuts
1-3/4 cups sugar
2 eggs
2 teaspoons vanilla
2/3 cup cooking oil
3 cups grated zucchini (May use blender)

Mix together wheat germ, flour, baking powder, cinnamon, and nuts. Beat eggs until light colored and fluffy. Beat in sugar, vanilla, and oil. Stir in zucchini. Gradually stir in wheat germ mixture. Turn into 2 greased and floured 8-1/2 x 4-1/2 x 2-1/2 inch loaf pans. Bake at 350 de-

grees for 1 hour. Test for doneness. Cool 10 minutes on rack.

Mrs. Stanley M. Lewis, Sussex, WI

COCONUT BREAD

Makes 1 loaf

2 cups pancake mix
1 cup coconut
1/4 cup sugar
3/4 cup chopped pecans
1 teaspoon cinnamon
2 eggs
1-1/2 cups milk
3 tablespoons margarine, melted

Grease a loaf pan and line bottom with wax paper, then grease again. Combine first 5 ingredients and mix well. Beat eggs in separate bowl. Add milk and melted margarine. Stir in dry ingredients; mix thoroughly until moistened. Pour batter into the prepared pan. Bake at 350 degrees for 50-55 minutes. Remove from pan and cool. Serve with whipped butter.

Whipped Butter:
1/2 cup butter or margarine
1/2 cup maple syrup

Beat butter until light and fluffy; gradually beat in syrup. Delicious!!

Jodi McCoy, Tulsa, OK

SIMPLE SOUR-CREAM CORNBREAD

Serves 6-8

3/4 cup yellow or white cornmeal
1 cup all-purpose flour
1/4 cup sugar
2 teaspoons baking powder
1/2 teaspoon salt
1 cup sour cream
1/4 cup milk
1 egg, beaten lightly
2 tablespoons vegetable oil

Mix all ingredients, just enough to blend well. Pour into a greased 8-inch square pan. Bake at 425 degrees for about 20 minutes. Serve piping hot with butter, jelly, jam, or maple syrup.

Gwen Campbell, Sterling, Va.

ANGEL BISCUITS

Makes 5 dozen

1 package dry yeast
1/2 cup lukewarm water
3 cups flour
2 tablespoons sugar
2 teaspoons baking powder
1 teaspoon baking soda
1 teaspoon salt
3/4 cup shortening
2 cups buttermilk

Dissolve yeast in water. Sift flour and remaining dry ingredients together in large mixing bowl. Add shortening, buttermilk, and yeast; mix well. Turn out onto floured board; knead well. Cover; refrigerate. When ready to bake, pinch off as much dough as needed. Return remaining dough to refrigerator. Roll out the amount you are using to about 1/2 inch thickness. Let sit in pan to rise for 15-20 minutes. Bake in 375 degree oven until brown, about 20-25 minutes.

Betty Peel, Milford, Ohio

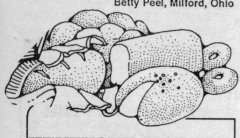

KENTUCKY BISCUITS

Makes 1 dozen

1-1/2 cups flour
1 tablespoon baking powder
1 tablespoon sugar
1 teaspoon salt
1/2 cup milk
1/3 cup softened shortening or lard

Stir together flour, baking powder, sugar, and salt. Make a well in the center; add milk and shortening; stir with a fork only until well mixed. Turn onto lightly floured surface; knead 6-8 times, then pat out until 1/2-inch thick. Cut out 1-3/4-inch round biscuits and place on ungreased baking sheet.

Bake in preheated 450 degree oven 10-12 minutes or until golden brown.
Mrs. Jerry E. Jones, Gas City, Ind.

CINNAMON-SUGAR BISCUITS

Makes 1 dozen

2 cups Basic Campers' Mix
2 tablespoons cinnamon-sugar mix
1/2 cup milk

Combine Basic Campers' Mix and cinnamon-sugar combination. Add milk, stirring lightly until moistened. Pat out to form 2-inch rounds. Sauté biscuits in butter in covered skillet, over low coals until brown on bottom for about 5 minutes. Turn; brown tops in covered skillet about 5 additional minutes. To serve, brush tops with melted butter and sprinkle with additional cinnamon-sugar.

LIGHT TASTY BISCUITS

2 cups all-purpose flour
2-1/2 teaspoons baking powder
1/2 teaspoon salt
1/3 cup shortening
3/4 cup milk
Butter or margarine

Sift together flour, baking powder, and salt. Cut in shortening with fork until mixture resembles coarse cornmeal. Add milk and blend lightly with fork only until flour is moistened and dough pulls away from sides of bowl. Turn out onto lightly floured board. Knead lightly (30 seconds) and roll 3/4-inch thick. Cut as desired. Place on lightly greased pan and brush tops of biscuits with butter or margarine. Bake at 475 degrees for 12-15 minutes.
Elizabeth Hunter, Pasadena, Md.

POTATO BISCUITS

cup potato water
1/2 cup mashed potato
1/2 cup water, lukewarm
1/2 cup sugar
1 yeast cake
1 teaspoon salt

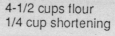

4-1/2 cups flour
1/4 cup shortening

Crumble yeast, adding salt, sugar, and water. Add potato and potato water. Stir in flour to make a stiff sponge. Add melted shortening. Add remainder of flour; knead until smooth. Put into greased bowl. Let rise for 2 hours. Knead. Let rise for 45 minutes. Shape into round balls and put in muffin pans. Let rise again about 35 minutes and bake in a hot 425-degree oven for 25 minutes.
Suzan L. Wiener, Spring Hill, Fla.

ONE-RISE CINNAMON ROLLS

Topping:
1 cup heavy whipping cream
  (do not substitute)
1 cup brown sugar

Rolls:
3 to 3-1/2 cups flour
1 package yeast
1/4 cup sugar
1 teaspoon salt
1 cup hot tap water
2 tablespoons butter, softened
1 egg

Filling:
1/2 cup granulated sugar
2 teaspoons cinnamon
1/2 cup butter, softened

First, mix brown sugar and heavy cream in 9 x 13-inch greased baking pan. In large bowl, blend 1-1/2 cups flour and the next 6 ingredients. Beat 3 minutes with electric mixer at medium speed. Stir in remaining 1-1/2 to 2 cups flour. Knead on floured surface for 1 minute. Roll dough into 15 x 7-inch rectangle. Spread filling over dough starting at long side; roll tightly in jelly roll fashion; seal edges. Cut into 16 to 20 rolls. Place cut side down on cream mixture. Cover and let rise until double in bulk, about 35-45 minutes. Bake in preheated 400 degree oven for 20-25 minutes. Cool 10-15 minutes before inverting on serving tray.
Ruth Eichholz, Blairsville, GA

CALIFORNIA ROLLS

Mix together and let stand 30 minutes:

1 package yeast
1/2 cup sugar
1 cup milk

Add:

2 eggs, well-beaten
4 cups flour
1 teaspoon salt
1/2 cup melted butter

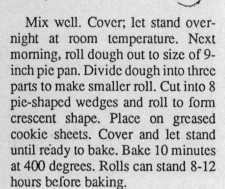

Mix well. Cover; let stand overnight at room temperature. Next morning, roll dough out to size of 9-inch pie pan. Divide dough into three parts to make smaller roll. Cut into 8 pie-shaped wedges and roll to form crescent shape. Place on greased cookie sheets. Cover and let stand until ready to bake. Bake 10 minutes at 400 degrees. Rolls can stand 8-12 hours before baking.

Betty Ireton, Kingston, OH

BISQUICK YEAST ROLLS

Makes 16 rolls

1 package yeast
1 teaspoon sugar
3/4 cup warm water
2-1/2 cups Bisquick

Dissolve yeast and sugar in water. Add Bisquick and mix well. Turn onto floured surface and knead until smooth. Form into rolls and place in greased baking pan. Cover; let rise 1 hour. Bake at 400 degrees for 10-15 minutes.

ZUCCHINI YEAST ROLLS

1/2 cup zucchini, cooked and mashed
1/4 cup sugar
1/4 cup shortening
1/2 teaspoon salt

1/2 cup scalded milk
1 cake yeast
1/4 cup lukewarm water
2-1/2 cups flour

Combine squash, sugar, salt, and shortening with milk; heat to lukewarm. Dissolve yeast in lukewarm water and add to milk mixture. Add flour and mix well. Dough will be soft. Let rise until double in bulk. Knead and shape into rolls and let rise again. Bake at 400 degrees for 15-20 minutes.

Sue Thomas, Casa Grande, Ariz.

DINNER ROLLS

Sweet Dough recipe
1/4 cup margarine, melted

Using the Sweet Dough recipe, roll dough on a well-floured board. Spread with margarine. Roll up, beginning with wide side and cut into slices. Place in a 15x9-inch rectangle pan and drizzle with remaining margarine. Bake at 375 degrees for 20 minutes.

EASY DANISH ROLLS

1 loaf (1 pound) frozen bread dough
1/4 cup melted butter
1/4 cup sugar
1 teaspoon cinnamon
1 cup raisins

Thaw dough completely. On a floured surface, roll dough out in a rectangular shape; about 10x6 inches. With a pastry brush, spread melted butter evenly over surface. Combine sugar and cinnamon; sprinkle over butter. Add raisins. Roll dough up jelly-roll fashion. Use a sharp knife and slice roll into 3/4-inch slices. Place individual rolls on a greased cookie sheet and let rise until doubled in size. Bake at 375 degrees about 15-20 minutes. When cool, glaze.

Glaze:

Combine 1/2 cup powdered sugar and 1 or 2 tablespoons orange juice; mix to a smooth consistency.

Shirley Viscosi, Worcester, Mass.

APPLE ROLLS

4 cups diced, pared apples
1 cup coarsely chopped pecans
2 cups sugar
3 cups flour
2 teaspoons baking soda
1/4 teaspoon salt
1/4 teaspoon allspice
1/4 teaspoon nutmeg
3/4 teaspoon cinnamon
1 cup butter, melted
2 teaspoons vanilla
2 eggs, lightly beaten

Stir together apples, nuts, and sugar. Let stand, stirring often, until juicy—about 1 hour.

Stir together flour, soda, salt, and spices. Add apple mixture and stir well. Stir in butter and vanilla. Add eggs. Turn into two greased and floured 1-pound coffee cans. Tie 2-inch-wide band of double foil around top. Bake at 325 degrees for about 1 hour and 15 minutes or until tester comes out clean.

Cool on rack 10 minutes. Remove foil; turn out. Serve warm with pudding sauce or cold as cake or tea bread.

June Harding, Ferndale, Mich.

PEANUT BUTTER LOAF

1-3/4 cups sifted enriched flour
2 teaspoons baking powder
1/2 teaspoon salt
1/4 teaspoon baking soda
1/3 cup shortening
3/4 cup crunchy peanut butter
2/3 cup sugar
2 eggs, slightly beaten
1 cup mashed ripe bananas

Set oven for moderate, 350 degrees. Mix and sift first four ingredients. Cream shortening and peanut butter; add sugar gradually. Continue creaming until light and fluffy. Add eggs; beat well. Stir in dry ingredients alternately with mashed bananas; mix well; do not beat. Spoon batter into well greased loaf pan 8x4x3-inch. Bake for 1 hour.

Peggy Fowler Revels, Woodruff, S.C.

NUT KUCHEN

Sweet Dough recipe
1/4 cup melted margarine
1/2 cup brown sugar
1/2 cup chopped nuts
1 teaspoon cinnamon

Using the Sweet Dough recipe, roll dough on a well-floured board into a rectangle shape 1/2 inch thick. Brush with melted margarine, spread with brown sugar, nuts, and cinnamon mixture. Roll tightly, placing into a 15x9-inch pan shaping into a circle. Make small incisions 1/2 inch long with knife, across top, about 1 inch apart. Let rise about 1-1/2 hours. Bake at 375 degrees for 25 minutes.

HUSH PUPPIES
Makes 3 to 3-1/2 dozen

1-1/2 cups cornmeal
1/2 cup flour
1/2 teaspoon baking soda
3/4 cup buttermilk
2 teaspoons salt
1 large, finely-diced onion

Combine cornmeal, flour, and baking soda in a mixing bowl. Stir in buttermilk and beat until batter is smooth. Stir in salt and onion. Drop heaping tablespoons of batter into a deep fryer; fry until golden brown. Drain on paper toweling before serving.

Marcella Swigert, Monroe City, MO

BREAD DUMPLINGS
Makes 14-16

3 cups 1/2-inch stale bread, trimmed of crusts
1/4 cup unsifted flour
1 teaspoon salt
1/8 teaspoon pepper
1/4 teaspoon baking powder
1/8 teaspoon nutmeg
1 tablespoon minced parsley
2 tablespoons minced yellow onion
1/4 cup milk

1 egg, lightly beaten
1 tablespoon melted butter or margarine

Mix all ingredients together; let stand 5 minutes, and mix again. Drop by rounded teaspoonfuls into a little flour, then roll into balls. Drop into *just* boiling soup or stew; simmer, uncovered, 5 minutes. Cover and simmer 2-3 minutes longer. Do not cook more than 1 layer deep at a time.

SWEET DOUGH

2 cakes yeast
1/4 cup lukewarm water
1 cup milk
1/2 cup margarine
1 teaspoon vanilla
1/2 cup sugar
1 teaspoon salt
2 eggs
3-1/2 cups flour

Soften yeast in lukewarm water; set aside. Scald milk. Add margarine, vanilla, sugar, and salt; cool. Add enough flour to make a thick batter. Add yeast and eggs. Beat. Knead about 10 minutes. Place in greased bowl and let rise about 1-1/2 hours. Punch down and work into desired shapes.

CRUSTY CRACKLIN' BREAD SQUARES
Serves 4

1 cup cooked crisp bacon, crumbled
1-1/2 teaspoons baking powder
1/4 teaspoon salt
1 egg, beaten
1/2 teaspoon baking soda
2 cups white stone-ground cornmeal
1 cup buttermilk

Have bacon cooked and crumbled. Sift dry ingredients. In a separate bowl mix buttermilk, egg, and bacon; mix well. The dough will be stiff. Pat batter evenly into a 9x13-inch, well-greased pan; bake at 375 degrees for 35 minutes. To serve: Cut the bread into squares.

Gwen Campbell, Sterling, Va.

EASTER EGG TWIST

1 (1-pound loaf) frozen white bread dough
1 tablespoon grated orange peel
1/2 teaspoon anise seed
6 eggs
1 tablespoon water
Food coloring
Vanilla icing

Thaw dough according to package directions. Sprinkle orange peel and anise seed on flattened dough piece; work in well. Divide dough in half. Roll each piece into a 24-inch rope. On a greased baking sheet, loosely twist ropes and shape into a circle; sealing the ends. Place 5 eggs between ropes in twist. Cover and let rise until double in size. Beat 1 egg with water and brush the loaf. Bake in preheated 350 degree oven for 30-35 minutes or until done. Cool on rack. Brush eggs with food coloring and drizzle with vanilla icing.

Diantha Hibbard, Rochester, N.Y.

BANANA-NUT MUFFINS
Makes 2 dozen

2 cups flour
1/2 teaspoon salt
1 cup sugar
1-1/3 cups mashed bananas (3 medium)
3 teaspoons baking powder
1/2 cup shortening
2 eggs
1 cup chopped walnuts

Sift together flour, salt and baking powder. Cream shortening and sugar in bowl until fluffy. Beat in eggs, one at a time. Stir in bananas. Add flour, salt, sugar, and baking powder. Do not overbeat. Mix in nuts. Fill greased muffin-tins 2/3 full. Bake at 350 degrees for 20 minutes.

Mrs. L. Mayer, Richmond, Va.

BRAN MUFFIN MIX

1-1/2 cups sugar
1/2 cup shortening
2 eggs
1 cup boiling water
3 cups 100% bran
2-1/2 cups flour
1-1/2 teaspoons salt
2 teaspoons soda
1 pint buttermilk

Mix sugar, shortening, and eggs with beater. Add water and bran; mix. Stir in dry ingredients and milk. Fill muffin cups 2/3 full and bake at 375 degrees for 15-20 minutes. Batter keeps 1 month in refrigerator. Can also bake muffins in microwave, about 1-1/2 to 2 minutes each.

Cheryl Santefert, Thornton, IL

ZUCCHINI NUT MUFFINS
Makes 18

2 eggs
1/2 cup brown sugar
1/2 cup honey
1/2 cup melted margarine
1 teaspoon vanilla
1 3/4 cups flour
1 teaspoon soda
1 teaspoon salt
1/2 teaspoon baking powder
1/2 teaspoon nutmeg
2 teaspoons cinnamon
1 cup rolled oats
1/2 cup chopped nuts
1/2 cup raisins
2 cups shredded zucchini

In a large bowl, beat eggs, then beat in sugar, honey, margarine and vanilla. In another bowl, mix flour, soda, salt, baking powder, nutmeg and cinnamon. Add to egg mixture and stir until moist. Stir in oats, nuts, raisins and zucchini. Spoon into well-greased muffin tins (or use paper liners), filling 3/4 full. Bake at 350 degrees for 25 minutes, or until toothpick comes out clean . Serve warm. Freezes very well, but cool completely first. Nice to have on hand for breakfast.

Vicki Hardekopf, Canyonville, OR

BLUEBERRY MUFFINS

2 cups sifted flour
3 teaspoons baking powder
1/2 teaspoon salt
1/3 cup sugar
1 egg beaten
3/4 cup milk
3 tablespoons melted butter
1 cup fresh blueberries

Sift flour, baking powder, salt and sugar together. Add the egg, milk, and butter. Fold in blueberries. Fill greased muffin tins 2/3 full. Bake at 350 degrees for 20 minutes.

HONEY OATMEAL MUFFINS

2/3 cup milk
1/3 cup vegetable oil
1 egg, beaten
1/4 cup honey
1-1/2 cups oatmeal
1 cup sifted flour
1/3 cup brown sugar
1 tablespoon baking powder
1/4 teaspoon salt
1/2 cup chopped nuts

Combine milk, vegetable oil, egg, and honey. Mix well and set aside. Mix oatmeal, flour, brown sugar, baking powder, and salt together. Blend all ingredients together; add nuts. Fill greased muffin tins 2/3 full. Bake at 375 degrees for about 20 minutes.

MAPLE BRAN MUFFINS
Makes 1 dozen

3/4 cup wheat bran
1/2 cup milk
1/2 cup maple syrup
1 egg, slightly beaten
1/4 cup vegetable oil
1-1/2 cups whole wheat flour

3 teaspoons baking powder
1/2 teaspoon salt
1/3 cup nuts, chopped

Glaze:
1 tablespoon butter
1/2 cup confectioners' sugar
1 tablespoon maple syrup

Combine bran, milk, and maple syrup. Mix in egg and oil. Combine remaining muffin ingredients. Add maple mixture; stir until just moistened. Spoon batter into greased muffin tins. Bake at 400 degrees for 18-20 minutes. Mix glaze ingredients and spread on warm muffins. Great when served warm!

Mrs. H.W. Walker, Richmond, Va.

CRUNCH APPLE MUFFINS
Makes 1 dozen

2 cups sifted all-purpose flour
1/3 cup instant nonfat dry milk
1/3 cup granulated sugar
3/4 cup water
1/4 cup vegetable oil
1 teaspoon cinnamon
1 cup finely chopped, peeled apples
4 teaspoons baking powder
1 teaspoon salt
1 egg

Crunch Topping:
1/3 cup firmly packed brown sugar
1/2 teaspoon cinnamon
1/3 cup chopped nuts

Sift flour; add nonfat dry milk, sugar, baking powder, salt, and cinnamon in bowl. Stir in apples. Combine water, oil, and egg. Stir into flour mixture. Do not over-mix. Spoon into 12 well-greased muffin cups. Combine ingredients for topping. Sprinkle over batter in each cup. Bake in preheated 400-degree oven for 20 minutes or until done. Serve warm.

Sandra Russell, Gainesville, Fla.

APPLE CRUMB MUFFINS
Makes 16

1 cup chopped pared apples
1 teaspoon lemon juice
1-1/2 cups all-purpose flour
1 cup whole wheat flour
1/2 cup firmly-packed dark brown sugar
4 teaspoons baking powder
1/2 teaspoon salt
1 cup milk
1 egg
1/4 cup margarine, melted
2 tablespoons granulated sugar
1/2 teaspoon ground cinnamon

Toss apples with lemon juice in small bowl. Stir together all-purpose flour, whole wheat flour, brown sugar, baking powder, and salt in medium-size bowl until well blended. Whisk milk, egg, and margarine in small bowl; pour over flour mixture. Add apples; gently stir until dry ingredients are moistened. Spoon mixture into greased muffin cups. Combine 2 tablespoons granulated sugar and cinnamon; sprinkle over dough.

Bake in preheated oven at 400 degrees for 25 minutes or until browned.

Esther Kaylor, Young, AZ

GINGER MUFFINS

1 cup margarine
1 cup sugar
4 eggs
1 cup molasses
1 cup buttermilk
4 cups flour
2 teaspoons soda
1/2 teaspoon cinnamon
2 teaspoons ginger
1/2 teaspoon salt
1/2 cup raisins
1 cup walnut meats

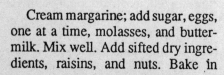

Cream margarine; add sugar, eggs, one at a time, molasses, and buttermilk. Mix well. Add sifted dry ingredients, raisins, and nuts. Bake in

greased muffin pans at 350 degrees for 20-25 minutes. This batter may be kept in the refrigerator and used as needed.

Barbara Beauregard-Smith, Northfield, S.A., Australia

BEST YET ZUCCHINI MUFFINS
Makes 2 dozen

2 eggs
1 cup sugar
1/2 cup oil
1 tablespoon vanilla
2 cups unpeeled shredded zucchini
2 cups flour
1 teaspoon soda
1/4 teaspoon baking powder
1/2 teaspoon salt
1-1/2 teaspoons cinnamon
1 cup raisins
1/2 cup chopped nuts

Combine first four ingredients, mixing well. Stir in zucchini; set aside. Combine next five ingredients. Reserve 1/4 cup flour mixture and toss with raisins and nuts.

Make a well in center of flour mixture. Add zucchini mixture to dry ingredients, stirring just until moistened. Stir in raisins and nuts. Spoon into greased muffin cups, filling 2/3 full. Bake at 350 degrees for 20 minutes.

Margaret Hamfeldt, Louisville, KY

RICE MUFFINS
Makes 1 dozen

1 cup cold cooked rice
1 cup milk
1 cup flour
4 teaspoons baking powder
1/2 teaspoon salt
2 eggs, beaten

Combine rice, milk, and eggs. Sift together flour, baking powder, and salt. Add to rice and eggs. Pour into greased muffin cups or paper liners. Bake at 400 degrees for 30 minutes.

Zenana Warren, Bloomville, OH

LEMON MUFFINS
Makes 2 dozen

1 cup butter or margarine
1 cup sugar
4 eggs, separated, whites beaten
2 cups flour
2 teaspoons baking powder
1 teaspoon salt
1/2 cup lemon juice
2 teaspoons grated lemon peel

In a bowl cream butter or margarine and sugar until smooth. Add egg yolks, beat until light. Sift flour with baking powder and salt; add alternately with lemon juice, mixing after each addition. Do not overmix. Fold in stiffly-beaten egg whites and grated lemon peel. Fill buttered muffin pans 3/4 full; bake in 375-degree oven for 20 minutes or until done.

Alice McNamara, Eucha, OK

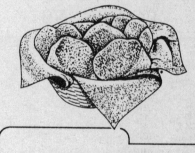

BLUEBERRY YOGURT MUFFINS
Makes 12

1 egg
1 cup (8 ounces) yogurt (lemon, vanilla, or honey-flavored)
3 tablespoons melted margarine
2-1/2 cups biscuit mix
1 cup blueberries

In medium bowl, lightly beat egg; gently blend in yogurt and margarine. Add biscuit mix; stir just until well moistened. Stir in blueberries. Fill 12 greased or paper-lined muffin cups, 2/3 full. Bake in preheated 400 degree oven for 15 minutes or until lightly browned. Remove from pan immediately. Serve hot.

These are so easy to make and the yogurt contributes to the flavor and delicate texture.

Shirley Viscosi, Worcester, MA

Casseroles
CREATIVE

CHEESEBURGER CASSEROLE

1 pound ground beef
1/4 cup diced onion
1 (8-ounce) can tomato sauce
1/4 cup ketchup
1/4 pound sliced American cheese
1 package - 8 Pillsbury crescent rolls dough

Brown ground beef; add onion, and cook 10 minutes. Add tomato sauce, ketchup, salt, and pepper. Cook 5 minutes. Spoon into a 9 x 9-inch baking dish. Arrange slices of cheese and top with crescent dough. Bake at 350 degrees until dough is light brown, about 20-25 minutes.

Eleanor Condrick, Hazleton, PA

TATO TACO CASSEROLE
Serves 4-6

Crust:
1-1/2 cups Hungry Jack mashed potato flakes
1 (8-ounce) container dairy sour cream
2/3 cup water

Filling:
1 pound ground beef
1/2 cup taco sauce
4 ounces (1 cup) shredded Cheddar cheese

Topping:
1-1/2 cups shredded lettuce
1 cup (1 large) chopped tomato
1 cup slightly crushed tortilla chips

Heat oven to 350 degrees. Combine crust ingredients. Press into 1-1/2 quart casserole. Bake at 350 degrees for 25-30 minutes. In skillet, brown ground beef; drain. Stir in taco sauce; heat through. Combine meat mixture and cheese; spread over baked crust. Arrange lettuce and tomato on top of beef mixture around outside edge. Sprinkle tortilla chips over lettuce and tomato. Serve with additional taco sauce if desired.

Theresa Guillaume, Mosinee, WI

CALICO MACARONI
Serves 4-6

1/4 cup chopped carrots
1/4 cup chopped onion
1/4 cup chopped green pepper
2 tablespoons margarine
1 (7-ounce) package elbow macaroni, cooked and drained
1 (8-ounce) jar Cheese Whiz

Cook carrots, onion, and green pepper in margarine until tender. Combine cooked veggies with cooked macaroni and Cheese Whiz; stir until blended. Heat on top of stove or in oven until hot.

Jodie McCoy, Tulsa, Okla.

GARDEN CASSEROLE

3 tsps butter or margarine
1 large onion, sliced (1 cup)
1 large red pepper, cut in 1-inch strips (1 cup)
2 large cloves garlic, minced
1/4 cup flour
2 cups (1/2 pound) shredded Swiss cheese, divided
6 small Idaho® potatoes, unpared, thinly sliced
1 package (10 oz) frozen cut green beans, thawed
1 cup half and half or light cream
1/2 teaspoon dried leaf rosemary
1/2 teaspoon salt
1/4 teaspoon pepper

In large skillet melt butter saute onion, red pepper and garlic until tender. Stir in flour cook 1 minute. Spoon half the vegetable mixture into a 3-quart casserole. Sprinkle with one-third of the cheese. Layer poatoes and green beans; sprinkle with one-third of the cheese. Top with remaining vegetables and cheese. Combine half and half, rosemary, salt and pepper; pour mixture over vegetables. Cover. Bake in a 375 degree oven 45 minutes or until potatoes are tender. Uncover, place under broiler until top is golden.

SPINACH NOODLE CASSEROLE

serves 10-12

1 pound package noodles
2 (10-ounce) packages frozen chopped spinach
1 pound fresh mushrooms, sliced
1/2 onion, chopped
2-4 tablespoons margarine
1 (10-ounce) can cream of chicken soup
1 (10-ounce) can cream of mushroom soup
1 cup sour cream
2 tablespoons Worcestershire sauce
2 tablespoons margarine
Salt & pepper to taste

Cook noodles and drain. Cook spinach and drain well. Sauté mushrooms and onion in margarine. Mix together all ingredients, except 2 tablespoons margarine. Place in large greased casserole. Dot with margarine. Bake at 350 degrees for 30 minutes or until bubbly.

Note: Recipe may be halved. Omit either can of soup. For a variation you may add 1 (7-ounce) can tuna or 1 pound ground beef, cooked and drained, before baking.

Mrs. George Franks, Millerton, Pa.

MACARONI AND SAUSAGE BAKE

Serves 6

1 pound bulk pork sausage
1/2 cup chopped onion
1 cup elbow macaroni
1 (10-1/2 ounce) can cream of celery soup
2/3 cup milk
3 beaten eggs
1-1/2 cups shredded processed American cheese

Cook macaroni according to package directions. Cook sausage and onion until browned. Drain off excess fat. Combine sausage mixture, macaroni, soup, milk, eggs, and cheese. Place in 2-quart casserole. Bake at 350 degrees for 40-45 minutes.

Sharon M. Crider, Evansville, Wis.

BROCCOLI CASSEROLE

Serves 8

1/4 cup chopped onion
6 tablespoons butter or margarine
1/2 cup water
2 tablespoons flour
8 ounces processed cheese spread
2 packages frozen chopped broccoli, thawed and drained
3 eggs, well beaten
1/2 cup cracker crumbs

Sauté onion in 4 tablespoons butter until soft; stir in flour and add water. Cook over low heat, stirring, until mixture thickens and comes to a boil. Blend in cheese. Combine sauce and broccoli. Add eggs; mix gently until blended. Turn into a 1-1/2 quart casserole; cover with crumbs and dot with remaining butter. Bake at 325 degrees for 30 minutes.

Agnes Ward, Erie, PA

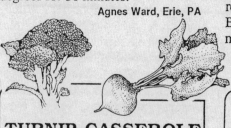

TURNIP CASSEROLE

Serves 4

1 1/2 lbs. turnips, peeled and thinly sliced
2 tablespoons butter
1 onion, thinly sliced
2/3 cup chopped celery
2 tablespoons flour
1 cup milk
1/2 cup grated sharp cheese
Salt and pepper to taste
3 tbsps. bread crumbs

Cook turnips in boiling, salted water to cover until just tender. Drain. Saute in butter the oinion, green pepper, and celery until tender. Sprinkle with flour and cook 1 minute. Add milk and stir until thickened. Stir in cheese, salt and pepper. Combine cheese sauce with turnips, place in baking dish and top with curmbs. Brown under broiler. May be prepared ahead and place-dunder broiler just before serving.

Marcella Swigert, Monroe City, MO

YELLOW SQUASH CASSEROLE

2 pounds yellow squash
1 large onion
1 can cream of chicken soup
1 jar pimientos (optional)
1 cup sour cream
1 teaspoon salt
1/4 teaspoon pepper
1 stick margarine
1 (8-ounce) package Pepperidge Farms herbal dressing

Boil squash until tender; drain and mash. Chop onion; sauté in a half stick margarine until tender. Add soup, chopped pimiento, sour cream, salt, and pepper. Melt the remaining margarine and add to dressing crumbs. Put half of dressing in bottom of baking dish. Mix all ingredients together. Pour on dressing. Spread remaining half of the dressing on top. Bake at 350 degrees for approximately 1 hour.

Mildred Beckham, Edgar, FL

PARSNIP CASSEROLE

2 pounds parsnips
2 tablespoons butter
1/4 teaspoon fresh or dried rosemary
2 tablespoons flour
1/4 cup grated Parmesan cheese
2 cups light cream or half-and-half
1/2 cup cracker crumbs
1/4 cup melted butter

Peel parsnips. Cook in boiling, salted water until tender. Drain; cut each in half lengthwise, or slice in rounds, if parsnips are large. Arrange half the parsnips in bottom of greased 1-1/2 quart baking dish. Dot with half the butter; sprinkle with half the rosemary, flour, and cheese. Drizzle with half the cream. Repeat layers. Mix cracker crumbs with melted butter; sprinkle over casserole. Bake, uncovered, in 400 degree oven for 20 minutes.

Diantha Hibbard, Rochester, NY

CHEESY SPAGHETTI

1 (12-ounce) package thin spaghetti
1/4 pound bacon, cut in small pieces
1 large onion, chopped
1 pound ground beef
2 cups (2 8-ounce cans) tomato
    sauce
1 (4-ounce) can sliced mushrooms,
    drained
1 teaspoon salt
1/2 teaspoon Italian seasoning
1/2 teaspoon garlic salt
1/8 teaspoon pepper
1 cup (4 ounces) shredded cheese
1/2 cup shredded Provolone cheese

Cook spaghetti; drain. Fry bacon slowly until browned. Drain off grease. Add onion and beef; cook until meat is brown; mix in tomato sauce and seasonings. Simmer 15 minutes. In large bowl, combine sauce and spaghetti. Place half of mixture in a buttered 2 quart casserole. Top with half of the Cheddar and half of the Provolone cheese. Repeat layers. Bake in pre-heated 375 degree oven for 20-25 minutes.

Betty L. Perkins, Hot Springs, AR

PORK CHOP CASSEROLE

6 pork chops
1 cup uncooked brown rice
6 slices onion
6 tomato slices
6 green pepper rings
1 teaspoon salt
1/8 teaspoon pepper
2 cups tomato juice

Spray 12-inch skillet with vegetable cooking spray. Brown pork chops on each side. Transfer to plate.
Place rice over bottom of skillet. Arrange chops on top. Stack slices of onion, tomato, and green pepper on top of each chop. Sprinkle with salt and pepper. Pour tomato juice over chops. Cover; simmer 45 minutes or until chops are tender.

Ella Evanicky, Fayetteville, TX

BACON AND RICE CREOLE

1 pound bacon
1 green pepper, diced
3 small onions, chopped
2-1/2 teaspoons salt
1/8 teaspoon pepper·
2 cups canned tomatoes
1 cup raw rice (not quick-cooking)

Simmer vegetables and spices in a sauce pan. At the same time, fry the bacon. When bacon is done, remove from pan and crumble into small pieces. Drain off all but 3 tablespoons of fat, to which add the raw rice. Let rice brown lightly. Add the vegetables and bacon; let simmer over very low heat for 30 minutes. Check after 20 minutes to see if it is drying out, if so, add more tomatoes, or some water, or a combination of both.

Linda Taylor, New Lenox, IL

FIESTA CORN CASSEROLE
Serves 4-6

3 tablespoons butter
3 cups corn flakes
1 pound lean ground beef
3/4 teaspoon seasoned salt
1 (8-ounce) can tomato sauce
1 (1-1/4 ounce) package Lawry's
    Taco Seasoning Mix
1 (17-ounce) can whole kernel corn,
    drained (save 1/4 cup liquid)
2 cups grated Cheddar cheese.

Combine butter and 2 cups corn flakes in bottom of a shallow 1-1/2 quart baking dish. Crush remaining corn flakes; set aside. In skillet, brown beef until crumbly; drain. Add seasoned salt, tomato sauce, taco seasoning mix, and reserved liquid from corn; mix well. Layer 1/2 each; corn, meat mixture, and cheese over buttered corn flakes in baking dish; repeat layers. Sprinkle crushed corn flakes over top in diagonal strips.

Agnes Ward, Erie, PA

CHICKEN ALMOND CASSEROLE

5 cups diced, cooked chicken
    breasts
2 cups diced celery
3 cups cooked rice
1 (8-ounce) can sliced water chest-
    nuts
2 cans cream of chicken soup
1/2 cup sour cream
1/2 cup mayonnaise
2 tablespoons chopped onion
2 tablespoons lemon juice
1 tablespoon salt
3/4 teaspoon white pepper
1 cup sliced almonds

Mix above ingredients and put into buttered 9x13 inch baking dish.

Topping:
1/2 cup sliced almonds
3 cups crumbled corn flakes
2/3 cup butter

Mix above ingredients and sprinkle on top of casserole. Bake at 350 degrees for 35-45 minutes. Can be prepared ahead and refrigerated until baking.

Sharon Sisson, Longview, Was

GERMAN SUPPER
Serves 4-5

5-6 potatoes, scrubbed (not peeled)
1/4 cup chopped onion
1/4 teaspoon garlic powder
1/2 teaspoon salt
1/3 teaspoon pepper
3 cups cubed beef Hillshire Farms
    sausage or Eckrich smoked
    sausage
1 (7-ounce) can sauerkraut

Cut potatoes into thumb-size pieces. Add onion, garlic powder, salt, and pepper. Brown in a small amount of oil for 25 minutes until tender. Add sausage; heat; stir occasionally. Drain kraut and spread on top surface. Do not stir. Cover and heat.
Ann Sterzer, Lynch, Neb.

FRESH CORN CASSEROLE

Preheat oven to 350 degrees. Generously butter a 2-quart rectangular baking dish. In blender puree:

1 cup corn (fresh or frozen, thawed)
1/2 cup butter, softened
2 eggs

Pour into bowl; blend in:

1 cup corn
4-ounce can green chilies; drained, seeded, and chopped
1 cup sour cream
1 cup diced Monterey Jack cheese
1/2 cup cornmeal
1-1/2 teaspoons salt

Spread above ingredients in baking dish. Bake 50 - 60 minutes. Serve with sliced tomatoes. This is delicious and very light!

Patricia Staley, Westmont, IL

STUFFED SHELLS

Serves 8-10

1 (12-ounce) package jumbo shells for stuffing
2 tablespoons butter
1 clove garlic, crushed
1/2 cup finely-chopped onion
2 beaten eggs
2 pounds Ricotta cheese
1/2 cup Parmesan and Romano cheese, mixed
1/3 cup parsley flakes
1/8 teaspoon nutmeg
1 cup shredded Mozzarella cheese (4 ounces)
2-3 pounds Italian meat sauce
1/2 cup Parmesan and Romano, mixed for topping

Preheat oven to 350 degrees. Cook shells according to package directions. Rinse with cold water; drain. Melt butter; sauté garlic and onion until soft. Mix together onion, garlic, eggs, ricotta, Parmesan, Romano, parsley, and nutmeg. Stir in Mozzarella, stuff shells with filling. (At this point, the shells may be frozen for future use).

Cover the bottoms of two 13x9x2-inch baking dishes with meat sauce.

Place shells on top of sauce and sprinkle with Parmesan and Romano. Bake, covered with foil, at 350 degrees for 30-40 minutes or until hot and bubbly.

This is a dish that is easy to prepare; and receives many compliments at potluck dinners.
Betty Perkins, Hot Springs, Ark.

DEVILED HAM AND RICE CASSEROLE

Serves 6

1 medium onion, chopped
1/2 medium green pepper, chopped
1/2 cup finely diced celery
2 tablespoons butter or margarine
1 cup raw rice
2 chicken bouillon cubes
2 (4-1/2 ounce) cans deviled ham
3 cups boiling water
Chopped parsley

Sauté first 3 ingredients in butter for 2-3 minutes. Place mixture in 1-1/2 quart casserole with remaining ingredients, except parsley. Mix with fork. Cover and bake for 45 minutes in pre-heated moderate oven at 350 degrees, stirring twice at 15-minute intervals, or until rice is tender. Sprinkle with parsley.

Mrs. Robert Shaffer, Middleburg, PA

ANOTHER HAMBURGER CASSEROLE

1 pound hamburger
1 green pepper, chopped
1 (8-ounce) package of 1/4 inch noodles, cooked
1 can cream of mushroom soup
1 can evaporated milk

Fry hamburger with green pepper, then blend in soup and milk. Combine with cooked noodles and bake 45-60 minutes at 350 degrees. Do not alter any of these ingredients. It takes this combination for the special flavor.

Linda Taylor, New Lenox, IL

CHICKEN LIVER CASSEROLE

Serves 5-6

2 (10-ounce) packages frozen French-style green beans
4 slices bacon, diced
1 pound chicken livers, cut in half
1/2 teaspoon seasoning salt
2 tablespoons sherry
1 (10-ounce) can cream of mushroom soup
1/2 cup sour cream
3/4 cup crushed barbecue potato chips

Cook green beans according to directions. Drain and spread in greased 9x6 or 8x8 inch baking dish. Sauté bacon until crisp; scatter over beans. Stir-fry chicken livers in bacon fat until pinkness disappears. Add next 4 ingredients, as soon as heated; pour over bacon. Top with potato chips. Bake at 375 degrees for 15 minutes, or until bubbly.

This is a very tasty dish and easy to make!

Lillian Smith, Montreal, Que., Canada

ZUCCHINI CASSEROLE

Serves 12

2 cups bread crumbs
1/4 cup butter or margarine, melted
1/4 teaspoon Italian seasonings
1/4 cup Parmesan cheese
2 pounds zucchini; sliced, parboiled, and drained
1 medium carrot, shredded
10-1/2-ounce can cream of chicken soup
1 cup sour cream
1/4 cup chopped green onion

Combine crumbs, butter, seasonings, and cheese, spread half in bottom of 13 x 9 x 2-inch pan. Combine zucchini and carrot; spread over crumbs. Mix soup, sour cream, and onion; pour over vegetables. Top with remaining crumbs. Bake at 350 degrees for 1 hour.

Lisa Varner, Baton Rouge, LA

HAM, POTATO, AND ONION CASSEROLE
Serves 8-10

6 tablespoons ham drippings or butter
6 tablespoons enriched flour
3 cups milk
2 teaspoons salt
1/4 teaspoon pepper
1/4 pound Cheddar cheese, grated
1 pound diced cooked ham
4 cups cubed cooked potatoes
12 small cooked onions
1/2 cup buttered bread crumbs

Melt drippings or butter. Blend in flour and add milk, stirring constantly. Cook mixture until thickened, boiling about 3 minutes. Add seasonings and grated cheese. Cook slowly until cheese melts. Add cooked ham, potatoes, and onions. Pour mixture into a greased casserole. Sprinkle with buttered bread crumbs. Bake, uncovered, in a 350-degree oven for 30-40 minutes or until crumbs are lightly browned.

Ruby Walsh, West Chicago, Ill.

VEGETABLE CASSEROLE

1 can whole kernel corn, drained
1 can French green beans, drained
1 cup finely chopped celery
1 cup finely chopped onion
1/2 cup green pepper, finely chopped
4 cups grated sharp cheese
1 container sour cream
1 can cream of celery soup

Mix well and pour into a very large casserole.

Topping:
3/4 box Cheese-It crackers, crumbled into 3/4 stick melted margarine. You may add a can of slivered almonds. Bake at 350 degrees for 45 minutes. This makes a large amount. Great for a covered-dish supper!!

Peggy Fowler, Woodruff, SC

CHICKEN-PASTA HOT DISH
Serves 6-8

1/2 pound elbow or spiral pasta (2 cups uncooked)
1/4 cup butter or margarine
1/4 cup finely chopped onion
3 tablespoons all-purpose flour
1-1/2 teaspoons salt
1/8 teaspoon pepper
3 cups milk
3 cups shredded cheddar cheese
2 cups diced cooked chicken or turkey
1 (9-ounce) package frozen Italian-cut green beans, thawed and drained
1 (2-ounce) jar diced pimiento, drained
3 tablespoons cornflake crumbs

Cook pasta according to package directions; drain. In large saucepan, melt butter; add onion and cook until tender. Stir in flour, salt, and pepper. Blend in milk. Cook, stirring constantly, until thickened and bubbly. Add cheese; stir until melted. Combine pasta, cheese sauce, chicken, green beans, and pimiento; mix well. Pour into a 3-quart casserole. Top with cornflake crumbs. Bake in a 350-degree oven until hot, about 30 minutes. Refrigerate leftovers.

* * National Pasta Association

ONE-POT TUNA PASTA
Serves 4

3-1/2 cups water
4 chicken bouillon cubes
1/8 teaspoon pepper
1 teaspoon basil leaves
2 cups (8 ounces) elbow pasta or spiral pasta
1 (4-ounce) jar pimiento
1 (9-ounce) package frozen cut green beans
2 cups milk
1 cup (4 ounces) process American cheese
1 (7-ounce) can tuna, drained and broken into chunks

1/4 cup chopped parsley

Bring water, bouillon cubes, pepper and basil leaves to a boil in a 4-quart pot. Gradually add uncooked pasta so that water continues to boil. Cover and simmer for 7 minutes, stirring occasionally.

Meanwhile, dice pimiento. Stir diced pimiento, beans, and milk into pot; cover and simmer 6 to 8 minutes longer or until pasta and beans are tender. Stir in cheese, tuna, and parsley until cheese is melted. Serve from pot or turn into serving dish. Serve immediately.

ONION CASSEROLE
Serves 2

2 large or 3 medium onions
1/4 teaspoon salt
Dash of pepper
2 or 3 tablespoons whipping cream (see directions)
1/3 cup buttered bread crumbs
Garlic powder (optional)

Grease or spray with pan release, a small baking dish, about 2-cup capacity.

Peel onions; cut in half lengthwise; place cut-side down on board; cut in 1/4-inch slices. Use your hands to separate layers. Drop into saucepan of cold salted water. Bring to boil over high heat; boil until onions are transparent but barely fork tender, about 3 minutes. Drain thoroughly. (If doing ahead, set aside.) Return to pan. Sprinkle on salt and pepper. Add 2 tablespoons cream; toss to mix; if onions seem dry, add another tablespoon cream (this depends on how well drained onions were). Spread evenly in prepared dish. Top with crumbs; sprinkle crumbs lightly with garlic powder, if desired.

Bake at 325 or 350 degrees (depending on what else may be cooking in the oven) until heated through and crumbs are golden. 20 to 25 minutes.

WINTER SQUASH CASSEROLE
Serves 2

1 cup mashed squash, thawed if frozen
1 or 2 slices bacon (use two if you can afford the calories)
1/4 cup chopped onion
1/3 cup grated Cheddar cheese
1/4 teaspoon salt
Dash Tabasco or use black pepper
1/4 cup buttered bread crumbs

Grease or spray with pan release a small baking dish, one quart or smaller. Put squash into medium bowl. Fry bacon until crisp; crumble into squash. Leave about 1 tablespoon drippings in skillet. Fry onions in drippings until transparent; add to squash. Add cheese (I grate it directly into the bowl, estimating the measure). Add salt and Tabasco or pepper; mix well. Transfer to prepared baking dish; top with bread crumbs.

Bake at 325 or 350 degrees (depending on what else may be cooking in the oven) until heated through and crumbs begin to brown, 25 to 30 minutes.

TAGLIARINA

1 pound hamburger
1 onion, chopped
2 tablespoons butter
1 (8-ounce) can tomato sauce
1-1/2 cups water
2 cups uncooked noodles
1 (1-cup) can corn
1 large jar whole mushrooms
1 (No. 2) can pitted ripe olives
1 cup Parmesan cheese
Salt to taste

Mince and brown onion in butter in large skillet. Add meat and brown. Add tomato sauce, water and noodles; stir until noodles are tender. Add more water, if needed. Add salt and rest of ingredients. Pour into 11x11x2-inch glass baking dish and sprinkle with Parmesan cheese. Bake 45 minutes in 350 degree oven. Let stand in oven with door open for 15 minutes before serving.

MOCK OYSTER CASSEROLE

1 medium eggplant
1 stick margarine
1-1/2 cups Ritz cracker crumbs
1 egg, beaten
1 (6-1/2 ounce) can minced clams, drained (reserve liquid)
Salt, pepper, Tabasco sauce to taste

Peel eggplant; cut into 1-inch cubes and parboil 3 minutes. Drain well; set aside. Melt margarine and add Ritz crackers; mix well. Reserve 1/3 cup cracker crumb mixture for topping.

Gently mix beaten eggs, drained clams, and eggplant. Add crumbs, salt, pepper, and Tabasco sauce. Then add enough clam liquid to make quite moist, but not soupy. Pour into buttered casserole. Top with remaining crumbs and bake at 350 degrees for 45 minutes.

Rebecca Preston, Weare, N.H.

LUNCHMEAT AND NOODLE CASSEROLE

1/4 cup margarine
1/4 cup all-purpose flour
1/2 teaspoon salt
Dash of pepper
2-1/2 cups milk
1 can lunch meat, cubed
2 cups cooked noodles
1 teaspoon mustard
3/4 cup bread crumbs
2 tablespoons melted margarine
1 (16-ounce) can peas and carrots

Preheat oven to 375 degrees. Melt margarine in a skillet. Blend in flour, salt, pepper, and gradually stir in milk. Cook over medium heat, stirring constantly, until mixture is smooth and thick.

Add meat, noodles, mustard, and peas and carrots. Mix well. Spoon into a greased 1-1/2 quart casserole. Combine crumbs and melted butter; sprinkle over noodles. Bake 25 minutes.

Alpha Wilson, Roswell, N.M.

CORNED BEEF SCALLOP CASSEROLE

1 (3-ounce) package potato soup mix
1-1/2 cups milk
1 cup water
1 cup American cheese, grated
1/2 teaspoon Worcestershire sauce
1 (12-ounce) can corned beef, shredded
3/4 cup carrots, sliced and cooked
1/2 cup celery, sliced and cooked
1/4 cup green peas, cooked
2 tablespoons pimiento, chopped
1 teaspoon parsley, chopped
3/4 cup soft bread crumbs

Empty potato soup mix into saucepan; add milk and water; stir constantly until blended. Cook until mixture comes to a boil; remove from heat. Add cheese and Worcestershire sauce; mix well. Stir in corned beef shreds, carrots, celery, green peas, and pimiento. Turn into a well-greased 1-1/2 quart ovenproof casserole. Sprinkle parsley over the top, then bread crumbs; cover. Bake 350 degrees for 20 minutes; uncover; bake 12 minutes longer until top is golden.

Gwen Campbell, Sterling, Va.

MAIN DISH NOODLES
Serves 2

2-1/2 cups uncooked medium noodles
2 tablespoons butter or margarine
2 tablespoons half-and-half or cream
2 tablespoons Parmesan cheese
1 (6-ounce) can boneless salmon or tuna

Cook noodles in boiling, salted water according to directions on package.

Meanwhile, in a medium saucepan, melt butter. Stir in half-and-half and cheese; leave over low heat. Drain fish; break into lumps; add to butter mixture. Drain cooked noodles; immediately add to saucepan; toss to mix. Serve with additional Parmesan cheese.

LADIES' LUNCHEON LAYERED DISH

1 cup crushed potato chips
4 hard-cooked eggs, sliced
1 onion, sliced thin and separated into rings
1/3 cup parsley, chopped
1 (10-1/2-ounce) can cream of mushroom soup
1/4 cup sour cream
3/4 cup milk
1/2 teaspoon paprika

Spread 1/3 of potato chips in bottom of a greased 1-1/2 quart ovenproof baking dish. Cover with 1/3 of the egg slices, 1/3 of the onion rings and chopped parsley. Repeat layers until potato chips, egg slices and onion rings are all used. Combine soup with sour cream, milk, and paprika; mix well; pour over all; cover. Bake 350 degrees for 30 minutes; uncover, bake 10 minutes longer until hot, bubbly, and golden.

Gwen Campbell, Sterling, Va.

BAKED RICE WITH HERBS
Serves 4-6

2 tablespoons butter
1 green onion, minced
1/4 cup parsley, chopped fine
1/4 teaspoon thyme
1/4 teaspoon sage
Salt and pepper to taste
1 cup brown rice
2-1/2 cups water
1/2 teaspoon garlic powder

Preheat oven to 350 degrees. Place butter in ovenproof baking dish with lid. Heat butter and sauté green onion until golden. Add parsley, thyme, and sage. Sprinkle with salt and pepper; add rice. Pour 2-1/2 cups water over rice and then stir in garlic powder. Bring to a boil for about 45 minutes or until liquid is absorbed and rice is tender.

This rice goes well with turkey, goose, or duck.

Suzan L. Wiener, Spring Hill, Fla.

LASAGNA SURPRISE
Serves 6-8

3/4 cup chopped onion
2 cloves garlic, finely chopped
2 tablespoons vegetable oil
2 (26-ounce) jars prepared spaghetti/pasta sauce or prepare about 2 quarts of your own tomato-based spaghetti/lasagna sauce recipe (add ground meat or sausage, if desired)
1 (15- or 16-ounce) container ricotta or cottage cheese
1 (10-ounce) package frozen chopped spinach, thawed and well-drained
1 pound mozzarella cheese, shredded
1/2 cup grated Parmesan cheese
2 eggs
1 (1-pound) package lasagna noodles, cooked according to package directions

In a large pan, cook onion and garlic in oil. Add prepared pasta sauce. (If you cook your own sauce, it may not be necessary to add more onion and garlic.) Simmer 15 minutes. In bowl, mix ricotta, spinach, and 1 cup mozzarella, all the Parmesan, and eggs. In 15x9-inch baking dish (or smaller dishes as needed), layer 2 cups sauce, half the lasagna, half the remaining sauce, all the spinach mixture, half the mozzarella, remaining lasagna and sauce. Cover; bake at 350 degrees for 45 minutes or until hot. Uncover; top with remaining mozzarella. Bake 15 minutes. Let stand 15 minutes before serving.

PORK PAGODA

1 cup diced cooked pork
1/2 cup sliced celery
1 cup cooked bean sprouts
1/2 cup sliced mushrooms
1/2 cup sliced carrots
1/4 cup sliced green onions
2 tablespoons oil

1 (10-ounce) can condensed cream of asparagas soup
1/4 cup water
2 teaspoons soy sauce
1 (10-ounce) box frozen chopped spinach, thawed and squeezed dry.

In large skillet, sauté pork and all the vegetables in oil until meat is brown and vegetables are tender. Blend in soup, water, soy sauce, and spinach. Heat, stirring occasionally. Serve hot over chow mein noodles. I have substituted beef for the pork and any other creamed soup, also.

Mrs. Laura Hicks, Troy, Mont.

CROWD PLEASER CASSEROLE
Serves 10-12

1 (20-ounce) package frozen broccoli flowerets
1 (20-ounce) package frozen cauliflower flowerets
4 tablespoons butter or margarine
3 tablespoons flour
3 cups milk
6 ounces (or 1-1/2 cups) shredded cheddar cheese
1 cup Parmesan cheese, shredded or grated
1/2 teaspoon salt
3 cups chopped ham
3 cups fresh bread crumbs tossed with 4 tablespoons butter

Cook broccoli and cauliflower in slightly salted water. Cook slightly underdone. Drain; set aside. Melt 4 tablespoons butter in a 1-quart saucepan; add flour; blend well. Add milk, stirring constantly, until thickened. Add cheddar, Parmesan, and salt. Stir over low heat until cheese melts. Place vegetables in an ungreased 4-quart casserole. Sprinkle with chopped ham. Pour cheese sauce mixture over ham. Make a border of buttered bread crumbs around edge of casserole. Bake uncovered at 350 degrees for 30 minutes.

PIZZA CASSEROLE

1/3 cup butter or margarine
1 large onion, finely chopped (about 1-1/2 cups)
2 (8-ounce) cans tomato sauce
1/4 pound mushrooms, sliced (about 1-2/3 cups)
1 large garlic clove, minced
1 teaspoon oregano
1/2 teaspoon dried basil, crumbled
1 (8-ounce) package spaghetti, cooked and drained
1 (4-ounce) package thinly sliced pepperoni
8 ounces mozzarella cheese, grated (about 2 cups)
3-1/2 ounces Swiss cheese, grated (about 1 cup)

Preheat oven to 350 degrees. Lightly grease 9x13-inch baking dish. Melt butter in heavy medium skillet. Add onion and cook over medium-high heat until translucent, about 6 minutes. Remove from skillet and set aside. Combine tomato sauce, mushrooms, garlic, oregano, basil, and onion; mix thoroughly. Arrange spaghetti in bottom of prepared pan. Top with half of tomato sauce mixture; dot with half of pepperoni and sprinkle with half of cheeses. Repeat layering with remaining tomato sauce mixture, pepperoni, and cheeses. May be prepared ahead to this point and refrigerated. Bake until heated through, about 25-30 minutes. Serve immediately.

Sharon Sisson, Longview, Wash.

SPAGHETTI PUFF
Serves 8

1-1/3 cups spaghetti, broken into 1-inch pieces
1 cup milk, scalded
1/4 cup butter, melted
3 egg yolks, beaten
1-1/2 cups cheese, grated
2/3 cup dry bread crumbs
1/4 cup onion, chopped
1 tablespoon parsley, chopped
1 tablespoon pimiento, chopped

1 teaspoon Worcestershire sauce
1/2 teaspoon salt
3 egg whites, stiffly beaten

Cook spaghetti in boiling, salted water and drain thoroughly in strainer. Combine milk and butter; gradually combine with egg yolks. Add spaghetti and remaining ingredients, except egg whites. Mix thoroughly and gently fold in egg whites.

Pour into greased 11-1/2 x 7-1/2 x 1-1/2-inch baking dish. Bake in slow oven, 325 degrees, for 1 hour, or until set.

Garnish with parsley in each corner and serve with green beans and sliced tomatoes. This is a good emergency recipe for one of those times when you haven't had a chance to go to the market. You probably still have all the ingredients on hand.

Eleanor V. Craycraft, Santa Monica, Calif.

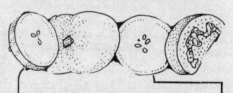

COUNTRY PIE

1/2 of 8-ounce can tomato sauce
1/2 cup bread crumbs
1 pound ground beef
1-1/2 teaspoons salt
1/4 cup chopped onion
1/4 cup chopped bell pepper
1/8 teaspoon oregano
1/8 teaspoon pepper

Combine ingredients and mix well. Pat mixture into 9-inch pie plate and pinch flutings around edges.

Filling:
1-1/4 cups Minute Rice
1-1/2 (8-ounce) cans tomato sauce
1 cup water
1/2 teaspoon salt
1 cup grated cheese

Combine all ingredients, except 1/2 cup grated cheese, which is reserved for topping. Spoon into pie shell. Cover closely with foil and bake 25 minutes at 350 degrees. Uncover; sprinkle with remaining 1/2 cu cheese; return to oven and bake, uncovered, 15 minutes. Serve in wedges.

Sharon McClatchey, Muskogee, Okla.

BAKED STUFFED SHELLS
Serves 6

1/2 (12-ounce size) package jumbo pasta shells
1 (1-pound) carton creamed small-curd cottage cheese
1 (3-ounce) package cream cheese, softened
1 (8-ounce) package shredded mozzarella cheese
1 large egg
1/4 cup packaged plain bread crumbs
1/4 cup chopped parsley
1/2 teaspoon salt
1 (32-ounce) jar spaghetti sauce

In a large pot, cook shells as package directs. In a bowl, combine cottage cheese, cream cheese, half of mozzarella, the egg, bread crumbs, parsley, and salt. Heat oven to 375 degrees. Drain shells. Spoon 1 cup spaghetti sauce into a 13x9x2-inch baking pan. Stuff cheese mixture into shells. Place stuffed shells, filling side up, in baking pan. Spoon remaining spaghetti sauce over shells. Sprinkle with remaining mozzarella cheese. Bake 25 minutes or until hot and bubbly.

Joy Shamway, Freeport, Ill.

PIGS IN THE BLANKET CASSEROLE
Serves 6

1 small head of cabbage
1 pound ground beef
1/2 cup chopped onion
1/2 cup cooked rice
1 can tomato soup
1-1/2 cups water
Salt and pepper to taste
1/4 cup grated cheese

Put a thick layer of cabbage in bottom of casserole. Brown meat and onion; add rice, salt and pepper; place over layer of cabbage. Repeat another layer of cabbage, then meat mixture; pour soup over all; sprinkle top surface with cheese. Bake at 350 degrees for 1-1/2 hours.

Mrs. Merle Mishler, Hollsopple, Pa.

PASTA PRIMAVERA
Makes 4-6 servings

8 ounces uncooked spaghetti
1 cup tender green beans, cut in
  1-inch pieces
2 small zucchini, sliced
2 small yellow squash, sliced
1 cup thinly sliced carrot
1 cup cauliflower flowerets
1 tablespoon olive oil
2 garlic cloves, minced
1/8 teaspoon crushed red pepper
  flakes
1/4 cup chicken broth
1/4 cup lightly packed fresh basil
  leaves, chopped
1/4 cup oil-packed, sun-dried
  tomatoes
3 tablespoons grated Parmesan
  cheese
1/4 cup chopped fresh parsley

Cook spaghetti according to package directions, drain and set aside. Steam vegetables only until crisp-tender, drain and chill. Sauté garlic in olive oil until light brown. Add crushed red pepper, stir; then add chicken broth and simmer 1 minute. Add chopped basil, spaghetti and vegetables; toss. Arrange on platter. Garnish with sun-dried tomatoes, Parmesan cheese and parsley. Serve at room temperature.
***Recipe provided by the courtesy of the National Pasta Association

BAKED MACARONI AND CHEESE WITH SOUR CREAM
Serves 2

3/4 cup macaroni, uncooked
1/3 cup sour cream
1 cup grated sharp Cheddar cheese
1/3 cup milk
Paprika

Preheat oven to 325 degrees. Cook macaroni in boiling, salted water according to package directions until barely tender. Drain well. Return to saucepan. Add sour cream, cheese, and milk; mix well. Turn into a small greased baking dish; sprinkle on paprika. Bake at 325 degrees for about 25 minutes.

HARVEST SWEET POTATO CASSEROLE
Serves 6

1 (23-ounce) can sweet potatoes or
  yams, drained, *or*
1 (18-ounce) can vacuum-packed
  sweet potatoes
7 tablespoons butter, melted
1 apple, cored and thinly sliced

Topping:
1/4 cup firmly packed brown sugar
1 tablespoon all-purpose flour
1/4 teaspoon cardamom
1 tablespoon cold butter
2 tablespoons chopped pecans

Preheat oven to 350 degrees. In 1-quart round casserole, mash sweet potatoes until smooth. Stir in the 7 tablespoons melted butter. In small bowl cut 1 tablespoon cold butter into brown sugar, flour, and cardamom. Stir in pecans and sprinkle one-half of the mixture over potatoes. Arrange apple slices on top. Sprinkle with remaining mixture. Bake for 35-40 minutes or until apples are crisp/tender.

POTATO AND HAM CASSEROLE
Serves 6-8

1 (5-1/2 ounce) package au gratin
  potatoes
2-1/2 cups diced cooked ham
1 cup canned or frozen peas
1 small onion, chopped
1 small green pepper, chopped
1/3 cup chopped celery
1 cup shredded Cheddar cheese

Preheat oven to 400 degrees. Mix potatoes as directed on package in a 2-quart ovenproof dish. Mix together ham, peas, onion, green pepper, celery, and add to casserole. Sprinkle cheese on top.
Bake 30 minutes and serve hot. This is a great dish for working women who have to cook "hurry-up" dinners.
Mrs. H. W. Walker, Richmond, Va.

REUBEN CASSEROLE

1 can corned beef—or 1 pound deli
1/2 cup thousand island dressing
1 can sauerkraut, drained
6 slices rye bread, cut in cubes or
  crumbled
1/2 pound Swiss cheese, grated
1/2 cup margarine, melted

Crumble corned beef into well-greased 12x8-inch glass dish. Spread dressing, then sauerkraut. Cover with cheese. Toss crumbled bread with melted margarine; sprinkle on top. Bake at 350 degrees for 30 minutes or until hot and bubbly.
Laura Morris, Bunnell, Fla.

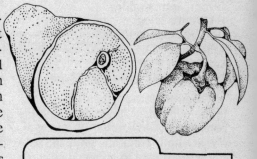

SAUCY SAUSAGE SUPPER
Serves 4

1 (16-ounce) can applesauce (2
  cups)
1 (16-ounce) can sauerkraut,
  drained and snipped (2 cups)
1/3 cup water
2 tablespoons brown sugar, packed
1/2 teaspoon salt
4 small onions, quartered
4 small potatoes, peeled and
  quartered
1 (12-ounce) Polish sausage, cut
  diagonally to desired lengths
Snipped parsley

In a 3-quart saucepan, combine applesauce, sauerkraut, water, brown sugar, and salt; add onions and potatoes. Cover and simmer 20 minutes, stirring occasionally. Add sausage; simmer, covered about 20 minutes longer, stirring occasionally. To serve, spoon sauerkraut mixture onto a platter and top with sausage. Sprinkle with parsley.
Agnes Ward, Erie, Pa.

Cakes
TO BAKE

CREAM CHEESE POUND CAKE

3/4 cup butter or margarine
1 (8-ounce) package cream cheese, room temperature
1-1/2 cups sugar
1-1/2 teaspoons vanilla
4 eggs
1-3/4 cups flour
1-1/2 teaspoons baking powder

Cream butter and cream cheese until light; add sugar gradually, beating constantly. Add vanilla. Beat in eggs, one at a time. Combine flour and baking powder; add to creamed mixture, beating well. Pour into greased 9x5-inch loaf pan. Bake at 350 degrees for 1 hour and 15 minutes or until wooden pick inserted in center comes out clean. Cool in pan 10 minutes. Turn onto a cake rack to cool completely.
Suzanne Dawson, Cypress, Tex.

OATMEAL CAKE

1 cup quick oatmeal
1 1/4 cups boiling water
1 stick butter or margarine
2 eggs, beater
1 cup white sugar
1 cup brown sugar
1 1/2 cups flour
1 teaspoon soda
1 teaspoon cinnamon
1/2 teaspoon salt
1 teaspoon vanilla

Stir together the oatmeal, boiling water and butter until butter melts. Let cool. Add the eggs and beat, then add sugar and beat mixture again. Sift together the flour, soda, cinnamon and salt and add to cake mixture with the vanilla. Beat all well.

Pour into greased and floured 9x13" pan. Bake at 350-degrees for about 32 minutes.

When done and still hot, spread with the following topping. Mix together in heavy pan 3/4 cup brown sugar, 3/4 cup pecan pieces (or other chopped nuts), 6 tablespoons butter and 1/2 cup condensed milk (1/2 cup coconut, optional). Cream and cook until thick (but not too long).Evenly place mixture on cake. Place cake under broiler until topping becomes bubbly.
Karen Shea Fedders, Dameron, Md.

GERMAN CHOCOLATE UPSIDE-DOWN CAKE

1 cup coconut
1 cup chopped pecans
1 oackage German Chocolate cake mix

Mix these two ingredients and put into a greased 9x13-inch pan. Mix 1 package German chocolate cake mix according to directions and pour on top of coconut pecan mixture.

In saucepan put 1 stick margarine and 1 (8-ounce) package cream cheese, softened. Heat until mixture is warm enough to stir in 1-pound box confectioners' sugar. Spoon over top of cake mix. Bake at 350 degrees for 35-40 minutes. Do not cut until cooled.
Hazel C. Jackson, Glade Spring, Va.

PINEAPPLE-ALMOND CREAM CHEESE CAKE
Serves 12

1 (8-ounce) package cream cheese, at room temperature
1/4 pound (1 stick) unsalted butter, at room temperature
1-1/2 cups sugar
2 eggs
1 teaspoon vanilla.
2 cups all-purpose flour
1 teaspoon baking powder
1 teaspoon baking soda
1/4 teaspoon salt
1/4 cup pineapple juice
1 (12-ounce) jar pineapple preserves
1/2 cup slivered almonds

Preheat oven to 350 degrees. In a large mixing bowl, cream together cream cheese, butter, and sugar until light and fluffy. Add eggs, one at a time, beating well after each addition. Stir in vanilla.

Sift together flour, baking powder, baking soda, and salt. Alternately, add flour mixture and pineapple juice to butter mixture. Pour half the batter into a greased 9x13-inch baking dish, spreading evenly. Combine pineapple preserves and almonds; spread evenly over batter. Cover with remaining batter. Bake 45-50 minutes, until a toothpick inserted in center comes out clean. Cut into squares and serve.
Mrs. L. Mayer, Richmond, Va.

GOOEY BUTTER CAKE

1/4 cup sugar
1/4 cup Crisco
1/4 teaspoon salt
1 egg
1 (6-ounce) cake of yeast
1/2 cup warm milk
2-1/2 cups all-purpose flour
1 tablespoon vanilla

Prepare a sweet dough by mixing sugar with Crisco and salt. Add egg and beat with electric mixer one minute until well blended. Dissolve yeast in warm milk. Add flour, then milk/yeast mixture, and vanilla to sweet dough batter. Mix 3 minutes with dough hooks or with hands. Turn dough onto floured board and knead for one minute. Place in a lightly-greased bowl; cover with a towel and let rise in a warm place for 1 hour.

M. Lanff, Philadelphia, Pa.

GOOEY BUTTER CAKE

1 yellow cake mix
4 eggs
1 stick butter, melted
1 pound box powdered sugar
1 (8-ounce) package cream cheese

Mix together the cake mix, 2 eggs, and butter. Spread batter into a 9 x 13 inch greased and floured pan. Batter will be thick. Blend remaining 2 eggs, powdered sugar, and cream cheese. Pour over batter. Bake at 350 degrees for 35 minutes or until top has a brown glaze and pulls from the sides of the pan.

Betty Ireton, Kingston, OH

APPLESAUCE CAKE

1-1/4 cups shortening (Crisco)
3 cups brown sugar
3 eggs
2-1/4 cups applesauce
4-1/2 cups sifted flour
1 teaspoon salt
2-1/4 teaspoons cinnamon
1 teaspoon ground cloves
2-1/4 teaspoons baking soda

Cream shortening, sugar, and eggs. Dissolve soda into the applesauce; add to egg mixture. Sift flour, salt, cinnamon, and cloves; add to egg mixture. Pour into tube pan; bake at 350 degrees for one hour. Let cool five minutes; invert on rack. No icing is needed.

Karin Shea Fedders, Dameron, MD

APPLE POUND CAKE

2 cups unsifted flour
1 teaspoon soda
1 teaspoon salt
1/2 teaspoon nutmeg
2 cups sugar
2 teaspoons vanilla
1 cup chopped pecans or walnuts
1/2 teaspoon cinnamon
1-1/2 cups corn oil
3 eggs
2 cups finely chopped apples
1/2 cup raisins

Preheat oven to 325 degrees. Combine flour, soda, salt, cinnamon, and nutmeg in a large bowl. With electric mixer at medium speed, beat together the oil, sugar, eggs, and vanilla until thoroughly combined. Gradually beat in the flour mixture until smooth. Fold in apples, pecans (or walnuts), and raisins. Turn into greased and floured 10-inch tube pan or bundt pan. Bake at 325 degrees for 1 hour and 15 minutes or until cake tester inserted in center comes out clean. Cool cake in pan on wire rack for 10 minutes, then remove from pan to cool completely. Store in air-tight container.

Mrs. H. W. Walker, Richmond, VA

MAPLE-FLAVORED GINGERBREAD
Serves 16

2-1/2 cups all-purpose flour
1-1/2 teaspoons soda
1 teaspoon ground cinnamon
1 teaspoon ground ginger
1/2 teaspoon ground cloves
1/2 teaspoon salt
1/2 cup shortening
1/2 cup sugar
1 egg
1/2 cup molasses
1/2 cup maple-flavored syrup
1 cup hot water
Whipped cream

Combine flour, soda, spices, and salt; set aside. Cream shortening and sugar until light and fluffy. Add egg, beating well. Gradually beat in molasses and syrup. Add dry ingredients alternately with hot water, beating well after each addition. Pour batter into greased 13 x 9 x 2 inch pan. Bake at 350 degrees for 30 minutes or until done. Cool thoroughly in pan. Serve with whipped cream.

Barbara Beauregard-Smith, Northfield, S. A. Australia

ONE-BOWL CHOCOLATE CAKE

Sift into large bowl:
3-1/2 cups flour
2 cups sugar
5 tablespoons cocoa
1 teaspoon cinnamon
2 teaspoons baking soda
1 teaspoon salt

To these 6 ingredients add:
1 cup cooking oil
2 teaspoons vinegar
2 teaspoons vanilla
2 cups water

Beat well. Pour into ungreased 9 x 13 inch pan. Bake at 350 degrees for 35-45 minutes. This is a very moist cake, easy to make, and no eggs needed.

Tom McNiel, Constantine, MI

$175,000 CAKE

Bottom Layer:
1 German chocolate cake mix
1 egg
1 stick butter

Middle Layer:
1 (12-ounce) package chocolate chips
1 cup chopped nuts

Top Layer:
1 (8-ounce) package cream cheese, softened
2 eggs
1 pound confectioners' sugar

Combine cake mix, egg, and butter. Press mixture into 9 x 13 inch pan. Sprinkle with chips and nuts for middle layer. For top layer, cream together cheese, eggs, and confectioners' sugar. Pour over chips and nuts.

Bake 350 degrees for 40-45 minutes. Cool 2 hours.

Mrs. Tom McNiel, Constantine, MI

BANANA CAKE

2-1/2 cups sifted flour
1-1/4 teaspoons baking powder
1 teaspoon salt
1/3 cup buttermilk
1-1/4 cups bananas (3 large)
Chopped nuts (optional)
1-2/3 cups granulated sugar
1-1/4 teaspoons baking soda
2/3 cup shortening
1/2 cup eggs (2 large)
Another 1/3 cup buttermilk

Preheat oven to 350 degrees. Grease and flour two 8-inch cake pans or one 13 x 9 x 2-inch pan. Cream sugar and shortening. Blend in eggs. Add sifted dry ingredients, alternately with first 1/3 cup buttermilk. Mash bananas and add along with remaining milk and nuts, if desired; mix. Bake at 350 degrees for approximately 30-40 minutes.

Sylvia K. Miller, Bechtelsville, PA

TOASTED BUTTER PECAN CAKE
Serves 12-16

2 cups chopped pecans
1/2 pound, plus 4 tablespoons butter
3 cups sifted flour
2 teaspoons baking powder
1 teaspoon salt
2 cups granulated sugar
4 eggs
1 cup milk
2 teaspoons vanilla extract
Toasted Butter Pecan Frosting (recipe follows)

Toast pecans in 4 tablespoons butter in 350-degree oven for 20-25 minutes, stirring frequently. Sift together flour, baking powder, and salt. Cream 1/2 pound butter; gradually add sugar, creaming well. Blend in eggs, one at a time, beating well after each. Add dry ingredients, alternately with milk, beginning and ending with flour. Blend well; add vanilla and 1-1/3 cups pecans. Pour batter into 3 greased, floured 8- or 9-inch round pans and bake at 350 degrees for 25-30 minutes. Cool. Prepare frosting.

Toasted Butter Pecan Frosting:
4 tablespoons butter
4 cups confectioners' sugar
1 teaspoon vanilla extract
1-2/3 tablespoons evaporated milk
2/3 cup of reserved, toasted pecans

Cream butter, then blend in confectioners' sugar, vanilla, and evaporated milk until frosting is of spreading consistency. Stir in reserved pecans. Spread over tops and sides of the three cooled layers.

Agnes Ward, Erie, PA

ORANGE-NUT CAKE

1 (6-ounce) can (3/4 cup) frozen orange juice concentrate, thawed
2 cups all-purpose flour, sifted
1 cup sugar
1 teaspoon soda
1 teaspoon salt
1/2 cup margarine or butter
1/2 cup milk
2 eggs
1 cup raisins
1/2 cup chopped walnuts or pecans

Preheat oven to 350 degrees. Grease and flour bottom of 13 x 9-inch pan. Combine 1/2 cup orange juice concentrate with remaining ingredients in large mixer bowl. Blend at lowest speed for 30 seconds. Beat 3 minutes at medium speed. Pour into pan. Bake at 350 degrees for 40-45 minutes, until cake is browned and tests done in middle. Remove from oven. Drizzle remaining orange juice concentrate over warm cake; sprinkle with topping.

Sugar-Nut Topping:
1/3 cup sugar
1/2 cup chopped walnuts or pecans
1 teaspoon cinnamon

Thoroughly combine all ingredients in small bowl and sprinkle evenly over drizzled cake. Cut into squares to serve. Serve warm or cold.

Mrs. L. Mayer, Richmond, VA

CHERRY CAKE

2 cups sugar
3/4 cup shortening
3 eggs, beaten
1/2 cup milk
3 cups all-purpose flour
1 teaspoon soda
1 teaspoon salt
1 teaspoon cinnamon
1/2 teaspoon nutmeg
1/4 teaspoon cloves
1 cup raisins
1 cup nut meats
1 quart Royal Ann cherries
1 teaspoon lemon extract

Cream sugar and shortening; add eggs. Add sifted dry ingredients, alternately with milk. Add lemon extract. Stir in nuts and fruit. Bake in large loaf pan at 350 degrees until it tests done.

Fay A. Duman, Eugene, OR

CREAM-FILLED RASPBERRY ROLL

3 eggs
1 cup granulated sugar
1/3 cup water
1 teaspoon vanilla
1 cup cake flour or 3/4 cup all-purpose flour
1 teaspoon baking powder
1/4 teaspoon salt
1/2 cup raspberry jelly, plus 1/3 cup for top of cake
Fluffy White Frosting (recipe follows)
Coconut
1 tablespoon raspberry gelatin powder

Heat oven to 375 degrees. Line jelly roll pan, 15x10x1-inch, with waxed paper; grease. Beat eggs in small mixer bowl on high speed until very thick and lemon colored, 3-5 minutes. Pour eggs into large mixing bowl; gradually beat in granulated sugar. On low speed, blend in water and vanilla. Gradually add flour, baking powder, and salt, beating just until batter is smooth. Pour into pan, spreading batter to corners. Bake until wooden pick inserted into center comes out clean, 12-15 minutes. Loosen cake from edges of pan; immediately invert onto towel generously sprinkled with powdered sugar. Carefully remove wax paper; trim stiff edges of cake, if necessary. While hot, roll cake and towel from narrow end. Cool on wire rack at least 30 minutes.

Unroll cake; remove towel. Beat jelly with fork just enough to soften; spread over cake. Carefully spread a layer of Fluffy White Frosting over jelly; roll up. Place coconut in a small jar (about 2/3 cup) with 1 tablespoon gelatin powder and shake to color coconut. Spread about 1/3 cup jelly over rolled up jelly roll and sprinkle coconut on top.

Fluffy White Frosting:
1/2 cup sugar
1/2 stick butter or margarine
1/2 cup shortening
1-1/2 tablespoons flour
1/3 cup warm milk (barely heated)
1 teaspoon vanilla

Cream sugar, butter, and shortening. Add flour, and gradually add milk and vanilla. Beat until thick. Has consistency of whipped cream.
Geneva Cullop, Ceres, Va.

COCONUT POUND CAKE

1 cup butter, softened
3 cups sugar
6 large eggs
3 cups all-purpose flour
1/4 teaspoon soda
1/4 teaspoon salt
8 ounces sour cream
1 cup frozen coconut, thawed
1 teaspoon vanilla
1 teaspoon coconut extract

Cream butter and add sugar. Beat until mix is light and fluffy. Add eggs, one at a time, beating well after each addition. Mix together flour, soda, salt; add flour mixture alternately with sour cream to creamed mixture, beginning and ending with flour. Stir in coconut and flavorings last. Grease and flour 10-inch tube pan. Bake at 350 degrees for 1 hour and 15 minutes. Remove from pan; cool completely; dust with powdered sugar. If you like pound cake you will love this!!

Renee Dennis Wells, Columbia, S.C.

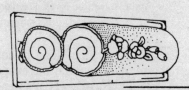

PINK AND PRETTY VALENTINE CAKE
(Serves 20)

1 cup sugar
3/4 cup butter or margarine, softened
2-1/3 cups cake flour
3/4 cup milk
2-1/2 teaspoons baking powder
1 teaspoon vanilla
3 eggs
1/2 teaspoon salt
Buttercream Frosting (recipe follows)
Chocolate Hearts (recipe follows)

1 cup raspberry preserves
3 tablespoons orange juice
Red food coloring

Preheat oven to 350 degrees. Grease and flour 10-inch springform pan. In large bowl, with mixer at high speed, beat sugar and butter until fluffy. At low speed, beat in flour, milk, baking powder, vanilla, eggs, and 1/2 teaspoon salt until blended. Beat 1 minute at medium speed. Spoon batter into pan. Bake 45 minutes or until toothpick inserted in center comes out clean. Cool in pan on rack 10 minutes. Remove side of pan. Cool completely.

Prepare Buttercream Frosting and Chocolate Hearts. Place raspberry preserves in bowl. Stir in orange juice.

Remove cake from pan bottom. Cut into 3 layers. Place 1 layer on cake plate. Spread with half of raspberry mixture. Top with another layer. Spread with remaining raspberry mixture. Top with remaining layer. Spread top and side of cake with about 2 cups frosting. Add coloring to remaining buttercream to tint pink. Place about 1/2 cup of pink buttercream in decorating bag with small writing tube. Use to pipe lattice on top of cake. Use remaining buttercream to pipe border around top and bottom of cake and decorate side. Attach chocolate hearts. Refrigerate.

Buttercream Frosting:
3 cups confectioners' sugar
1-1/2 cups butter or margarine, softened
4 egg yolks

In large bowl with mixer at low speed, beat sugar and softened butter until mixed. At high speed beat until fluffy. At medium speed beat in 4 egg yolks.

Chocolate Hearts:
1/4 cup semi-sweet chocolate pieces, melted

Spread chocolate pieces, melted, into 4x3-inch rectangle on waxed paper-lined cookie sheet. Refrigerate until firm. With heart-shaped cookie cutter, cut chocolate into hearts. Refrigerate.

PINEAPPLE UPSIDE DOWN CAKE ROLL

3 tablespoons margarine
3/4 cup brown sugar
1 (20-ounce) can crushed pineapple, drained
1/4 cup maraschino cherries, chopped and drained
3 eggs, room temperature
3/4 cup sugar
3 tablespoons orange juice
1 teaspoon vanilla
3/4 cup flour, sifted
1 teaspoon baking powder
1/2 teaspoon salt

Preheat oven to 375 degrees. Melt margarine in a 15x10 inch jelly roll pan. Sprinkle brown sugar over margarine. Cover with pineapple and cherries. Beat eggs until fluffy. Beat in sugar, a little at a time; blend well. Add juice and vanilla; beat. Sift flour, baking powder, and salt together. Fold in carefully by hand. Pour into pan, covering pineapple mixture. Bake 15 minutes. Turn out onto towel that has been dusted with confectioners' sugar. Roll up jelly roll style; cool in towel.

Mrs. E. Bartels, Howard Beach, N.Y.

POUND CAKE HEARTS

1 (10-1/4 or 16-ounce) prepared pound cake cut into 1/2-inch slices
3 (1-ounce) squares semisweet chocolate
1 tablespoon butter or margarine
1/4 teaspoon almond or vanilla extract

Cut cake into 1/2-inch slices. Using 2-inch heart-shaped cutter, cut one heart out of each slice. Set cake scraps aside for other use. In small heavy saucepan over very low heat, melt chocolate and butter, stirring frequently until blended and smooth. Remove from heat. Stir in flavoring. Dip one side of each pound cake heart into melted chocolate mixture. Use small metal spatula to smooth chocolate. Place hearts on wire rack about 15 minutes until chocolate is set.

NUTTY LEMON CAKE

3/4 cup softened butter or margarine
1-1/4 cups sugar
3 eggs
2-3/4 cups flour
1 teaspoon baking soda
1 cup undiluted evaporated milk
3 tablespoons lemon juice
1 cup chopped nuts
2 tablespoons freshly grated lemon rind
Chopped black walnuts
Shredded lemon rind
Icing (recipe follows)

Cream butter; gradually beat in sugar. Beat in eggs, one at a time. Stir together flour, baking powder, and baking soda. Combine evaporated milk and lemon juice. Alternately, add dry ingredients and evaporated milk mixture to butter mixture; beat until smooth. Stir in nuts and rind. Spoon into lightly greased 10 inch tube pan. Bake in slow oven of 325 degrees for 50-60 minutes or until toothpick inserted in center comes out clean. Cool 20 minutes in pan. Remove; cool completely. Drizzle with icing; sprinkle with nuts and shredded lemon rind.

Icing:
Stir together 1 cup powdered sugar and about 4 teaspoons lemon juice. Stir to a thick consistency.

Nina G. Hutton, Nashville, Tenn.

OLD FASHION CARROT CAKE

Serves 8

2 eggs
1/2 cup maple syrup
3/4 cup oil
1/2 cup dairy yogurt
3/4 cup sunflower seeds (shelled)
1-1/2 cups grated raw carrots, packed tightly
1/4 cup raisins
1/4 cup cashew nuts, chopped
1-1/4 cups whole wheat flour
1 teaspoon salt
1 teaspoon baking soda
1 teaspoon baking powder
1 tablespoon cinnamon
1 tablespoon nutmeg

Preheat oven to 300 degrees. Beat eggs and add maple syrup, oil, and yogurt. Blend well; then stir in seeds, nuts, raisins, and carrots. In another bowl, sift together flour, salt, baking soda, baking powder, cinnamon, and nutmeg. Fold these dry ingredients into carrot mixture. Blend well, but *do not beat*. Pour into greased 8x8 inch pan; bake for 1 hour. Remove from oven and cool in pan, until edges separate from sides. Turn out onto a rack and cool well before serving.

This recipe may be doubled and frozen.

Marie Fusaro, Manasquan, N.J.

CHOCOLATE CHERRY UPSIDE DOWN CAKE

1 (21-ounce) can cherry pie filling
2-1/4 cups all-purpose flour
1-1/2 cups sugar
3/4 cup unsweetened cocoa powder
1-1/2 teaspoons baking soda
3/4 teaspoon salt
1-1/2 cups water
1/4 cup cooking oil
1/4 cup vinegar
1-1/2 teaspoons vanilla

Spread cherry pie filling evenly over bottom of greased 13x9x2-inch pan. In large bowl, stir flour with sugar, cocoa, soda, and salt. In another bowl, combine water, oil, vinegar, and vanilla. Add liquid to dry mixture, all at once. Stir, just to moisten. Pour batter evenly in pan over cherry filling.

Bake in preheated 350 degree oven for 30-35 minutes. Cool 10 minutes in pan; invert onto plate and cool.

Corena J. Bennington, Whitestown, Ind.

COOKIE CRUST CRUNCH CAKE
(Makes 2 loaf cakes)

2-1/4 cups vanilla wafer crumbs
1-1/4 cups pecans, finely chopped
1/2 cup sugar
1/2 stick butter or margarine
1 (18-1/4-ounce) box yellow cake mix
3 large eggs
1 stick butter or margarine, softened
1 tablespoon orange extract
2/3 cup water

Combine vanilla wafer crumbs, pecans, and sugar in bowl. Add 1/4 cup butter; cut in until crumbs are fine. Divide evenly into 2 greased 9x5x3-inch loaf pans. In a large mixer bowl, combine cake mix, eggs, 1/2 cup butter, orange extract, and water. Mix cake as directed on package; divide batter evenly into pans. Bake at 350 degrees for 60 minutes or until tested done in center of cake. Cool in pans on rack 5 minutes; loosen cake from pans; turn upside down on rack; cool completely. These loaves freeze nicely.
Gwen Campbell, Sterling, Va.

ANGEL RIPPLE CAKE
(from prepared mix)
Serves 12-16

1 package angel food cake mix
1 tablespoon ground cinnamon

Cinnamon Cream Sauce:
3/4 cup whipping cream
1/2 cup milk
1/3 cup confectioner's sugar
1 teaspoon vanilla
1/2 teaspoon ground cinnamon

Preheat oven to 375-degrees. Mix cake as directed on package. Spoon 1/4 of batter into an ungreased 10-inch tube pan and spread evenly. With a fine small sieve, sprinkle 1/3 of cinnamon over batter. Repeat layering 2 or 3 times ending with cake batter. Bake and cool as directed.

For sauce, mix cream and milk in a chilled bowl. Beat with chilled beaters until thick. Blend in confectioner's sugar, vanilla and cinnamon. Serve sauce over cake slices.

EASTER RING CAKE

2 cups sifted flour
1-1/4 cups sugar
3 teaspoons baking powder
1 teaspoon baking soda
1/2 teaspoon salt
1/2 cup shortening
2/3 cup orange juice
1 cup sugar
2 eggs
1/4 cup sweet orange marmalade
Lemon Butter Fluff Icing (recipe follows)

Sift together flour, sugar, baking powder, soda, and salt; blend in shortening and 2/3 cup orange juice. Beat 2 minutes at medium speed of electric mixer. Blend in remaining orange juice with eggs, beat at medium speed 2 minutes. Fold in orange marmalade and turn into greased and lightly floured 9 inch tube pan. Bake in a 350 degree oven for 50-55 minutes or until tests done. Cool completely before removing from pan. Frost with Lemon Butter Fluff Icing, and decorate with flowers.

Lemon Butter Fluff Icing:
1 (3-ounce) package cream cheese
2 tablespoons cream
1/2 cup soft butter
4 cups powdered sugar
1 tablespoon lemon juice
2-3 teaspoons grated lemon rind
1 teaspoon vanilla

Soften cream cheese to room temperature; blend in cream and butter. Beat until soft and smooth. Gradually blend in powdered sugar, lemon juice, rind, and vanilla. Beat until light and fluffy. Tint mixture a delicate color, if desired.
NOTE: A bouquet of real spring flowers placed in center of this ring cake is a delightful touch.
Leona Teodori, Warren, Mich.

ANGEL CAKE DELIGHT
Serves 24

1 (20-ounce) can crushed pineapple
1 large angel food cake
8 cups prepared Dream Whip (may substitute Cool Whip)
2 envelopes Knox unflavored gelatin
3 tablespoons lemon juice
1 cup white granulated sugar
1 cup coconut

Pour four tablespoons cold water over gelatin. Stir and add 1 cup boiling water. Add pineapple, lemon juice, and sugar. Let stand until chilled. Prepare Dream Whip, or use Cool Whip. Mix with gelatin mixture. Add coconut. Pinch cake in fine pieces. Prepare cake, alternating with a layer of cake crumbs and a layer of Dream Whip mixture—ending with Dream Whip mixture. Chill. This cake keeps very well when prepared and stored in a lid-covered cake tray.
Great recipe for a party, a family gathering, or anytime!
Faye Wilson, Maysville, Ky.

ORANGE PEANUT BUTTER CAKE

2 oranges
1 package yellow cake mix (with or without pudding)
1-1/4 cups water
3 eggs
1/2 cup peanut butter (smooth or chunky)
1 teaspoon ground cinnamon
1/3 cup packed brown sugar

Grate peel from oranges; reserve. Peel oranges and cut into bite size pieces; drain well. In large bowl, combine cake mix, water, eggs, peanut butter, and cinnamon; beat according to package directions. Stir in orange pieces and peel. Pour batter into a greased and floured 13x9 inch cake pan. Sprinkle brown sugar over top. Bake 350 degrees for 35-40 minutes. Serve warm.
Mrs. Kit Rollins, Cedarburg, Wis.

JELLY BEAN CONFETTI CAKE

2 cups all-purpose flour
3/4 cup miniature jelly beans, cut in half (not licorice)
1 cup sugar
1 cup butter or margarine, softened
1 (8-ounce) package cream cheese, softened
1 teaspoon vanilla
3 eggs
1-1/2 teaspoons baking powder
1/4 teaspoon salt
Confectioners' sugar

Heat oven to 325 degrees. Generously grease and flour 12-cup fluted tube pan or angel-cake pan. Lightly spoon flour into measuring cup. Level off. In small bowl, toss jelly beans with 2 tablespoons of the flour. Set aside.

In large bowl, beat sugar, butter, cream cheese, and vanilla until well blended. Add eggs one at a time, beating well after each addition. Add remaining flour, baking powder, and salt. Blend well. Spoon 1 cup of batter evenly over bottom of prepared pan. Stir jelly beans into remaining batter; spoon into baking pan. Bake in a 325 degree oven for 50 to 60 minutes, or until toothpick inserted in center of cake comes out clean. Cool upright in pan 10 minutes. Invert on serving plate. Cool completely. Sprinkle with confectioners' sugar.

MOCK CRAB CAKES

2 cups zucchini squash, peeled and grated
1 cup seasoned bread crumbs
1 teaspoon Old Bay seasoning
1 egg, well beaten
1 tablespoon mayonnaise
Butter flavored Crisco

Mix all ingredients together. Form mixture into individual serving patties, then roll in bread crumbs. Fry patties in butter flavored Crisco until crispy and golden brown.
Peggy Fowler Revels, Woodruff, S.C.

APPLE CAKE WITH NUT TOPPING

3/4 cup cooking oil
2 cups sugar
2 eggs, beaten
3 cups flour
1-1/2 teaspoons soda
1 teaspoon salt
1 teaspoon vanilla
1 cup chopped walnuts
3 cups chopped apples (with peelings)

Mix oil, sugar, and eggs and blend well. Add dry ingredients and vanilla by hand. Blend in nuts and apples. Spoon batter into a well-greased tube or bundt pan. Bake at 350 degrees for 1 hour. Remove from oven and pour topping over cake. Return cake to oven and bake 15 minutes more. Cool on wire rack. Slide knife around cake to loosen.

Topping:
1 cup light brown sugar
1 stick butter or margarine
1/4 cup orange juice
Cook over low heat for 3 minutes after the mixture starts boiling. Pour over cake and continue as directed.
Mrs. P. B. Brothers, Richmond, Va.

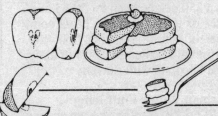

SOUR CREAM DEVILS FOOD CAKE

2 cups sour cream
2 teaspoons soda
4 eggs
1 teaspoon vanilla
2 cups sugar
2 cups flour
6 tablespoons cocoa

Beat sour cream, soda, eggs, and vanilla until foamy; add sugar, flour, and cocoa that has been sifted together. Pour into a greased and floured pan. Bake at 350 degrees for 30 minutes. Frost with your favorite frosting.
Mildred Sherrer, Bay City, Texas

CREAM CHEESE POUND CAKE

3/4 cup butter or margarine
1 (8-ounce) package cream cheese, room temperature
1-1/2 cups sugar
1-1/2 teaspoons vanilla
4 eggs
1-3/4 cups flour
1-1/2 teaspoons baking powder

Cream butter and cream cheese until light; add sugar gradually, beating constantly. Add vanilla. Beat in eggs, one at a time. Combine flour and baking powder; add to creamed mixture, beating well. Pour into greased 9x5-inch loaf pan. Bake at 350 degrees for 1 hour and 15 minutes or until wooden pick inserted in center comes out clean. Cool in pan 10 minutes. Turn onto a cake rack to cool completely.
Suzanne Dawson, Cypress, Tex.

RHUBARB CAKE

1-1/2 cups brown sugar
1/2 cup shortening
1 egg
1 teaspoon vanilla
2 cups flour
1 teaspoon soda
1/2 teaspoon salt
1 cup buttermilk or sour cream
1-3/4 cups chopped rhubarb, may use frozen
1/2 cup chocolate chips

Topping:
1/2 cup brown sugar
1 teaspoon cinnamon
1/2 cup chopped nuts
1/2 cup chocolate chips

Cream 1-1/2 cups brown sugar, 1/2 cup shortening; add egg and vanilla. Combine flour, soda, and salt together. Add flour mixture, alternating with buttermilk, beating after each addition. Stir in rhubarb and chocolate chips. Pour into greased 9x13-inch pan. Combine topping and sprinkle over cake mixture. Bake at 350 degrees for 45 minutes.

This is a delicious cake. Serve with ice cream, whipped cream, or just plain. You will get raving reviews.
Roselyn Finan, Fort Wayne, Ind.

SWISS CHOCOLATE CAKE

1 (6-ounce) package (1 cup) semi-
  sweet chocolate morsels
1/4 cup water
2-1/4 cups sifted flour
1 teaspoon baking soda
3/4 teaspoon salt
1-3/4 cups sugar
3/4 cup soft butter or margarine
1 teaspoon vanilla
3 eggs
1 cup buttermilk

Preheat oven to 375 degrees. Combine chocolate morsels and water; stir over low heat, until well blended. Sift together flour, baking soda, and salt; set aside.

Combine sugar, butter, and vanilla; beat until creamy. Beat in eggs, one at a time. Blend in semi-sweet chocolate mixture. Stir in, alternately in small amounts, the flour mixture and buttermilk. Pour into 3 greased and floured 8- or 9-inch layer cake pans. Bake at 375 degrees for 25-30 minutes. Cool. Frost with Creamy Chocolate Frosting (recipe follows).

Creamy Chocolate Frosting:

1 (8-ounce) package cream cheese,
  softened
1/3 cup soft butter or regular
  margarine
6 cups confectioners' sugar
1 cup cocoa
1/2 cup light cream

Cream together cream cheese and butter. Sift together confectioners' sugar and cocoa. Add to creamed mixture alternately with 1/2 cup light cream, blending well after each addition.

Note: This is my favorite chocolate cake recipe. It is a light chocolate cake (milk chocolate).

Barbara Beauregard-Smith, Northfield, S.A. Australia

EASY CARROT CAKE

4 eggs
2 cups flour
2 cups sugar
1 teaspoon salt
2 teaspoons soda
1-1/4 teaspoons cinnamon
1/4 cup salad oil
2 large jars baby food carrots

Place all ingredients in bowl. Beat until well combined. Pour into a 9x13-inch pan. Bake in preheated oven at 350 degrees for 25 minutes. Cool and remove from pan.

Frosting:

1 (3-ounce) package cream
  cheese, softened
1/4 cup margarine, softened
2 cups powdered sugar
1/2 cup chopped nuts

Place all ingredients in a large bowl and blend 3-4 minutes. Spread on cooled cake.

Doris Williams, Little Rock, Ark.

MAKE AHEAD UP-SIDE-DOWN CAKE

1/4 cup butter
1/2 cup brown sugar, packed
1 (16- or 17-ounce) can sliced
  peaches, drained
Maraschino cherries, cut in halves
1/4 cup nuts, chopped

Melt butter in 9- or 10-inch cake pan. Sprinkle sugar evenly over butter. Arrange peach slices and cherries in attractive pattern on top of sugar; sprinkle with nuts.

Cake Batter:

1-1/2 cups sifted cake flour
1 cup sugar
2 teaspoons baking powder
1/3 cup soft shortening
2/3 cup milk
1 teaspoon vanilla
1 egg

Sift dry ingredients together into bowl; add remaining ingredients except egg, and beat 2 minutes. Add egg and beat 2 additional minutes. Pour batter over fruit and bake 40-50 minutes in moderate 350 degree oven. Immediately turn upside-down on serving platter.

The positive reception of this masterpiece is most rewarding!!

Karin Shea Fedders, Dameron, Md.

SPICED CHOCOLATE CAKE

4 (1-ounce) squares unsweetened
  chocolate
2/3 cup shortening
2 cups sifted all-purpose flour
2 cups sugar
1 teaspoon baking powder
1 teaspoon soda
1 teaspoon salt
1 teaspoon cloves
1 teaspoon cinnamon
1 teaspoon instant coffee
1 cup buttermilk
1/2 cup buttermilk
3 eggs
1 teaspoon vanilla

Melt chocolate; set aside to cool. Stir shortening to soften. Sift in flour, sugar, baking powder, soda, salt, cloves, cinnamon and coffee. Add 1 cup buttermilk and mix until flour is dampened. Beat vigorously 2 minutes. Stir in 1/2 cup buttermilk, eggs, chocolate and vanilla. Beat 2 minutes longer. Pour into greased and floured 13x9x2 inch baking dish. Bake in moderate oven, 350 degrees for 40 minutes or until done. Cool; frost with 7-minute frosting.

Susan L. Wiener, Spring Hill, Fla.

NO EGG, MILK, OR BUTTER CAKE

1-1/4 cups brown sugar
1-1/4 cups vegetable oil
1/4 teaspoon salt
1-1/2 cups dark seedless raisins
1 teaspoon cinnamon
1/4 teaspoon nutmeg
1/2 teaspoon cloves
1 cup hot water
1/2 teaspoon baking soda
3 cups all-purpose flour

Combine first 8 ingredients; reserve 1 teaspoon hot water. Cook over medium heat to boiling point, stirring constantly. Remove from heat; cool completely. Dissolve soda in remaining teaspoon hot water. Add to mixture with flour; stir until well blended; turn into loaf pan. Bake 325 degrees for 45 minutes. Turn out of baking pan; cool on rack; slice thinly.

Gwen Campbell, Sterling, Va.

LEMON PUDDING CAKE

1 package white or yellow cake mix
1 package instant lemon pudding
3/4 cup vegetable oil
3/4 cup water
4 eggs
2 cups powdered sugar
3/4 cup orange juice
2 tablespoons melted butter
2 tablespoons water

In a large bowl, combine the cake mix, pudding mix, oil, and 3/4 cup water. Beat with electric mixer at medium speed for 2 minutes. Add eggs, one at a time, beating well after each addition. Pour into a greased and floured 9x13-inch pan and bake at 350 degrees for 35-40 minutes.

While cake is baking, mix powdered sugar, orange juice, butter, and 2 tablespoons water; mix well. When cake is done, take a serving fork and poke holes all over top of cake. Pour sugar-orange juice mixture over cake before it cools. Refrigerate before serving. May be garnished with Cool Whip.

Irene Donner, Jamestown, N.Y.

LEMON CAKE

1 box yellow cake mix
1 (3-ounce) box lemon gelatin
3/4 cup oil
3/4 cup water
2 eggs

Mix all ingredients well and pour into a greased 13x9-inch baking pan. Bake at 350 degrees for 40 minutes. Remove and punch holes all over top with a meat knife.

Glaze:

2 cups powdered sugar
2 tablespoons boiling water
2 tablespoons margarine
1/4 cup lemon juice

Mix all ingredients well, and spread over cake. Chill 2 hours before serving.

Lou Henri Baker, Killuck, Ohio

BEST BANANA CAKE

1/2 cup butter
1-1/2 cups sugar
2 large eggs
2 cups sifted flour
2 teaspoons baking powder
3/4 teaspoon soda
1/2 teaspoon salt
1/4 cup sour milk or buttermilk
1 teaspoon vanilla
1 cup mashed bananas

Cream together butter and sugar until light and fluffy; beat eggs lightly and add to creamed mixture. Sift together dry ingredients and add alternately with sour milk, beginning and ending with flour. Add vanilla, mixing thoroughly. Fold in bananas, stirring well. Pour into two greased and floured 9-inch layer pans or 1 (9-inch) tube pan and bake in preheated 350 degree oven for 50 minutes. Fill between layers and top with sliced bananas and sweetened whipped cream.

Agnes Ward, Erie, Pa.

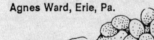

EASTER SPECIAL CAKE

1/2 cup Crisco
2 sticks margarine
2-3/4 cups sugar
6 eggs
3-1/4 cups unsifted flour
1 teaspoon baking powder
1/4 cup milk
3/4 cup undrained crushed pineapple
1 cup shredded coconut
1 cup chopped pecans
1 teaspoon vanilla

Cream Crisco, margarine, and sugar. Add eggs; mix well. Combine sifted flour with baking powder. Combine mixtures, alternating with milk. Stir in pineapple, coconut, pecans, and vanilla; blend well. Pour into bundt or tube pan. Bake at 325 degrees for 1-1/2 hours.

My family loves this cake at Easter. It is so fresh and delicious—like springtime!!

Muriel Cregger, Draper, Va.

OLD FASHIONED PEACH CAKE

1 package yellow cake mix
1 can peach pie filling
3 eggs
1/2 teaspoon lemon extract
1/2 cup chopped nuts

In a large bowl, combine dry cake mix, pie filling, eggs, 1/2 teaspoon extract, and nuts. Blend at low speed of electric mixer until completely moistened, about 1 minute. Beat 2 minutes at medium speed. Spread batter in a greased and floured 13x9x2-inch pan.

Topping:

In a medium bowl combine 1/2 cup sugar, 1/2 teaspoon lemon extract. Stir with a fork. Mixture will be crumbly. Sprinkle over cake batter. Bake for 40-45 minutes at 350 degrees.

Sharon M. Crider, Evansville, Wisc.

BANANA-CHOCOLATE CAKE

Makes 2 (9-inch) layers

2-1/4 cups sifted cake flour
1 teaspoon baking powder
3/4 teaspoon baking soda
1 teaspoon salt
2/3 cup shortening
1-1/2 cups sugar
1 teaspoon vanilla
2 eggs
2 ounces unsweetened chocolate, melted
1 cup mashed bananas
1/2 cup buttermilk

Sift together first 4 ingredients. Cream shortening, sugar, and vanilla together until fluffy. Add eggs, one at a time, beating well after each addition. Blend in chocolate. Add dry ingredients alternately with bananas and milk, beating until well-blended. Turn into greased layer pans and bake at 350 degrees for 30-40 minutes. Fill and frost cooled cakes with a butter frosting.

Agnes Ward, Erie, Pa.

Cookies
& BARS

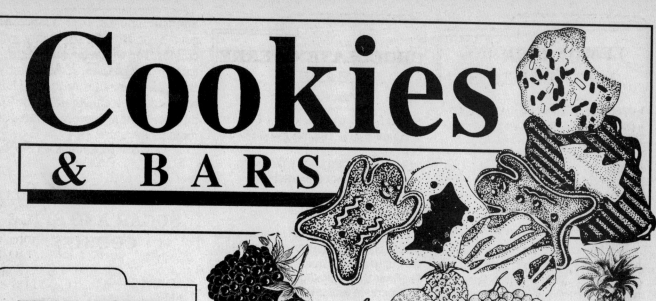

WRAP-AROUND CHERRY COOKIES

2 tablespoons white sugar
5 tablespoons powdered sugar
1/2 cup butter
1 cup all-purpose flour
Maraschino cherries

Mix together all ingredients, except cherries; wrap small amount of dough around well-drained maraschino cherries. Bake at 350 degrees for 12-15 minutes. Remove from pan; cool on rack. Use cherry juice to make powdered sugar icing or glaze.
Gwen Campbell, Sterling, Va.

PINEAPPLE COOKIES

1/2 cup shortening
1 cup sugar
1 egg
2 cups flour
1 teaspoon baking powder
1 teaspoon baking soda
1/2 cup raisins
1/2 cup chopped walnuts
1/2 cup crushed pineapple, drained
1 teaspoon vanilla

Cream together margarine and sugar; add egg and pineapple. Add dry ingredients, alternately, with pineapple and shortening mixture. Mix well; add vanilla. Drop by spoonfuls on greased cookie sheet. Bake at 375 degrees for 15 minutes or until done.

Judy Roberts, Bellingham, WA

CHOCOLATE SURPRISE COOKIES
Makes 4 dozen

1/2 cup butter or margarine
1/2 cup peanut butter
1-1/4 cups sugar
2 eggs
1-1/2 teaspoons vanilla
1/3 cup milk
2 cups all-purpose flour
1/2 cup cocoa
2 teaspoons baking powder
1/2 teaspoon salt

Cream together butter, peanut butter, and sugar. Add eggs, vanilla, and milk. Beat well. Mix flour, cocoa, baking powder, and salt with the creamed mixture. Drop by teaspoonfuls onto ungreased cookie sheet. Bake in a 375 degree oven for 8 minutes. Remove from oven and drop one miniature marshmallow in center of each cookie. Return to oven for 3-4 minutes.

Icing for cookies:
1/3 cup cocoa
1/3 cup hot coffee
1/3 cup butter or margarine
1 teaspoon vanilla
3 cups powdered sugar

Blend ingredients. Spread icing on cooled cookies.

Ann Norman, Chrisman, IL

MARSHMALLOW BANANA BARS

1-1/2 cups sifted flour
1 teaspoon baking powder
1/2 cup shortening
1 cup sugar
1 egg
1 teaspoon baking soda (dissolved in 1 tablespoon water)
1 teaspoon vanilla
1-1/3 cups mashed bananas
1 (7-ounce) jar marshmallow creme
Vanilla icing (recipe follows)

Sift together flour and baking powder. Cream shortening and sugar. Add egg; beat well. Stir in soda mixture and vanilla. Add dry ingredients, alternately, with bananas, beating well after each addition. Spread into greased 15x9-inch jelly roll pan. Bake at 350 degrees for 25-30 minutes. Remove from oven. Drop spoonfuls of marshmallow creme on bars. Let stand two minutes. Spread gently over surface of cake. Cool; frost with Vanilla Icing.

Vanilla Icing:
2 cups sifted confectioners' sugar
1 tablespoon butter
2 tablespoons milk
1 teaspoon vanilla
Few drops yellow food coloring

Blend ingredients until smooth.
Diantha Hibbard, Rochester, N.Y.

BANANA DROP COOKIES

Makes 4 dozen

2 ripe bananas, peeled
1 cup butter, softened
1 cup sugar
1/2 cup brown sugar, packed
2 eggs
1 teaspoon vanilla extract
2 cups flour
1 teaspoon ground cinnamon, optional
1 teaspoon baking soda
1/2 teaspoon salt
1 cup peanut butter chips
1 cup chopped walnuts
1 cup raisins

Preheat oven to 375 degrees. Mash bananas. Cream together butter and sugars. Beat in bananas, eggs, and vanilla. In separate bowl, combine flour, cinnamon, soda, and salt. Gradually beat dry ingredients into banana mixture. Fold in peanut butter chips, nuts, and raisins. Drop by tablespoon onto greased cookie sheets; bake 12 minutes or until golden brown. Remove to wire rack to cool.

Kit Rollins, Cedarburg, WI

LEMON-PINEAPPLE DROPS

Makes 4 dozen

1/2 cup shortening
2 eggs
1 (3-ounce) package lemon flavored gelatin
1 pound package cake mix
1 (8-1/4 ounce) can crushed pineapple, well drained

In mixing bowl, combine shortening and eggs. Blend in dry gelatin. Add half of dry cake mix. Beat at medium speed of mixer until fluffy. Add remaining cake mix. Blend on low speed, scraping sides of bowl constantly. Stir in pineapple. Drop rounded teaspoonfuls 2 inches apart on ungreased cookie sheet. Bake at 375 degrees for 10-12 minutes. Cool one minute on cookie sheet. Remove; cool on rack.

Shirley Viscosi, Worcester, Mass.

CHOCOLATE CHERRY BARS

Makes 3 dozen

1 (18.5-ounce) package Duncan Hines Butter Recipe Fudge Cake Mix
1 (21-ounce) can cherry pie filling
1 teaspoon almond extract
2 eggs, beaten

Frosting:

1 cup granulated sugar
5 tablespoons butter or margarine
1/3 cup milk
1 (6-ounce) package semi-sweet chocolate morsels

Preheat oven to 350 degrees. Using solid shortening or margarine (not oil), grease and flour 15 x 10-inch jelly roll or 13 x 9-inch pan. In large bowl, combine first 4 ingredients. By hand, stir until well mixed. Pour into prepared pan. Bake on jelly roll pan 20-30 minutes; 13 x 9-inch pan 25-30 minutes or until toothpick inserted into center comes out clean. While bars cool, prepare frosting. In small saucepan, combine sugar, butter, and milk. Boil 1 minute, stirring constantly. Remove from heat; stir in chocolate morsels until smooth. Pour over partially-cooled bars.

Christine E. Shamanoff, Fort Wayne, IN

SEVEN LAYER HEAVEN

Makes 24-36 bars

1/2 cup margarine or butter
1-1/2 cups graham cracker crumbs
1 (14-ounce) can Eagle Brand Sweetened Condensed Milk
1 (6-ounce) package semi-sweet chocolate chips
1 (6-ounce) package butterscotch flavored chips
1 (3-1/2 ounce) can flaked coconut (1-1/3 cups)
1 cup chopped nuts

Preheat oven to 350 degrees (325 degrees for glass dish). In 13 x 9-inch baking pan, melt margarine in oven.

Sprinkle crumbs over margarine; pour Eagle Brand milk evenly over crumbs. Top with remaining ingredients in layers; press down firmly. Bake 25-30 minutes or until lightly browned. Cool; chill thoroughly. Cut into bars. Store loosely covered at room temperature.

Mae Gianocca, Half Moon Bay, CA

SUGAR AND SPICE COOKIES

2/3 cup shortening
1 egg
3/4 cup sugar
2 cups flour
1 tablespoon plus 1 teaspoon milk
1-1/2 teaspoons baking powder
1/4 teaspoon salt
2 teaspoons ground cinnamon
3/4 teaspoon ground nutmeg
1 teaspoon vanilla

Cream shortening; gradually add sugar, beating until light and fluffy. Add egg and milk; beat well. Combine flour, baking powder, cinnamon, nutmeg, and salt. Add to creamed mixture, beating well. Stir in vanilla. Chill dough 1 hour.

Roll out dough onto floured board to 1/4 inch thickness. Use cookie cutter and place on a greased cookie sheet. Bake at 375 degrees for 6-8 minutes or until lightly browned.

Sheila Hoag, Salida, CO

TREASURE BALLS

3 tablespoons brown sugar
1 teaspoon vanilla
1 stick margarine
1 cup minus 2 tablespoons flour
1/2 cup chopped chocolate chips
Confectioners' sugar

Cream together brown sugar, vanilla, and margarine. Shape into balls and bake on ungreased cookie sheet at 350 degrees for 15-20 minutes. When cool, toss in a bag with confectioners' sugar.

Susan L. Wiener, Spring Hill, FL

PUMPKIN FILLED COOKIES

Filling:
1 cup pumpkin
1/2 cup sugar
1/2 teaspoon cinnamon
1/2 teaspoon ginger
1/4 teaspoon nutmeg
1/4 teaspoon salt

Blend ingredients together. Set aside.

Cookies:
3 cups flour
1 teaspoon salt
1/2 teaspoon baking soda
1/2 cup brown sugar
3/4 cup soft shortening
1 egg
1/4 cup molasses
1 cup rolled oats

Mix and sift together flour, salt, and baking soda. Combine sugar, shortening, egg, and molasses; mix well. Add oats. Chill 1/2 hour. Roll out 1/8 inch thick; place 1 tablespoon filling on 1 cookie and cover with second cookie. Press together; slit top. Bake 375 degrees for 15 minutes.

Agnes Ward, Erie, PA

CHOCOLATE BROWNIES

2 cups sugar
2 cups flour
1 teaspoon soda
2 eggs, beaten
1 cup buttermilk
1/4 pound margarine or butter
1/2 cup shortening
1/4 cup cocoa
1 cup water

Sift flour, sugar, and soda together in large bowl. Bring margarine, water, cocoa, and shortening to a boil. Pour over flour and sugar and mix well. Add remaining ingredients. Pour into greased 15-1/2x10-1/2x1-inch pan. Bake at 350 degrees for 20-30 minutes or until done.

Brownie Icing:
1 stick margarine or butter
1/4 cup cocoa
6 tablespoons milk
4 cups powdered sugar, sifted
1 teaspoon vanilla
1 cup nuts, chopped

Mix first five ingredients well with mixer; fold in chopped nuts, and spread on brownies while hot. The icing melts a bit, but firms up again as it all cools. Brownies stay moist and are delicious!!

Dolores Warner, Thomasboro, Ill.

BABY RUTH CANDY BROWNIES

2/3 cup margarine
1 cup brown sugar
1/4 cup light corn syrup
1/4 cup smooth peanut butter
1 teaspoon vanilla
1 cup quick oatmeal

Topping:
1 (12-ounce) package chocolate chips
1 (6-ounce) package butterscotch chips
2/3 cup smooth peanut butter
1 cup salted Spanish peanuts

Combine margarine, sugar, and syrup in saucepan. Stir over low heat until margarine melts and sugar dissolves. Add peanut butter and vanilla. Pour over the oatmeal; mix well. Press into a greased 13 x 9-inch pan and bake at 375 degrees for 12 minutes. Melt the chocolate and butterscotch bits. Add peanut butter and peanuts. Pour over baked mixture. Cool and cut into squares.

Shirley Viscosi, Worcester, MA

BUTTERFINGER COOKIES

2-2/3 cups flour
1 teaspoon baking soda
2/3 cup Crisco
1/2 teaspoon salt
1-1/2 cups sugar
2 eggs
4 Butterfinger candy bars, chopped

Cream Crisco and sugar; beat in eggs. Sift dry ingredients and sprinkle over candy pieces. Mix well. Stir into egg mixture. Shape dough into rolls. Cover with foil or plastic wrap. Chill rolls. Cut into thin slices. Place slices on greased cookie sheet; bake at 375 degrees for 12 minutes. Remove from pan immediately.

Sue Thomas, Casa Grande, Ariz

APRICOT-COCONUT BALLS
Makes 5 dozen

2 (6-ounce) packages dried apricots, ground
1 cup shredded coconut
2/3 cup sweetened condensed milk
Confectioners' sugar

Combine apricots and coconut; stir to mix. Add condensed milk and mix well. Shape into 1-inch balls and coat with confectioners' sugar.

Mrs. Bruce Fowler, Woodruff, SC

RICH SHORTBREAD COOKIES

2 cups butter
1-1/2 cups confectioners' sugar
2 teaspoons vanilla
4 cups flour
1 teaspoon salt
Candied cherries, if desired

Cream butter thoroughly. Add confectioners' sugar and vanilla; beat well. Add flour and salt; blend together. Form into several rolls and wrap each roll in waxed paper. Refrigerate overnight. Slice and put on ungreased baking sheets. At this point, you may decorate with red cherries. Bake for 20 minutes at 300 degrees.

Great for Valentine's Day festivities!!

Lillian Smith, Montreal, Que.

GRANDMA'S SUGAR-RAISIN COOKIES

Makes 6 dozen

1-1/2 cups seedless raisins
1-1/2 cups sugar
1 cup shortening
2 eggs
1 teaspoon vanilla
3 cups flour
1 teaspoon baking powder
1 teaspoon baking soda
1/2 teaspoon salt
1/2 teaspoon nutmeg
Sugar

Simmer raisins in water to barely cover, until water is all absorbed. Set aside to cool. Cream sugar and shortening; add eggs and vanilla; beat thoroughly. Sift together the dry ingredients, except last sugar, and add to creamed mixture. Stir in raisins. Roll dough into 1-inch balls; roll in sugar. Place balls 2 inches apart on greased cookie sheets; flatten with bottom of sugar-dipped glass. Bake at 400 degrees for 10 minutes until lightly browned.

Agnes Ward, Erie, PA

OLD FAMILY FAVORITE TOFFEE SQUARES

1 cup margarine *or* half margarine
   and half butter
1 cup brown sugar
1 egg yolk
1 teaspoon vanilla
2 cups flour
1 cup chocolate chips
1/4 cup Crisco
Ground walnuts

Cream shortening and sugar. Add egg yolk and vanilla; blend together. Add flour; mix together again. Spread this mixture onto a cookie sheet by pinching pieces of dough and pressing dough to cover the cookie sheet, working with your fingers. Bake 15 minutes at 325 degrees.

Melt chocolate chips. Add 1/4 teaspoon Crisco to chocolate to keep it soft.

After dough is baked, spread with chocolate, while warm. Thinly spread chocolate with your fingers instead of a knife. While chocolate is still warm, sprinkle with ground walnuts. After chocolate is set, cut cookies into 1-1/2 inch squares.

Luscious!!

CARROT COOKIES

Makes 3 dozen

1 cup flour
1/2 cup butter, softened
1/2 cup brown sugar
1 egg
1/2 cup sugar
1 cup oats, uncooked
3/4 cup chopped nuts
1/4 teaspoon baking powder
1/4 teaspoon soda
1/2 teaspoon vanilla
1/2 cup finely grated carrots, not
   packed down
1/2 cup flaked coconut

Preheat oven to 350 degrees. Grease 2 cookie sheets. Combine flour, baking powder, and baking soda. In mixer bowl, cream butter, sugars, and vanilla; beat in egg. Gradually stir in flour. Add carrots, oats, coconut, and nuts; blend well. Drop onto cookie sheets. Bake 12-15 minutes.

Ruth Morris, Lima, OH

FOREVER AMBERS

1 pound orange slices (chopped)
1 cup chopped nuts
2 cans Eagle Brand milk
1 (7-ounce) can Angel Flake coconut
1 teaspoon vanilla
Confectioners' sugar

Mix well; spread on cookie sheet and bake 30 minutes at 350 degrees. Let cool enough to handle and roll into balls. Roll the balls in confectioners' sugar.
Nene Jordan, Rome, Ga.

CHOCOLATE CHIP COCONUT BARS

1/3 cup margarine
1/2 cup granulated sugar
1/2 cup brown sugar packed
1 egg
1 teaspoon vanilla
1 tablespoon water
1 cup sifted flour
1-1/2 teaspoons baking powder
1/4 teaspoon salt
1/2 cup moist coconut
1 (6-ounce) package semi-sweet
   chocolate pieces
1/2 cup chopped nuts

Cream margarine and sugars. Add egg; mix well. Add vanilla and water; blend. Add flour, baking powder, and salt, which have been sifted together. Add coconut, chocolate pieces, and nuts. Press into a greased pan 7 x 11 inches or 9-inch square. Bake in a moderate oven 350 degrees for 30 minutes. Cool; cut into bars.

Carrie TreeChel, Johnson City, TN

LOW CHOLESTEROL OATMEAL COOKIES

1-1/2 cups brown sugar
1/2 cup corn oil
2 egg substitutes
2 cups flour
1 teaspoon baking powder
1/4 teaspoon salt
2 teaspoons baking soda dissolved in
   2 tablespoons hot water
1 teaspoon vanilla
2 cups oatmeal
1/2 cup raisins (optional)

Beat sugar, oil, and egg substitutes together. Mix flour, baking powder, and salt; add to egg mixture. Add baking soda mixture and vanilla. Mix well. Add oatmeal and raisins. Drop by heaping teaspoons onto greased cookie sheet. Bake at 325 degrees for 10-12 minutes or until very lightly browned.

Rosalie Buyce, Winter Haven, FL

CHOCO SURPRISE COOKIES

Makes 8 dozen

1 cup all-purpose flour
1 teaspoon baking powder
1 teaspoon cinnamon
1 cup peanut butter (creamy)
1/2 cup margarine, softened
1 cup firmly-packed brown sugar
2 eggs, well beaten
1 (16-ounce) package milk chocolate stars (or Hershey Kisses with tips cut off)
Confectioners' sugar

Combine first three ingredients and set aside. Combine and cream until fluffy, the peanut butter, margarine, brown sugar and eggs. Add dry ingredients. Cover dough; chill 1 hour or overnight.

Shape 1 teaspoon dough around star; place on lightly-greased cookie sheet or on Teflon cookie sheet. Bake at 350 degrees for 9-11 minutes or until lightly browned. Cool slightly on wire racks; then roll in powdered sugar. Cool completely before storing.

Mrs. Hobert Howell, Waco, TX

CHERRY NUT COOKIES

Makes 4-1/2 dozen

1/2 cup soft butter or margarine
1 cup light brown sugar, packed
1 egg, slightly beaten
1 teaspoon vanilla
2 cups all-purpose flour
1/2 teaspoon baking soda
1/4 teaspoon salt
1 cup chopped walnuts
1/3 cup chopped maraschino cherries

Cream together the butter and sugar. Beat in egg and vanilla until smooth. Blend in flour, baking soda, and salt. Stir in walnuts and cherries. Shape the dough into a roll about 14 inches long. Wrap in foil or plastic wrap and refrigerate overnight. With a sharp knife, cut dough into 1/4-inch slices. Place on ungreased cookie sheets. Bake at 375 degrees for about 10 minutes or until just golden brown. Remove from the cookie sheets while warm. Cool on rack. Store in air-tight containers.

Make the dough for these cookies the day before baking, so it can firm up in the refrigerator for thin slicing. The chunks of cherries and nuts make it a good choice to serve during February.

Ella Evanicky, Fayetteville, Texas.

EASTER BONNET COOKIES

You may use commercial, plain round cookies or make the following recipe, using a scalloped, circle cookie cutter.

Rolled Cookies:
3-1/2 cups all-purpose flour
1 teaspoon baking powder
1/2 teaspoon salt
1 cup shortening
1-1/2 cups sugar
2 well-beaten eggs
1-1/2 teaspoons vanilla

Sift flour, baking powder, and salt together. Cream shortening; add sugar gradually; beat until light. Add beaten eggs; blend well; add vanilla. Combine dry ingredients with creamed mixture. Chill. Roll out dough thin; cut with cookie cutter. Grease baking sheet. Bake at 400 degrees for 6-10 minutes. When cool, frost with yellow icing. Use tines of small fork to draw lines around edge of cookies. This simulates the appearance of a straw hat.

Frosting:
2 cups confectioners' sugar
2 tablespoons hot water or milk
1 teaspoon vanilla or almond flavoring

While frosting is still moist, place a colored marshmallow in center of cookie. May add colored sugar flowers. Dip underside of flowers in frosting and place on marshmallow crown or straw brim of hat. Sugar flowers can usually be found in a supermarket section where colored sugars and cake decorating icings are displayed.

Dorothy Stranix, Victoria B. C., Canada

FROSTED CHOCOLATE CHIP BARS

2-1/2 cups (1 pound) brown sugar
3 eggs
2/3 cup shortening (melted)
2-3/4 cups flour
2-1/2 teaspoons baking powder
1/2 teaspoon salt
1 cup salted nuts
1 (6-ounce) package chocolate chips

Cream sugar and eggs, one at a time, beating well after each one. Add melted shortening, then sifted dry ingredients. Mix well. Add nuts and chocolate chips. Batter will be thick. Grease a 10x15-1/2x3/4 inch pan. Bake at 350 degrees for 25-30 minutes. Frost with recipe below. Cut when cool.

Frosting:
Confectioners' Sugar (enough for spreading consistency desired)
2 tablespoons butter, melted
3 tablespoons milk
2 tablespoons cocoa

Blend butter, milk and cocoa, and add confectioners' sugar to spreading consistency. Add 1/2 teaspoon vanilla.

Ilene Ongman, Klamath Falls, Ore.

POTATO CHIP COOKIES

Makes 2 dozen

1 cup margarine (2 sticks)
1/2 cup sugar
1 teaspoon vanilla
1 cup crushed potato chips
1 cup all-purpose flour

Preheat oven to 350 degrees. Mix margarine, sugar, and vanilla together; blend well. Add potato chips and stir in flour. Form small balls from mixture and place on an ungreased cookie sheet. Press balls flat with the bottom of a glass that has been dipped in sugar. Bake 16-18 minutes, or until lightly browned.

Trenda Leigh, Richmond, VA

BUTTERMILK CHOCOLATE CHIP COOKIES
Makes 7 dozen

1 cup shortening
1 cup sugar
1 cup brown sugar, firmly packed
2 eggs
1-1/2 teaspoons vanilla
3 cups sifted flour
1 teaspoon baking soda
1/2 cup buttermilk
1 (6-ounce) package semisweet
  chocolate pieces
1 cup chopped pecans

Cream together shortening and sugars until light and fluffy. Beat in eggs, one at a time. Blend in vanilla. Sift together flour and baking soda. Add dry ingredients, alternately with buttermilk, to creamed mixture; mix well. Stir in chocolate pieces and pecans. Drop by teaspoonsful about 2 inches apart on greased baking sheets. Bake in 350-degree oven for 12-15 minutes or until done. Remove from baking sheets; cool on racks.

These are my favorite chocolate chip cookies. They are so fabulous!!
Barbara Beauregard-Smith, Northfield, South Australia

CHEESECAKE BARS

1 box Duncan Hines Golden Butter
  Recipe cake mix
1 egg
1 stick margarine
1 (8-ounce) package cream cheese
2 eggs
1 pound box powdered sugar

Blend together the first 3 ingredients. Crumble and press into greased oblong pan. Then mix next three ingredients together and spread on top of bottom layer. Bake at 350 degrees for 35-40 minutes or until golden brown. Cool completely and cut into bars.
Sue Hibbard, Rochester, N.Y.

PRIDE OF OHIO COOKIES

1 cup brown sugar
1 cup white sugar
1 cup shortening
1 cup flour
2 eggs
1 cup coconut
1 cup nut meats, chopped
1 teaspoon soda
1 teaspoon baking powder
1/2 teaspoon salt
3 cups quick rolled oats

Beat eggs in mixing bowl, add sugars and softened shortening. Blend well. Stir in coconut, nuts and vanilla. Sift flour and measure, then add soda, baking powder and salt, then sift again. Combine with other mixture. Stir in rolled oats, mix thoroughly by hand. Roll in small balls the size of a walnut and place on ungreased cookie sheet. Bake at 375-degrees for about 9 minutes or until nicely browned.
Marjorie Baxler, Greenfield, OH

MINCEMEAT COOKIES

2 cups shortening
5 eggs
1 teaspoon salt
6-1/2 cups flour
3 cups mincemeat
3 cups brown sugar
2 teaspoons soda
3 tablespoons hot water
1 cup nuts

Cream shortening. Add brown sugar and mix until well-blended. Add eggs and beat thoroughly. Mix salt and soda with the flour. Add water to first mixture. Add mincemeat and flour mixture alternately to first mixture. Add nuts. Mix thoroughly. Drop with a spoon onto greased baking sheet and bake 10 minutes in a moderately hot 375-degree oven.

These cookies don't last long in my house as they are really extra-delicious!
Suzan L. Wiener, Spring Hill, Fla.

ORANGE SLICE BAR COOKIES
Makes 2 dozen

4 eggs, lightly beaten
2 cups brown sugar, packed
2 cups flour
1 teaspoon baking powder
1 tablespoon cold water
1 teaspoon ground cinnamon
1 cup chopped walnuts or pecans
2 teaspoons vanilla
1/2 teaspoon salt
1 pound orange slice candy, finely
  cut up

Beat eggs lightly in large bowl. Add brown sugar, flour, baking powder, cold water, cinnamon, nuts, vanilla, salt, and candy pieces. Mix until blended. Spread in lightly greased and wax-paper-lined 13x9-inch baking pan.

Bake at 350 degrees for 30 minutes. Cool 10 minutes on rack then invert onto bread board. Spread with frosting. Cut into 3x1-1/2 inch bars.

Frosting:
1 cup powdered sugar
1 tablespoon soft butter
2 teaspoons grated orange peel
Orange juice

Combine powdered sugar with butter, orange peel, and enough orange juice to be of spreadable consistency.
Grace Lane, Redondo Beach, Calif.

MOON ROCKS

1 pound powdered sugar
1 stick margarine, melted
1 (6-ounce) can frozen orange
  concentrate, (thawed)
1 teaspoon grated orange peel
1 cup ground pecans
1 pound vanilla wafers, crushed
1 pound shredded coconut (divided
  into two portions)

Combine all ingredients, except half of coconut. Mix thoroughly. Shape into balls and roll into remaining coconut. Makes 96 confections. Store in covered container in refrigerator.
Dovie Lucy, McLoud, Okla.

SOFT SUGAR COOKIES

1/2 cup butter or margarine
1-1/2 cups white sugar
2 eggs
1 teaspoon vanilla
3 cups unsifted enriched flour
1 teaspoon salt
1/2 teaspoon baking powder
1/2 teaspoon baking soda
1 cup dairy sour cream

Cream butter or margarine with sugar; add vanilla. Add eggs and beat well. Mix flour, salt, baking powder, and baking soda. Add to creamed mixture alternately with sour cream. You may add chocolate chips or raisins, or sprinkle with colored sugar, or sugar and cinnamon before baking. Drop on greased and floured cookie sheets. Bake at 400 degrees for 10-12 minutes.

I have made these cookies for a number of years for my children, and now grandchildren. The recipe is fast and easy.

Doris Mustard, Xenia, Ohio

FRUIT-N-HONEY COOKIES

1/4 cup brown sugar
1/2 cup honey
1/2 cup butter or margarine
2 eggs
1-1/2 cups flour
1/2 teaspoon salt
1/2 teaspoon baking soda
1 teaspoon cinnamon
1/2 cup milk
1/2 cup raisins
1/2 cup ground nuts
1/4 cup coconut

Cream brown sugar, honey, and butter together in a mixing bowl. Add eggs. Sift together dry ingredients. Add to creamed mixture. alternately with milk. Mix well. Stir in raisins, nuts, and coconut. Drop by teaspoonfuls onto greased cookie sheet. Bake at 400 degrees for 6-8 minutes.
Mrs. E. O'Brien, Richmond, Va.

BANANA OATMEAL DROPS

Makes 4 dozen

3/4 cup shortening
1 cup sugar
1 egg
1 medium-size banana, mashed
1/2 teaspoon lemon juice
1-1/2 cups sifted flour
1/2 teaspoon soda
1 teaspoon salt
3/4 teaspoon cinnamon
1/4 teaspoon nutmeg
1-1/2 cups quick-cooking oats
1/2 cup chopped walnuts

Cream together shortening and sugar until light and fluffy. Beat in egg. Stir in banana and lemon juice. Sift together flour, soda, salt, cinnamon, and nutmeg. Stir into creamed mixture. Mix in oats and walnuts. Drop from a teaspoon onto greased baking sheets, about 2 inches apart. Bake in a moderate oven of 350 degrees for 12-15 minutes, or until edges turn golden.

Marcella Swigert, Monroe City, Mo.

GRAHAM AND FIG WAFERS

1 cup cream
3 tablespoons sugar
1/4 teaspoon salt
2 teaspoons baking powder
2-1/2 cups graham flour
1/2 pound figs or dates

Sift together sugar, salt, and baking powder. Add to cream. Add graham flour. Chill. Roll half the dough on floured board. Spread with chopped figs or dates. Roll other half of dough and put on layer of fruit. Roll top lightly. Cut into strips with sharp knife. Bake on greased baking sheets in a moderate 350-degree oven for 15 minutes.

Suzan Wiener, Spring Hill, Fla.

APPLE BROWNIES

1/2 cup butter
1/4 teaspoon salt
1 egg, beaten
1 cup sugar
3 medium apples, pared and diced
    or 1/2 cup applesauce
1/2 cup chopped walnuts
1 cup flour
1/2 teaspoon baking powder
1/2 teaspoon baking soda
1/2 teaspoon cinnamon

Preheat oven to 350 degrees. Cream together butter and salt, then add the egg and sugar; beat well. Stir in apples, nuts, and dry ingredients. Blend well. Pour mixture into a greased and floured 8 inch square pan. Bake for 40 minutes. When cool, cut into squares.

GINGERSNAPS

2 cups flour
1 tablespoon ground ginger
2 teaspoons baking soda
1 teaspoon cinnamon
1/2 teaspoon salt
3/4 cup shortening
1 cup sugar
1 egg
1/4 cup molasses

Measure flour, ginger, soda, cinnamon, and salt; put aside. Cream shortening until soft. Gradually add sugar, creaming until light and fluffy. Beat in egg and molasses. Add dry ingredients over creamed mixture; blend well. Form teaspoonsful of dough into small balls by rolling them lightly between palms of hands. Roll dough balls in granulated sugar to cover entire surface. Place 2 inches apart on ungreased cookie sheet. Bake at 350 degrees for 12 to 15 minutes until tops are crackly and cookies are brown.

A good, old-fashioned cookie!
Mrs. George Franks, Millerton, Pa.

CHOCO–PEANUT YUMMIES

1 cup shortening
1/2 cup firmly packed brown sugar
1 cup sugar
2 eggs
1 teaspoon vanilla extract
2-1/4 cups all-purpose flour
1 teaspoon baking soda
1/2 teaspoon salt
1 (6-ounce) package peanut–butter
   morsels
1 (6-ounce) package semisweet
   chocolate morsels

Cream butter and shortening; add sugars and beat until light and fluffy. Combine flour, soda, and salt; add to creamed mixture; mix well. Drop dough by heaping teaspoonsful onto ungreased cookie sheets. Bake at 350 degrees for 12 minutes.

Mrs. Bruce Fowler, Woodruff, S.C.

PEANUT BUTTER COOKIES

2 cups sifted all-purpose flour
2 teaspoons baking powder
1/2 teaspoon salt
2/3 cup peanut butter
1 egg, slightly beaten
1-1/2 cups (1 can) sweetened
   condensed milk
1 teaspoon vanilla
1/2 cup finely chopped nut meats
   (optional)

Sift blended dry ingredients. In large mixing bowl, blend peanut butter and egg. Stir in one half of the condensed milk; blend in one half of the dry ingredients. Repeat; stir in vanilla and nuts. Drop by tablespoon about 2 inches apart onto well-greased cookie sheet. Bake at 350 degrees for 10-12 minutes, or until cookie edges are lightly browned. Remove at once from cookie sheet.

Karin Shea Fedders, Dameron, Md.

THE WORLD'S BEST COOKIES
Makes 8 dozen

1 cup butter
1 cup sugar
1 cup brown sugar, firmly packed
1 egg
1 cup salad oil
1-1/2 cups rolled oats, regular
1 cup crushed Grape-Nut flakes
1 cup shredded coconut
3/4 cup chopped walnuts or
   pecans
3-1/2 cups sifted all-purpose flour
1 teaspoon soda
1 teaspoon vanilla
1/2 teaspoon coconut extract
1/2 teaspoon salt

Preheat oven to 325 degrees. Cream together butter and sugars until light and fluffy. Add egg, mixing well, then salad oil, mixing well. Add oats, Grape Nut flakes, coconut, and nuts, stirring well. Add flour, soda, salt, and flavoring. Mix well and form into balls the size of small walnuts and place on ungreased cookie sheet. Flatten with a fork dipped in water. Position a pecan half on top surface of each cookie. Bake for 10-12 minutes. Allow to cool on cookie sheet for a few minutes before removing.

Chris Bryant, Johnson City, Tn.

STRAWBERRY BROWNIES

1/2 cup margarine
8 tablespoons Strawberry Quick
   flavored-milk mix
3/4 cup flour
1/3 cup sugar
2 eggs, slightly beaten
1 teaspoon vanilla

Melt margarine and mix in the Strawberry Quick. Combine flour and sugar; add the margarine/Quick mixture. Add eggs and vanilla. Stir until ingredients are combined. Pour into greased 9-inch square pan. Bake at 350 degrees for 20-25 minutes.

Anne Sherman, Orangeburg, S.C.

WALNUT MERINGUE BARS
Makes 4 dozen

2-1/2 cups all-purpose flour
5 eggs, separated
6 tablespoons sugar
1 cup sweet butter
2 teaspoons vanilla
2 cups apricot jam
1 cup sugar
3 cups ground walnuts
Confectioners' sugar

In a bowl, combine flour, egg yolks, sugar, butter and vanilla. Blend with fork until dough comes away from sides of bowl. Press dough into an 11x16-inch pan. Spread with jam. Beat egg whites until stiff, gradually beating in 1 cup sugar. Fold in nuts. Spread over dough. Bake at 350 degrees for 40 minutes. Sprinkle with confectioners' sugar. Cool and cut into bars.

Any kind of jam can be substituted for the apricot. The cookie is very rich, so make the bars small.

Ella Evanisky, Fayetteville, Texas

DELUXE FUDGY BROWNIES

4 squares unsweetened chocolate
1/2 cup butter or margarine
4 eggs
2 cups sugar
1 cup sifted flour
1 teaspoon vanilla
1 cup coarsely chopped nuts

Melt chocolate and butter together over hot water. Cool slightly. Beat eggs until foamy; gradually add sugar, beating thoroughly after each addition. Add chocolate mixture and blend. Stir in flour. Then add vanilla and nuts. Spread in greased 9x9x2-inch pan. Bake at 325 degrees for 40-50 minutes. Cool in pan, then cut into squares or bars. Will have crunchy top and bottom crust with a center almost like chocolate cream. Delicious served straight from the freezer.

Ruth Morris, Bradenton, Fla.

ROCKY ROAD S'MORES BARS

1/2 cup margarine
1/2 cup packed brown sugar
1 cup flour
1/2 cup graham cracker crumbs
2 cups miniature marshmallows
1 (6-ounce) package semisweet
    chocolate pieces
1/2 cup chopped walnuts (optional)

Beat margarine and brown sugar until light and fluffy. Add combined flour and crumbs; mix well. Press onto bottom of greased 9-inch square pan. Sprinkle with remaining ingredients. Bake at 375 degrees for 15-20 minutes or until golden brown. Cool; cut into bars.

Loriann Johnson, Gobles, Mich.

EASY COOKIES
Makes 4 dozen

3/4 cup Bisquick
1 small package instant pudding
1/4 cup salad oil
1 egg

Preheat oven to 350 degrees. Mix together all ingredients. Shape dough into balls, using 1 teaspoon of dough. Place dough balls on an ungreased cookie sheet and press flat. Bake for 8 minutes. Remove from cookie sheet to a flat surface to cool.

Other easy treats sure to please kids of any age are:

Popcorn.— Simply add butter or for a special treat; mix in peanut butter when melting butter to pour over popcorn;

Party Mix — Combine cereals, nuts, chocolate chips, coconut, pretzels, raisins, dry fruits, granola.

Send a large thermos of fruit juice or hot chocolate — a great way to wash down all the other treats.

PEEK-A-BOOS
Makes 24 squares

1-1/2 cups sugar
1 cup butter, softened
4 eggs
2 cups flour
1 teaspoon vanilla
1 large can fruit pie filling

Preheat oven to 325 degrees. Cream together butter and sugar, then add the eggs. Stir in flour and vanilla until mixture is well-blended. (Do not use an electric mixer for any part of this recipe.) Pour the mixture into a greased and floured 13x9x2-inch pan. Score the top of the dough before baking to form squares. Place 1 tablespoon of fruit pie filling on each square. Bake at 325 degrees for 25-30 minutes or until golden brown. As the cake bakes, the fruit filling will pop up through the dough. Cut into squares. Serve warm, if possible, with powdered sugar on top.

HONEY OATMEAL COOKIES
Makes 3 dozen

2 tablespoons butter (room temperature)
1 tablespoon oil
1/2 cup brown sugar
1/4 cup honey
1 egg
1 tablespoon water
1/2 cup flour
1/2 teaspoon salt
1/4 teaspoon baking soda
1-1/2 cups quick rolled oats
Fruits, nuts, or chocolate bits (optional)

Grease cookie sheets; set aside. Preheat oven to 350 degrees. Blend butter, oil, brown sugar, honey, egg, and water thoroughly. In another bowl, mix flour, salt, and baking soda; add rolled oats. Stir and blend two mixtures together. Add fruits, nuts, or chocolate bits (if desired). Drop by teaspoonfuls onto prepared cookie sheets. Bake at 350 degrees for 10-12 minutes.

Mrs. E. O'Brien, Richmond, Va.

SHORTBREAD COOKIES
Makes 4 dozen

1 cup butter or margarine, softened
1/2 cup sugar
1 teaspoon vanilla
2-1/4 cups flour

Preheat oven to 325 degrees. Cream together the butter and sugar, then add vanilla and blend until light and fluffy. Stir in flour until well-mixed. Place dough on a floured surface and knead until smooth (do not overwork). Place dough in refrigerator until chilled.

Remove a small portion of dough at a time so the rest will remain chilled. Roll the dough to 1/4" thickness and cut with cookie cutters. Place cookies on an ungreased cookie sheet and bake for 12-15 minutes or until the cookies are light brown. Remove cookies to a flat surface to cool. Sprinkle cinnamon/sugar or colored sugars on top of cookies before baking, if desired.

BLUEBERRY NUT DROPS
Makes 2-1/2 dozen

2 cups flour
2 teaspoons baking powder
1 teaspoon cinnamon
3/4 cup blueberries
1 cup sugar
1/2 cup margarine
1 egg
1 teaspoon vanilla
1/4 cup milk
1/4 cup chopped walnuts

Sift together flour, baking powder, and cinnamon. Stir in blueberries. In mixing bowl cream margarine and sugar together; beat in egg and vanilla. Add flour-berry mixture alternately with milk; beat with spoon until blended. Fold in nuts. Drop by heaping teaspoonsful onto greased cookie sheet, 2 inches apart. Bake at 375 degrees for 12-14 minutes, until lightly browned and firm.

OATMEAL-RAISIN COOKIES

3 eggs, well beaten
1 cup raisins
1 teaspoon vanilla
1 cup shortening
1 cup brown sugar
1 cup granulated sugar
2-1/2 cups flour
1 teaspoon salt
2 teaspoons soda
1 teaspoon cinnamon
2 cups oatmeal
1/2 cup chopped nuts

Combine eggs, raisins and vanilla. Let mixture stand for 1 hour or more. Thoroughly cream together shortening, brown and white sugar. Sift flour, salt, soda, and cinnamon. Mix well; blend in egg/raisin mixture, oats, and nuts. (Dough will be very stiff.) Roll the dough into balls, the size of a large walnut; roll the balls in a cinnamon-sugar mixture (1 teaspoon cinnamon mixed with 1 cup sugar). Place on cookie sheet about 3 inches apart. Bake at 350 degrees for 10-12 minutes or until lightly browned. Remove from oven and let cool a few minutes before removing from cookie sheet. These will keep several weeks, stored in a tightly covered container. Put waxed paper between layers of cookies. Let cool *completely* before closing container.

Jean Vincent, Grand Blanc, Mich.

COCO-CRISPIE BALLS

Makes 36 balls

1 cup sifted confectioners' sugar
1/2 cup light corn syrup
1/2 cup peanut butter
2 cups Cocoa Krispies cereal or a combination of 1 cup Cocoa Krispies and 1 cup regular Rice Krispies

Put sugar, corn syrup, and peanut butter into a large bowl and mix well. Add the cereal and mix to coat it. With clean hands, shape mixture into balls. Roll balls in extra cereal that has been slightly crushed, flaked coconut, or sifted confectioners' sugar. Place on a cookie sheet and put in a cool place until firm.

PECAN BUTTER-SCOTCH BROWNIES

Makes 24 squares

1/4 cup vegetable oil
1 tablespoon dark molasses
1/2 cup brown sugar, firmly packed
1/2 cup pecans, chopped
2 cups all-purpose flour
2 eggs
2 teaspoons vanilla
1/4 teaspoon salt
1/2 cup milk
1/2 teaspoon baking powder

Combine all ingredients; spread in a greased 8x8x2-inch pan. Bake at 350 degrees for 30 minutes; turn out of pan; cut into squares or bars while hot; place a whole pecan on each square.

Gwen Campbell, Sterling, Va.

PEANUT-BUTTER DUMP BARS

Makes 3 dozen

1 package yellow cake mix
2/3 cup evaporated milk
1/2 cup peanut-butter chips
1/2 cup chopped pecans
1/4 cup melted margarine
1/2 cup chocolate syrup

Preheat oven to 350 degrees and grease a 13x9x2-inch baking pan. In a large bowl, combine dry cake mix and pecans with milk and margarine. Pour half the mixture in the pan and bake for 10-12 minutes. Remove from oven and sprinkle with chips, then pour the syrup over. Top with spoonsful of remaining cake mixture. Return to oven for 20-25 minutes more. Cool; cut and remove from pan.

Linda Hutton, Hayden, Idaho

PEANUT-BUTTER CHOCOLATE-CHIP COOKIES

2 eggs
1/3 cup water
1/4 cup margarine, softened
1 cup peanut butter
1 package yellow cake mix
1 (12-ounce) package semisweet chocolate pieces

Heat oven to 375 degrees. Beat eggs, water, margarine, and half of dry cake mix until smooth. Beat in remaining cake mix and peanut butter. Stir in chocolate chips.

Spread dough in greased and floured 9x13-inch pan. Bake for 20 minutes. Cool; cut into bars.

Easy and delicious!!

Mrs. Howard Leslie, Youngstown, Ohio

BUTTER PECAN COOKIES

Makes 8 dozen

2 cups butter
1 cup brown sugar
2 egg yolks
5 cups flour
1/2 teaspoon salt
1 teaspoon vanilla

Topping:
1 egg
1/4 cup milk
1 cup pecan halves

Cream butter until light and fluffy. Gradually add brown sugar and cream well. Add unbeaten egg yolks; blend. Fold flour and salt into mixture. Add vanilla. Roll in balls the size of a marble and place on greased pan. Press down with a fork dipped in egg and milk mixture. Place a pecan half on each cookie. Bake at 350 degrees for 12-15 minutes.

This is a great recipe for a picnic or party.

Mrs. L. Mayer, Richmond, Va.

Cooking
FOR TWO

OVEN PORK CHOPS
Serves 2

(A time-saving recipe—chops are not skillet-browned first.)

4 small pork chops
Garlic salt
1/4 cup catsup
1 tablespoon brown sugar
1/2 teaspoon prepared mustard

Preheat oven to 350 degrees.

Grease or spray with pan release a shallow baking dish which will accommodate chops in a single layer. Sprinkle chops with garlic salt; arrange in baking dish. Stir together catsup, brown sugar, and mustard.

BREADED VEAL SCALLOPS
(also known as Wiener Schnitzel)
Serves 2

1/2 pound veal scallops (or 2 boned and skinned chicken breasts)
Salt and pepper
Flour
1 egg
About 1/3 cup fine dry bread crumbs
1-1/2 teaspoons butter or margarine

Pound veal (or chicken) until very thin according to directions given above. Sprinkle with salt, pepper, and a light dusting of flour. Whisk egg; pour onto a rimmed plate. Have a thin layer of bread crumbs on another plate.

Dip meat into egg; turn to coat; place on bread crumbs; sprinkle crumbs on top; turn and sprinkle on crumbs until well coated. If the rest of the meal is not ready, leave meat on waxed paper, in a single layer, uncovered.

In a large skillet, melt butter over high heat. Sauté meat on high 2 minutes per side, until crumbs are golden.

Serve with lemon wedges to squeeze over meat, if desired.

ORANGE CHICKEN WINGS
Serves 2

8 chicken wings, tips removed
Onion powder
Garlic salt
Pepper
1/4 cup orange marmalade
2 teaspoons cider vinegar

Preheat oven to 425 degrees. Sprinkle chicken wings with onion powder, garlic salt, and pepper. Arrange skin-side *up* on a rack on pan prepared as directed in italics at beginning of this article. Bake 35 minutes. Meanwhile, stir together marmalade and vinegar. Spoon the thick sauce on top of chicken wings; bake 15 minutes longer.

Good served with buttered white or brown rice.

STEAK ROLL
Serves 4

Good hot or cold—leftover meat makes great sandwiches.

1 pound round steak
1 tablespoon butter or margarine
1 tablespoon blue cheese
1 tablespoon fine dry bread crumbs
1/2 teaspoon salt
1/8 teaspoon black pepper
1/4 teaspoon dried thyme
1/4 teaspoon dried basil
1/4 teaspoon dried oregano
1 green onion
1/2 clove garlic
1 slice bacon
6 fresh mushrooms (optional)

Preheat oven to 275 degrees.

Trim steak; remove bone; score one side of meat by making long shallow cuts across the surface in a diamond pattern.

Into a small bowl measure butter, blue cheese, bread crumbs, salt and pepper. Rub thyme, basil, and oregano in palm of hand to release flavor; add to butter. With scissors snip in onion; crush garlic into mixture. Rub together with back of a spoon until a paste. Spread on scored side of meat pushing down into the cuts where meat was scored. Roll meat so that butter mixture is on inside; tie with string. (If possible refrigerate several hours.) Place on roasting pan (I spray it first with Pam). Top with slice of bacon to baste the beef roll. Bake uncovered at 275 degrees for 1-1/2 hours.

Remove meat to platter. Add 3 tablespoons hot water to pan drippings. Set over medium heat on top of stove; slice in mushrooms, if using. Bring to boil while stirring to scrape up brown bits in pan. Serve in a bowl to spoon over meat slices.

HOLIDAY CORNISH HENS
Serves 2

Sometimes 22-ounce hens are the smallest available. They are too large for us but the leftover meat makes good sandwiches.

2 Rock Cornish game hens
2 juice oranges
1 large clove garlic
1/4 teaspoon salt
Pinch black pepper
2 tablespoons brown sugar

Line a shallow baking pan with foil. Place two pieces of crushed foil on pan as racks for hens (without racks hens will stick and burn on the bottom due to sugar in the glaze).

Preheat oven to 450 degrees.

Rinse cavity and outside of hens; pat dry with paper towel. Thickly slice one orange; cut slices in half; reserve several center slices for serving decoration. Stuff half of remaining orange slices and half of garlic clove into the cavity of each hen. Place hens breast side up on prepared pan.

Squeeze remaining orange. Combine orange juice (about 1/3 cup), salt, pepper, and brown sugar; stir until sugar dissolves. Brush hens all over with orange sauce. Roast at 450 degrees for 15 minutes, brushing once with sauce. Reduce oven temperature to 350 degrees; roast 50 minutes longer, brushing several times with remaining sauce. Remove orange slices and garlic from cavity. Serve with reserved orange slices on the side.

SWISS VEAL
Serves 2

3/4 pound veal cutlet (or 2 boned and skinned chicken breasts)
3 tablespoons butter
Salt and pepper
Flour
2 thin slices onion, chopped
1/8 teaspoon dried tarragon
1/4 cup dry white wine (use chicken broth if you do not have wine)
1-1/2 teaspoons lemon juice
1/4 cup sour cream

Trim away fat and bone from veal. Cut veal (or chicken) into narrow strips about one inch long. Sprinkle with salt, pepper, and a light dusting of flour.

In a medium skillet heat butter until bubbly. Over medium heat cook meat until evenly brown. Add onions; cook just until soft. Add tarragon and wine; cover; cook on low heat 4 to 5 minutes, until meat tests done with a fork. Drizzle on lemon juice; toss to mix. Stir in sour cream; cook just until sour cream is hot, not boiling.

Serve with buttered noodles.

VEAL IN CREAM
Serves 2

1/2 pound veal scallops (or 2 boned and skinned chicken breasts)
2 tablespoons flour
1/2 teaspoon salt
1/4 teaspoon pepper
1/4 teaspoon paprika
1 tablespoon butter or margarine
1/2 tablespoon cooking oil
1/4 cup whipping cream

Pound veal (or chicken) until very thin according to directions given above.

Mix flour, salt, pepper and paprika; spread on waxed paper or large plate. Coat meat on both sides with mixture; leave on paper in a single layer until needed.

In a large skillet heat butter and oil until bubbly. Add meat, single layer, and cook over medium heat until brown on both sides. Reduce heat to low; cover skillet; cook until tender, 3 to 5 minutes. Add cream; cook uncovered a few minutes until cream has thickened to sauce consistency.

Serve with mashed potatoes or buttered noodles.

LEMON CHICKEN WINGS
Serves 2

3 tablespoons oil
1/2 teaspoon grated lemon peel
1 tablespoon lemon juice
1/2 teaspoon dried oregano leaves
1/2 teaspoon garlic salt
8 chicken wings, tips removed

Measure oil into a medium bowl. Grate lemon peel onto foil; add 1/2 teaspoon to oil; store remaining peel in foil; freeze for later use. Squeeze lemon; add 1 tablespoon juice to oil; chill or freeze remaining juice for another use. Add oregano and garlic salt to oil; whisk until blended. Add chicken wings, toss well; cover and refrigerate up to 24 hours.

Preheat oven to 425 degrees. Place chicken wings, skin-side down, on rack on pan prepared as directed in italics at beginning of this article. Reserve marinade. Bake 20 minutes; brush with marinade, turn; brush other side. Bake until brown and tender, about 30 minutes longer.

CHINESE PLUM CHICKEN
Serves 2

3 red plums, rinsed
2 tablespoons sugar
2 tablespoons orange juice
1/2 teaspoon lemon juice
1/2 teaspoon salt
1 teaspoon flour
1 whole chicken breast, halved

Preheat oven to 350 degrees.

Slice plums into small bowl. Mix in sugar, orange juice, lemon juice, salt, and flour. Spread in center of a square of foil (Use 18-inch heavy-duty foil for this).

Remove skin from chicken and score (make long shallow cuts in a diamond pattern in the flesh). Place cut side down on plum mixture. Fold foil to make a secure package. Place foil package on shallow baking pan (just in case). Bake until fork tender, about 45 minutes. Flip the package over and back, once during baking, to distribute the juices.

To serve, spoon plum sauce over chicken.

OVEN BARBECUED CHICKEN WINGS
Serves 2

4 tablespoons ketchup
2 tablespoons vinegar
2 tablespoons water
1 teaspoon Worcestershire sauce
1 teaspoon sugar
1/2 teaspoon salt
1/4 teaspoon dry mustard
1/4 teaspoon chili powder
1/8 teaspoon pepper or dash Tabasco sauce
8 chicken wings, tips removed

Measure all ingredients, except chicken wings, into medium size bowl; whisk until well blended. To do ahead, add chicken wings; toss well; cover and refrigerate up to 24 hours.

For last-minute preparation, dip chicken wings in sauce to coat; place skin-side down on rack on pan prepared as directed in italics at beginning of this article. Bake at 425 degrees for 20 minutes. Brush with sauce; turn; brush other side; bake until brown and tender, about 30 minutes longer.

BEEF PAPRIKA
Serves 4

Freeze half for another meal.
1-1/2 pounds boneless round steak
1/4 cup flour
1 teaspoon salt
1/4 teaspoon black pepper
1 medium onion
1 clove garlic
4 tablespoons oil
1 cup beef broth (Swanson's works well)
3 drops Tabasco sauce
1 teaspoon paprika
1 tablespoon sour cream

Trim meat; cut into four serving-size pieces. Place meat on cutting board; pound with a mallet on both sides until about 3/8 inch thick. Measure flour, salt, and pepper onto a plate; mix with a fork; coat meat on both sides with flour; set aside.

Slice onion thinly; mince garlic. Heat 1 tablespoon oil in a 12-inch skillet. Cook onions and garlic until transparent. Remove from skillet. Add remaining 3 tablespoons oil to skillet; when hot add meat in single layer. Brown on both sides. Add onions, garlic, broth, Tabasco sauce, and paprika. Stir; bring to boiling; partially cover; cook on low heat until meat is tender, 10 to 15 minutes.

Remove half of meat and sauce to freeze. Stir sour cream into remaining sauce. Set over low heat until sauce is warm.

Serve with noodles. (I cook 2 cups dry noodles for us. Drain cooked noodles; return to warm pan; stir in a large spoonful of paprika sauce to flavor noodles and to prevent them from sticking together.)

For another meal thaw frozen beef in refrigerator. Reheat; stir in 1 tablespoon sour cream just before serving

SUMMER SPAGHETTI
Serves 2

1 large or 2 medium ripe tomatoes
1-1/2 tablespoons olive oil
1 small clove garlic, crushed
5 fresh basil leaves, slivered (or 1/2 teaspoon crushed dried basil)
1 tablespoon minced parsley
Dash hot pepper sauce
Grinding or pinch black pepper
1/4 teaspoon salt
3 black olives, slivered (optional, but a real flavor boost)
2 to 3 ounces thin spaghetti

Peel tomato. Cut in half crosswise; remove and discard juicy seed sections (I use my thumb to scoop them out). Cut tomato into small chunks; set aside in strainer to drain.

In a small bowl combine oil, garlic, basil, parsley, hot sauce, pepper, salt, and olives if using. Add tomato chunks; mix well. Cover; set aside up to two hours on counter. Refrigerate for longer storage, but set out to warm to room temperature before serving.

Cook spaghetti according to package directions (I snap it in half before cooking). Quickly drain in a strainer; return to hot cooking pan; add tomato mixture; toss well. Serve immediately—with slotted spoon to drain, if necessary.

TOMATO-CHEESE BULGUR*
2 servings

A hearty Tex-Mex-flavored side dish to serve with beef or lamb patties, sausage links, roast pork, or lamb.

1-1/2 tablespoons margarine
1/2 onion, chopped
1 clove garlic, minced
1/4 green pepper, chopped
1/2 cup bulgur wheat
1/4 teaspoon dried basil
1/4 teaspoon chili powder
1/4 teaspoon salt
1/2 teaspoon sugar
1 cup tomato juice
1/2 cup shredded sharp Cheddar cheese

In medium skillet melt margarine on low heat. Add onion, garlic, and green pepper as you chop them. Cook until onion and green pepper are soft. Add bulgur. Cook one minute, stirring, on medium heat. Remove from heat. Measure in oregano, basil, chili powder, salt, and sugar, then stir in tomato juice. (If skillet is too hot when tomato juice is added, the dish will have a burned taste.) Over medium heat, stir to mix well. Bring to boiling; cover; reduce heat; simmer until all liquid is absorbed, about 20 minutes. Remove from heat; add cheese; stir until melted and serve.

BULGUR SALAD

2 servings

This do-ahead salad is an American version of Tabouli (or Tabbouleh). The mint leaves are optional, but an especially good addition if served with lamb.

1/3 cup bulgur wheat
Water
1 clove garlic
2 tablespoons olive oil
1 tablespoon lemon juice
1/2 teaspoon salt
Dash black pepper
2 sprigs parsley
1 green onion
4 mint leaves (optional)
1 large tomato

Measure bulgur into a small bowl; add hot tap water to cover. Split garlic clove; push down into bulgur; let stand about 20 minutes.

Meanwhile, in a medium bowl, whisk together oil, lemon juice, salt, and pepper. With scissors snip in parsley, green onion, and mint, if using. Chop tomato (on a plate to save juice); add tomato and juice to dressing.

Remove garlic from bulgur; drain in a strainer; press out excess water with back of spoon; add to tomato mixture. Mix well; cover; refrigerate several hours to overnight. (I usually make it in the morning for the evening meal.)

BULGUR PILAF

2 Servings

1 tablespoon butter
1 green onion
1/3 cup bulgur wheat
3/4 cup chicken or beef broth

In medium saucepan melt butter. With scissors snip in onion; cook until soft. Add bulgur; stir over medium heat about one minute. Remove from heat; stir in broth; bring to boiling over high heat; cover; reduce heat; simmer until all liquid is absorbed, 15 to 20 minutes. Taste for salt. Lighten with a fork. Sprinkle with chopped parsley, chives, or other fresh herb if desired. Try adding cooked (or leftover) peas just before serving.

If cooked ahead, add a little water to reheat.

PIEROGI ONE-DISH

12 potatoes, boiled and mashed
1 cup shredded cheddar cheese
1-1/2 cups butter (or margarine)
1 onion, minced
2 cups cooked noodles

Mash potatoes and mix in cheddar cheese. Sauté onions in margarine. Cook noodles and allow to cool. In a well-greased casserole, place a layer of noodles, potatoes, then onions. Repeat with second layer. Cover and bake at 325 degrees for 25 minutes.

FILLING

CHEESE 'N CHIVE

1/2 cup cottage cheese
3 eggs, beaten
1 teaspoon sugar
2 tablespoons chives

Combine all ingredients and mix well. Place by small teaspoonsful on pierogies and seal edges well.

FILLING

CABBAGE 'N BACON

1/2 head cabbage, chopped
1/2 pound bacon
1 small onion, minced

Steam cabbage and place in a meat grinder, cutting until very fine. Meanwhile, fry bacon and crumble. Add bacon and onion to cabbage and blend well.

FILLING

MUSHROOMS

1 cup mushrooms, chopped
2 tablespoons butter
2 egg yolks

Melt butter and sauté mushrooms. Remove from heat and add egg yolks for firmness. Mix well.

BLENDER PIEROGI DOUGH

2 cups cottage cheese
1 tablespoon butter
3 eggs, separated
1 teaspoon salt
1 teaspoon sugar
2-1/2 cups flour

In a blender, mix cottage cheese until smooth. Add egg yolks, salt, sugar and flour. Beat until light. Add egg whites and fold in. Knead on a floured board for about 15 minutes. Roll out as thin as possible and cut with biscuit cutter. Place filling in center of dough and fold. Moisten with water. Carefully place in boiling water until they rise to the top.

PIEROGI DOUGH

3 cups sifted flour
1 teaspoon salt
1/3 cup butter
2 eggs, beaten
3/4 cup warm water

Sift flour and salt together. Use a fork to work in butter (batter will be lumpy). Add eggs and water; stir until smooth. Place dough on well-floured board and knead until smooth, about 15 minutes. Set aside for 15 minutes.

Roll out dough as thin as possible. Cut dough with biscuit cutter. Spoon a small teaspoon of filling onto the center of each piece of pierogi dough.

Fold dough in half and pinch edges together by sealing with water. Carefully place in salted boiling water, cooking about 7 minutes, *or until they rise to the top.* Drain and serve with melted butter.

DESSERT PLUM SAUCE
Plenty for 2 sundaes

2 tablespoons sugar
1/2 teaspoon cornstarch
Pinch salt
2 large red plums
1/2 teaspoon lemon juice, if you have it
Few drops almond flavoring (optional)

In a small dry saucepan mix sugar, cornstarch, and salt until cornstarch disappears using a small whisk. Slice plums into saucepan. Stir gently over medium heat until boiling; reduce heat; simmer until sauce is thickened and clear, about 4 minutes. Stir in lemon juice and almond flavoring, if using. Set aside to cool completely. Serve over vanilla ice cream.

PINEAPPLE BUTTERMILK SHERBET

There is nothing more refreshing on a blistering hot day.

2 cups buttermilk
1/3 cup sugar
1 teaspoon vanilla
1 (8-ounce) can crushed pineapple, undrained (preferably in heavy syrup)

Measure buttermilk into a medium bowl. (I use a stainless steel bowl so that I can put it into the freezer.) Whisk in sugar and vanilla; stir in pineapple. Freeze until mushy. This takes about 2 hours. Whisk well; return bowl to freezer for about 2 hours, stirring now and then for a creamy sherbet.

Leftover sherbet will freeze solid—transfer to refrigerator to soften before serving.

LIME SORBET
Serves 2

A cool lime-flavored ice.

1/3 cup sugar
2/3 cup water
1 lime
Few grains salt

Place a one-quart freezer-safe bowl in freezer.

Combine sugar and water in a small saucepan. Stir over medium heat until sugar dissolves. When it comes to a boil, reduce heat and simmer for 6 minutes.

Roll lime on counter top to release juice; squeeze lime; add juice and salt to sweet syrup. Transfer to chilled bowl and freeze until mushy. It usually takes about 2 hours. Whisk thoroughly; freeze until barely firm. Serve in chilled dishes.

SHORTCAKE
(Two servings)

1/2 cup flour, spoon lightly into cup
3/4 teaspoon baking powder
1/8 teaspoon salt
1 tablespoons sugar
2 tablespoon shortening (I use half butter)
3 tablespoons milk

Preheat oven to 425-degrees. Measure flour, baking powder, salt and sugar into small bowl. Mix with pastry blender. Add shortening; cut in with pastry blender. When like fine crumbs, add milk; mix lightly with fork until it comes together (it will be a sticky ball). Drop into two mounds on small ungreased baking sheet. Use a fork to gently flatten and shape to a thick 3-inch biscuit. Sprinkle with sugar. Bake until beginning to brown, 10 to 12 minutes. Transfer to cooking rack. Split as soon as cool enough to handle, Serve warm or cold.

To assemble strawberry shortcake, spread bottom of shortcake with sweetened whipped cream; spoon on sliced, sweetened strawberries; cover with biscuit top, remaining whipped cream and berries.

SHORTCUT BREAD PUDDING WITH BOURBON SAUCE
Serves 2

Using cinnamon raisin bread is the shortcut. Expect a firm pudding because it is served with sauce.

1 tablespoon butter or margarine
2-1/2 slices cinnamon raisin bread
1 large egg
3/4 cup half-and-half or milk
1/4 cup sugar
1/8 teaspoon salt
1/2 teaspoon vanilla

Preheat oven to 350 degrees. Grease or spray a 1-quart casserole or souffle dish with pan release. Spread butter on one side of bread; cut into 1-inch squares. (1-1/2 cups loosely packed).

In a medium bowl, whisk egg to blend; whisk in half-and-half or milk, sugar, salt and vanilla. Add bread squares; stir until coated. (Let set a few minutes.) Pour into prepared dish. Set dish in pan containing 1/2 inch warm tap water. Bake until a rinsed knife inserted half way to center comes out clean, not milky, 35-40 minutes. Remove dish from hot water; cool at least 20 minutes before serving. Spoon into dessert dishes; pour on Bourbon Sauce.

Bourbon Sauce:
1/4 cup light brown sugar
1-1/2 teaspoons cornstarch
Few grains salt
1/3 cup water
1 to 2 tablespoons bourbon
1 tablespoon butter
1/4 teaspoon vanilla

Use brandy or dark rum instead of bourbon, if you prefer—one tablespoon for a mild-flavored sauce, two tablespoons for a powerful flavor.

In a small saucepan mix brown sugar, cornstarch, and salt. Stir in water; mix until smooth. With a rubber spatula stir over medium heat until boiling. Cook over low heat about 4 minutes, stirring often. Remove from heat; add bourbon; stir 1 minute over high heat (to evaporate the alcohol—empty calories); take off heat; stir in butter and vanilla. If made ahead, cover when cool and leave on counter. Serve sauce warm, or at room temperature, if dessert is hot.

Desserts
DELICIOUS

ICE-CREAM DESSERT
Serves 12-15

1/2 cup butter, melted
1 (10-ounce) package shortbread cookies, crushed
2 (3-ounce) packages instant vanilla pudding
2 cups milk
1 teaspoon vanilla
4 cups vanilla ice cream
1 (4-1/2-ounce) container frozen whipped topping
3 Heath candy bars, crushed

Combine butter and cookie crumbs. Pat into a 9x13-inch pan. Bake at 350 degrees for 15 minutes. Cool. With electric mixer blend pudding, milk, and vanilla. Add ice cream and mix well. Spread over cooled crust. Let set until firm. Cover with whipped topping and sprinkle with crushed candy bars. Refrigerate until serving.

Ida Bloedow, Madison, Wis.

CHERRY EMPANADAS
Makes 12-14

1-1/2 cups flour
1 teaspoon baking powder
1/2 teaspoon salt
8 tablespoons shortening
4-6 teaspoons water
1 small can cherry pie filling (or filling of your choice)
Confectioners' sugar
Cinnamon

Mix flour, baking powder, and salt; cut in shortening. Add water and mix. Roll out 1/8 inch thick and cut into 3-inch circular pieces. Fill each half round piece with fruit filling. Moisten edges; fold over and seal. Bake in 400-degree oven for 15 minutes. Cool slightly; roll each cooked empanada in confectioners' sugar mixed with cinnamon.

PINEAPPLE RICE PUDDING
Serves 6-8

3 cups cooked rice
3 cups milk
1/4 cup sugar
1 tablespoon margarine
3 eggs, separated
1 (15-1/4-ounce) can crushed pineapple
1 teaspoon cinnamon
1/2 cup flaked coconut

In saucepan, combine rice, milk, sugar, and margarine. Cook over medium heat, stirring occasionally, about 25 minutes, until thick and creamy. Beat egg yolks; blend a little creamed rice into yolks. Stir yolks into the creamed rice and cook 2 minutes longer.

Remove from heat; add pineapple and cinnamon. Cool. Beat egg whites until stiff; fold into cooled rice. Turn into greased 9-inch square baking pan. Sprinkle coconut on top. Bake at 325 degrees for 25 minutes.

June Harding, Ferndale, Mich.

CRANBERRY FLUFF
Serves 6

1 can whole cranberry sauce
1-1/2 cups finely crushed vanilla-wafer crumbs (about 20 wafers)
1 cup heavy cream, whipped

With fork, break up cranberry sauce. Blend in crumbs. Fold in whipped cream. Pile lightly in sherbet glasses; refrigerate 30 to 60 minutes.

Suzan L. Wiener, Spring Hill, Fla.

WHIPPED DESSERT TOPPING
Makes 1-2/3 cups

1/2 cup instant non-fat dry milk
1/2 cup ice water
2 tablespoons lemon juice
1/4 cup sugar
1/2 teaspoon vanilla

In a bowl combine nonfat dry milk, ice water, and lemon juice. Use an electric mixer and beat until mixture is very stiff. Beat in sugar and vanilla; beat until sugar is dissolved and mixture is smooth and creamy. Serve at once. Use as topping for desserts.

Variations: Make as directed, then blend in 2 tablespoons cocoa; or make as above and fold in 1/4 cup flaked coconut.

Marsha Miller, Hilliard, Ohio

CRANBERRY APPLE CRISP
Serves 9

5 cups sliced tart apples (about 6 medium apples)
1-1/2 cups Ocean Spray fresh or frozen cranberries
1/3 cup granulated sugar
1/2 cup all-purpose flour
1/2 cup brown sugar
1 teaspoon cinnamon
1/4 cup butter or margarine

Preheat oven to 375 degrees. Lightly grease a 9-inch square baking pan. Layer apple slices and cranberries in pan, sprinkling with granulated sugar as you layer. In a bowl, cut and mix together flour, brown sugar, and cinnamon. Cut in butter until light and crumbly. Sprinkle topping evenly over apples and cranberries. Bake 45 minutes, until apples are tender.

RHUBARB CRISP
Serves 6-8

1 cup flour
3/4 cup oatmeal
1 cup brown sugar
1 teaspoon cinnamon
1/2 cup margarine, melted
4 cups diced rhubarb

Sauce:
1 cup white sugar
2 tablespoons cornstarch
1 cup water
1 teaspoon vanilla

Preheat oven to 350 degrees. Mix flour, oatmeal, brown sugar, cinnamon, and melted margarine until crumbly. Divide in half, press one half of mixture into bottom of 9x9-inch pan. Cover bottom layer with 4 cups diced rhubarb.

In medium saucepan, combine white sugar, cornstarch, water, and vanilla. Cook until thickened and clear. Pour over rhubarb. Pat remaining crumb mixture on top. Bake at 350 degrees for 1 hour.
Judith L. Bailey, Lima, Ohio

PARADISE DESSERT
Serves 8

1 box regular-size lemon gelatin
1 pint boiling water
1/2 cup blanched almonds
12 large marshmallows, diced small
12 maraschino cherries, chopped
6 crushed macaroon cookies
4 tablespoons sugar
1/4 teaspoon salt
1-1/2 cups Cool Whip

Dissolve gelatin in boiling water and chill. When thickened beat until consistency of whipped cream. Combine next 6 ingredients and add to gelatin mixture. Fold in Cool Whip and turn into a 7x5-inch loaf pan and chill until firm. Unmold and slice into 3/4-inch slices to serve.
Jodie McCoy, Tulsa, Okla.

RASPBERRY REFRIGERATOR DESSERT
Serves 15-18

2 (10-ounce) packages frozen red raspberries
1 cup water
1/2 cup sugar
2 teaspoons lemon juice
4 tablespoons cornstarch
1/4 cup cold water
50 large marshmallows
1 cup milk
2 cups heavy cream or 2 packages Dream Whip
1-1/4 cups graham cracker crumbs
1/4 cup chopped nuts
1/4 cup melted butter or margarine

Heat raspberries with water, sugar, and lemon juice. Dissolve cornstarch in 1/4 cup water; stir into raspberries and cook until thickened and clear. Cool. Melt marshmallows in milk over boiling water in a double boiler. Cool thoroughly. Whip cream or Dream Whip and fold into marshmallow mixture. Mix graham cracker crumbs, nuts, and butter in a 13x9x2-1/2 inch pan. Press firmly into bottom of pan. Spread marshmallow cream mixture over crumbs. Spread raspberry mixture over top. Refrigerate until firm.
Marcelia Swigert, Monroe City, Mo.

EASY PEACH BUTTERSCOTCH CRISP
Serves 6

2 (16-ounce) cans sliced peaches, well drained
1/4 cup raisins
1 (3-3/4 ounce) package instant butterscotch pudding mix
1/2 cup flour
1/3 cup chopped dry roasted peanuts
1/4 cup old fashioned rolled oats
1/2 cup butter or margarine

Heat oven to 400 degrees. In an 8-inch square baking pan place peaches and raisins; set aside. In small bowl combine remaining ingredients, cutting in the butter or margarine until mixture is crumbly. Sprinkle crumbly mixture over peaches and raisins. Bake 15-20 minutes or until bubbly around edges. Serve with ice cream.
Diantha Hibbard, Rochester, N.Y.

STRAWBERRY CHEESE DELIGHT

2 (3-ounce) packages lady fingers
2 (10-ounce) packages frozen strawberries
1/4 cup cold water
1-1/2 tablespoons cornstarch
1 (8-ounce) package cream cheese, softened
1 cup confectioners' sugar
1 pint whipping cream, whipped
1 teaspoon vanilla

In 2 quart saucepan, bring berries to a gentle boil. Mix the cold water and cornstarch in a cup and slowly pour into the berries, stirring until thickened. Set aside to cool.

In mixing bowl beat softened cream cheese with confectioners' sugar until smooth. Fold in whipped cream and vanilla; set aside.

Line bottom of 13x9 inch pan with lady fingers. Top with cream cheese mixture. Finally top with the strawberry mixture. Refrigerate until ready to serve.
Jane Ann Weimann, Woodstock, Conn.

RHUBARB BERRY DELIGHT

Filling:
1-1/2 cups fresh or frozen chopped rhubarb
1 cup fresh or frozen, sliced strawberries
1/2 cup granulated sugar
1 tablespoon corn starch

Mix all ingredients well in a large bowl. Fill a 10-inch glass pie plate with the fruit mixture. Set aside while preparing topping.

Topping:
1/2 cup brown sugar
1/2 cup dry oats
1/2 cup all-purpose flour
1/2 cup butter or margarine

Mix all ingredients until crumbly. Sprinkle over fruit mixture until covered. Bake at 350 degrees for 20 minutes until fruit is tender and topping is golden brown. Serve warm with fresh whipped cream for a decorative touch.

BLUEBERRY SWIRL ICE CREAM
Makes 1-1/2 quarts

1 recipe Cheesecake Ice Cream (see above)
1/2 cup water
1/4 cup sugar
1 teaspoon cornstarch
1 tablespoon lemon juice
1 cup fresh or frozen blueberries, unsweetened
1/8 teaspoon cinnamon

Combine water and sugar in a saucepan. Bring to a boil, stirring to dissolve sugar. Dissolve cornstarch in lemon juice. Add to ingredients in pan, stirring until thickened. Add blueberries and cinnamon. Boil for about 2 minutes, mashing the berries slightly with the back of a large spoon or potato masher. Remove from heat. Chill thoroughly. Swirl into soft Cheesecake Ice Cream after removing it from freezer. Refreeze until firm.

BUTTERFINGER ICE CREAM

1 can Eagle Brand milk
8 eggs (or Egg Beaters)
1/2 cup peanut butter
1 can evaporated milk
3 cups sugar
Milk to fill freezer
4 King-size Butterfinger candy bars or 8 (11-ounce) size

Mix first 6 ingredients, then add chopped or broken Butterfingers. Freeze in 1-1/2 gallon ice cream freezer.

Sue Thomas, Casa Grande, Ariz.

BUTTERSCOTCH ICE CREAM
Makes 1 quart

1 quart vanilla ice cream, softened
1/2 cup butterscotch-flavored morsels
1/2 cup toasted walnuts
1/2 cup chopped toasted coconut

In large bowl, combine ice cream, butterscotch-flavored morsels, walnuts, and coconut. Stir until well blended. Pour into airtight container; freeze until firm.

Peggy Fowler Revels, Woodruff, S.C.

CHOCOLATY CHOCOLATE ICE CREAM
Serves 4

3 tablespoons cocoa
3/4 cup whole milk
1/2 cup water
2 teaspoons sugar
1/2 teaspoon vanilla

In mixing bowl mix milk and cocoa thoroughly. Add sugar, water, and vanilla; beat well. Pour into refrigerator tray and freeze until firm.

Susan L. Wiener, Spring Hill, Fla.

STRAWBERRY ICE CREAM

1 (14-ounce) can sweetened condensed milk
1 (10-ounce) package frozen strawberries in syrup, thawed
2 cups whipping cream

Whirl thawed strawberries in blender until smooth. Combine strawberries with condensed milk, then fold in whipped cream, and freeze, according to the directions for Chocolate Ice Cream (recipe follows).

NO-FUSS CHOCOLATE ICE CREAM
Makes 1-1/2 quarts

1 (14-ounce) can sweetened condensed milk
2/3 cup chocolate syrup
2 cups whipping cream

In large bowl, stir together the condensed milk and chocolate syrup. Whip cream until stiff. Gently fold into chocolate/condensed milk mixture. Line a 9 x 5-inch loaf pan (or other 2-quart container) with aluminum foil. Pour ice cream mixture into lined pan and cover with foil. Freeze for 6 hours or until firm. To serve, scoop ice cream directly from pan or remove from pan in one piece; peel off foil, and slice.

"COOKIES AND CREAM" ICE CREAM
Makes 1-1/2 quarts

3 egg yolks
1 (14-ounce) can sweetened condensed milk
2 tablespoons water
4 teaspoons vanilla extract
1 cup coarsely-crushed chocolate sandwich cookies
2 cups whipping cream

In large bowl, beat egg yolks. Stir in milk, water, and vanilla. Fold in cookies and whipped cream. Pour into aluminum foil-lined 9 x 5-inch loaf pan or other 2-quart container. Cover. Freeze 6 hours or until firm.

CHOCOLATE ICE CREAM
Makes 4 servings

3/4 cup milk powder
3 tablespoons cocoa
1/2 cup water
8 teaspoons sugar
1/2 teaspoon vanilla

Mix milk powder and cocoa thoroughly. Add sugar, water, and vanilla. Beat until smooth and pour into refrigerator tray. Freeze until firm.

Susan L. Wiener, Spring Hill, Fla.

WHITE CHOCOLATE ICE CREAM
Makes 1 quart

1 cup water
3/4 cup sugar
6 egg yolks
1 tablespoon vanilla
10 ounces Swiss or French white chocolate, melted
2 cups whipping cream

In heavy medium-size saucepan, blend water and sugar. Cook over low heat until sugar dissolves, swirling pan occasionally. Bring to a boil. Let boil 5 minutes. Meanwhile, combine egg yolks and vanilla in large bowl of electric mixer and beat at high speed until light and fluffy, about 7 minutes. Slowly, add hot syrup to yolk mixture, beating constantly until thickened and completely cooked, about 10 minutes. Gradually add white chocolate and continue beating until cooked, about 7 minutes. Stir in cream. Cover and freeze until set, at least 5 or 6 hours, or overnight.

CHEESECAKE ICE CREAM
Makes about 2 quarts

2 egg yolks
1 cup sugar, divided
1 cup half-and-half
2 (8-ounce) packages cream cheese
1/2 teaspoon grated lemon rind
1/2 teaspoon grated orange rind
1 tablespoon lemon juice

1/2 teaspoon vanilla
1 pint plain yogurt

In heavy saucepan, beat egg yolks with 1/2 cup sugar. Beat in half-and-half. Cook over low heat, stirring constantly, until just thick enough to coat back of spoon. Do not boil. Remove from heat. Chill thoroughly. Beat cream cheese until light. Add remaining sugar, lemon, and orange rinds, lemon juice, and vanilla. Continue to beat until smooth. Freeze in flat trays, then beat with rotary beater or in food processor.

LEMON ICE CREAM
Serves 6

2 eggs
1/2 cup sugar
1/2 cup light corn syrup
1-1/4 cups milk
1 cup whipping cream or Dream Whip
1/4 cup lemon juice
2 teaspoons grated lemon peel (2 lemons)

Beat eggs until light and lemon-colored. Add sugar gradually, beating constantly. Add corn syrup, milk, whipping cream, lemon juice, and grated lemon peel. Mix well. Put in 9x5-inch loaf pan. Freeze until firm, about 9 hours (covering with aluminum foil). Turn out into chilled bowl; beat until light. Return to 9x5-inch loaf pan. Cover; freeze until firm, 9 hours.

Mrs. Albert Foley, Lemoyne, Pa.

FRESH PEACH ICE CREAM
Makes about 2 quarts

2 eggs
3/4 cup sugar
1/8 teaspoon salt
3/4 cup light corn syrup
1 cup heavy cream

1 cup milk
3 cups peeled and sliced fresh ripe peaches
1 tablespoon, plus 2 teaspoons lemon juice
1/8 teaspoon almond extract

In large bowl of mixer beat eggs, sugar, and salt until thick and light-colored. Beat in corn syrup and cream until well blended. In blender, whirl until smooth, milk, peaches, lemon juice, and almond extract. Beat into cream mixture until well-blended. Freeze until almost firm. Beat until smooth. Freeze again, then beat again. Turn into chilled 9 x 9-inch baking pan or 9 x 5 x 3-inch loaf pan. Freeze until firm, then cover airtight.

PEPPERMINT ICE CREAM
Serves 6

1 envelope unflavored gelatin
1/2 cup cold milk
1-1/4 cups crushed peppermint candy
2 cups whipped whipping cream
1-1/2 cups scalded milk

Soften gelatin in cold milk; dissolve in hot milk. Add 1 cup candy and dissolve. Freeze. Break up and beat until smooth. Fold in cream and 1/4 cup candy. Freeze.

Kenneth McAdams, El Dorado, Ark.

RASPBERRY ICE CREAM
Makes 2 quarts

1 (10-ounce) package frozen raspberries, thawed
1/2 cup sugar
2-1/2 cups milk
1-1/2 cups whipping cream
1-1/2 teaspoons vanilla extract

Process undrained raspberries with food mill to remove seeds. Combine raspberries and remaining ingredients. Stir until sugar is dissolved. Pour mixture into 1 gallon freezer can. Freeze according to manufacturer's instructions. Let ripen at least 1 hour. Delicious!!

Mrs. Bruce Fowler, Woodruff, S.C.

VANILLA ICE CREAM
Serves 6

2 eggs
1/2 cup sugar
1/8 teaspoon salt
1/2 cup light corn syrup
1-1/3 cups heavy cream
2/3 cup milk
1 teaspoon lemon juice
Seeds scraped from split 6-inch
   vanilla bean

In large bowl of electric mixer beat eggs, sugar, and salt until thick and light-colored. Beat in remaining ingredients until well blended. Freeze until almost firm. Beat until smooth. Freeze again, then beat again. Turn into chilled 9 x 9-inch baking pan or 9 x 5 x 3-inch loaf pan. Freeze until firm, then cover airtight. Makes about 1 quart.

PEACH SHERBET

1 (1-pound) can peaches
1 tablespoon Tang powder
Pinch of salt
1/4 cup ice water

Empty can of peaches into freezer tray to freeze. When frozen, break into small pieces. Combine ingredients in blender and blend until smooth. Pour into chilled sherbet glasses, or freeze until ready to serve.

Mrs. Melvin Habiger, Spearville, Kan.

RASPBERRY SHERBET
Makes 1-1/2 pints

3/4 cup sugar
1/4 cup water
1 cup raspberry juice
1/4 cup lemon juice
Pinch of salt
1 cup evaporated milk

Boil sugar and water to a thin syrup. Add fruit juices and salt. Chill milk in ice cream can. Pour cold fruit juice mixture slowly into the milk. Freeze with ratio 1:8 salt-ice mixture.

Marcella Swigert, Monroe City, Mo.

APPLE-CHEESE PUDDING
Serves 6

2 cups firmly packed dark brown
   sugar
1 quart water
1 stick cinnamon
1 clove
6 slices stale bread, toasted and
   cubed
3 apples, pared, cored, and sliced
1 cup raisins
1 cup chopped blanched almonds
1/2 pound Monterey Jack or similar
   cheese, cubed

Put brown sugar, water, cinnamon, and clove into a saucepan and bring to boiling; reduce heat and simmer until a light syrup is formed. Discard spices; set syrup aside. Meanwhile, arrange a layer of toast cubes in a buttered casserole. Cover with a layer of apples, raisins, almonds, and cheese. Repeat until all ingredients are used. Pour syrup over all. Bake at 350 degrees for 30 minutes. Serve hot.

SOUR-CREAM APPLE PUDDING

5 large apples
1 cup brown sugar
1/4 cup butter
1 cup graham-cracker crumbs
1/2 cup flour
1 teaspoon cinnamon
1 cup sour cream

Peel and cut apples. Mix flour, sugar, and cinnamon together; combine with apples. Cut butter over surface of apples. Top with sour cream.Sprinkle the top surface with graham-cracker crumbs. Bake at 375 degrees for 20-25 minutes.

Mildred Sherrer, Bay City, Texas

BLACK BREAD PUDDING
Serves 6

6 eggs, separated
1/2 cup sugar
1/4 teaspoon salt
1 cup stale bread crumbs (made from
   rye, pumpernickel or whole wheat
   bread)
3/4 teaspoon cinnamon
1/4 teaspoon cloves
2 tablespoons melted butter
Stale dry bread crumbs, fine

Beat egg yolks at high speed in a small bowl until thick. Gradually beat in sugar. Continue beating at high speed until mixture is very thick and piles softly. Using clean beaters and a large bowl, beat egg whites with salt until stiff, not dry, peaks form. Fold bread crumbs, cinnamon, and cloves into beaten yolks. Then fold in 1 tablespoon melted butter. Fold in egg whites. Brush a 2-quart deep casserole with remaining 1 tablespoon melted butter. Coat dish with bread crumbs. Gently turn soufflé mixture into prepared dish. Bake at 350 degrees for 25-30 minutes, or until set in center.

BAKED RICE PUDDING
Serves 6-8

1 cup sugar
1-1/2 teaspoons cornstarch
1/8 teaspoon ground nutmeg
3 eggs, beaten
2 cups milk
1 cup raisins
2/3 cup cooked regular rice
1/2 teaspoon vanilla extract

Combine sugar, cornstarch, and nutmeg in a medium mixing bowl. Add eggs, beating until well-combined. Add milk, raisins, rice, and vanilla, stirring until well-blended. Pour mixture into a greased 8-inch square pan. Place prepared pan in a 13x9x2-inch baking pan; add boiling water to a depth of 1 inch. Bake at 325 degrees for 1 hour or until a knife inserted in center comes out clean. Spoon into individual serving bowls. Serve hot! This recipe is great for leftover rice.

Marilyn Jones, Indianapolis, Ind.

OLD-FASHIONED RICE PUDDING
Serves 6

1 quart skim milk
1 teaspoon Sweet 'N Low sugar
   substitute
1/4 cup raw white rice
1 tablespoon butter
1/4 teaspoon salt
1/4 teaspoon nutmeg
1 teaspoon vanilla

Preheat oven at 325 degrees. In a lightly greased 1-1/2 quart casserole, combine all ingredients. Bake uncovered, stirring frequently, for the first hour. The complete cooking time is 2-1/2 hours. This may be served topped with low-calorie whipped cream or crushed fruit. (115 calories per serving)

Judy Codenys, LaGrange, Texas

FIGGY PUDDING
Serves 8-10

1-1/2 cups all-purpose flour
1 teaspoon baking powder
1/2 teaspoon baking soda
1/2 teaspoon cinnamon
1/2 teaspoon nutmeg
1/2 teaspoon ginger
1 cup chopped cranberries
1 cup shredded carrots
1 cup packed brown sugar
1/2 cup cooking oil
1/2 cup honey
2 beaten eggs

In a large bowl, combine dry ingredients. In a bowl, combine carrots, cranberries, brown sugar, oil, honey, and eggs. Add carrot mixture to dry ingredients. Pour into greased 7-cup mold. Bake in a 325-degree oven for 30 to 40 minutes or until it tests done. Serve with Orange Hard Sauce (recipe follows).

Orange Hard Sauce:
Makes 1/2 cup
1/4 cup butter, softened
1 cup sifted confectioners' sugar
1/4 teaspoon shredded orange peel
1 tablespoon orange juice

Beat butter and sugar together in a small bowl. Beat in peel and juice until well-blended. Spoon into small serving bowl. Chill.

Marcella Swigert, Monroe City, Mo.

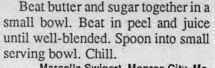

PARTY PUNCH BOWL DESSERT

1 box yellow cake mix
2 large boxes strawberry gelatin
2 large containers Cool Whip
2 large (10-ounce) packages frozen
   sliced strawberries
2 large packages regular vanilla
   pudding (*not* instant)
Fresh strawberries for garnish

Use 2 (8-inch) round layer cake pans and a clear glass punch bowl. Make cake according to box directions. Cool; cut layers horizontally by pulling string through so you have 4 layers. Make vanilla pudding according to package directions and let cool. Mix 2-1/2 cups boiling water with 2 packages strawberry gelatin to dissolve. Add the 2 packages of partially thawed berries. Put in refrigerator until mixture thickens—but do not let it get too firm.

To assemble:
In the punch bowl add 1/4 of the gelatin mixture.
First layer of cake, 1/4 more gelatin, spread a layer of Cool Whip, then a layer of pudding.
Second layer of cake, gelatin, Cool Whip, pudding
Third layer of cake, gelatin, Cool Whip, pudding
Fourth layer of cake only, topped with thick layer of Cool Whip. Garnish with fresh, sliced berries. You can make this the night before but *do not* put last layer of Cool Whip on until an hour or so before serving. Use large serving spoon to scoop out servings. Prepare for raving reviews on appearance and taste!

Mary Fuller, Warren, Ohio

CARAMEL TOPPED RICE CUSTARD
Serves 6

12 caramel candies
2-1/4 cups milk, divided
2 cups cooked rice, cooled
4 eggs
1/3 cup packed brown sugar
1 teaspoon vanilla extract
1/4 teaspoon salt

Combine caramels and 1/4 cup milk in small saucepan. Cook, stirring, over medium-low heat until caramels melt. Pour equal amounts into 6 buttered, 3/4-cup custard cups. Spoon 1/3 cup rice into each cup. Blend remaining ingredients; pour evenly into each cup. Place cups in shallow pan, containing 1 inch water. Bake at 350 degrees for 45 minutes, or until custard is set. Loosen custard with knife and invert onto dessert plates. Garnish with chopped nuts or coconut, if desired. Serve warm.

STRAWBERRIES WITH SOUR CREAM CUSTARD

1/2 cup sugar
2-1/2 tablespoons cornstarch
1-1/2 cups milk
4 eggs, beaten
1/2 cup sour cream
1-1/2 teaspoons vanilla
1-2 pints fresh strawberries
   (washed, hulled and halved)

Combine sugar and cornstarch in medium saucepan. Gradually, stir in milk and cook over medium heat, stirring constantly until it boils. Boil and stir 1 minute. Remove from heat. Blend milk mixture *into egg mixture* in saucepan. Add sour cream and vanilla; beat with whisk until well blended. Cool *immediately* by placing in a bowl of ice cold water for a few minutes. Cover and chill thoroughly. To serve, spoon custard sauce over strawberries. Will literally melt in your mouth.
Strawberry Almond Fritters are also completely different from the usual.

BUTTERSCOTCH TAPIOCA

Serves 4

3 tablespoons quick-cooking tapioca
1/8 teaspoon salt
2 cups milk
1 tablespoon butter
1/2 cup dark brown sugar
1/4 cup finely chopped pecans

Mix tapioca, salt, and milk in a pan and let stand for 5 minutes. Cook over moderate heat, stirring constantly, for about 6 minutes, until mixture comes to a full boil. Remove from heat. Melt butter in a small skillet and stir in brown sugar. Cook over moderate heat, stirring until sugar melts and bubbles for 1 minute. Stir into tapioca mixture and add pecans. Serve warm or chilled.

Lucille Roehr, Hammond, Ind.

ELEGANT CHOCOLATE ANGEL TORTE

Serves 12

1/3 cup Hershey's cocoa
1 (14.5 ounce) package angel food cake mix
2.8-ounce package (2 envelopes) whipped topping mix
1 cup *cold* milk
1 teaspoon vanilla
1 cup strawberry purée*
Strawberries

Combine cocoa and contents of cake flour packet. Proceed with mixing cake as directed on package. Bake and cool as directed. Slice cooled cake crosswise into four 1-inch slices. Combine topping mix, cold milk, and vanilla in large mixer bowl; prepare according to package directions. Blend in strawberry puree. Place bottom cake slice on serving plate; spread with one-fourth of topping.

Stack next cake layer; spread with topping. Continue layering cake and topping. Garnish with strawberries. Refrigerate. To serve, use sharp serrated knife and cut with a gentle sawing motion.
*Mash or puree 2 cups sliced fresh strawberries (or frozen berries, thawed) in blender or food processor to measure 1 cup.

BUTTERSCOTCH TORTE

Serves 8

1 package fluffy white frosting mix (for 2-layer cake)
1 teaspoon vanilla
1 cup graham-cracker crumbs
1 (6-ounce) package butterscotch chips
1/2 cup coconut
1/2 cup chopped pecans

Prepare frosting mix according to package directions. Add vanilla. Fold in all other ingredients carefully, and spread in a greased 9-inch plate. Bake in a 350-degree oven for 30 minutes or until lightly browned. Serve with vanilla ice cream or a dab of whipped cream, if desired.

Agnes Ward, Erie, Pa.

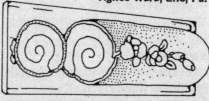

APPLE CHEESE TORTE

1/2 cup butter, softened
2/3 cup sugar, plus 1/4 cup sugar
3/4 teaspoon vanilla
1 cup flour
1 (8-ounce) package cream cheese, softened
1 egg
1/2 teaspoon cinnamon
4 cups peeled, sliced apples
1/4 cup sliced almonds

Preheat oven to 450 degrees. Cream butter, 1/3 cup sugar, and 1/4 tea-

spoon vanilla. Blend in flour. Spread dough onto bottom and 1-1/2 inches up the sides of a 9-inch spring-form pan.

Combine cream cheese and 1/4 cup sugar. Mix well. Add egg and remaining 1/2 teaspoon vanilla. Pour into pastry-lined pan. Combine 1/3 cup sugar and cinnamon. Add apples, spoon over cheese layer. Sprinkle with sliced almonds. Bake at 450 degrees for 10 minutes; reduce heat to 400 degrees and bake for 35 minutes. Cool before removing from pan.
Shirley Viscosi, Worcester, Mass.

CHOCOLATE ECLAIR TORTE

Serves 12-16

2 (6-ounce) packages instant vanilla pudding
3 cups milk
1 (10-ounce) container whipped topping
Graham crackers

Beat pudding and milk for two minutes. Add whipped topping. Line bottom of 9x13-inch pan with whole graham crackers. Pour half of pudding mixture over crackers. Put another layer of whole graham crackers and the rest of pudding mixture. Then top with last layer of whole graham crackers. Frost with Eclair Frosting (recipe follows).

Eclair Frosting:
4 (1-ounce) packages Nestle's Chocobake or 4 squares melted semisweet chocolate
1-1/2 cups confectioners' sugar
2 tablespoons butter or margarine
2 tablespoons white corn syrup
1 teaspoon vanilla
3 tablespoons milk

Mix thoroughly. Place on top of torte. Refrigerate overnight before serving.

Ida Bloedow, Madison, Wis.

STRAWBERRY MERINGUE TORTE

3 egg whites
1/2 teaspoon baking powder
1 cup sugar
10 squares or 10 soda crackers
  rolled fine
1/2 cup pecans, rolled fine
3 cups sliced strawberries
Cool Whip

Beat egg whites and baking powder until frothy. Gradually beat in sugar until whites are stiff. Fold in crackers and pecans. Spread in 9-inch pie pan, which has been greased thoroughly with butter. Bake 30 minutes in 300 degree oven.

Fill meringue tart with strawberries; top with Cool Whip when ready to serve.

Ruth Arnett, Fort Recovery, Ohio

STRAWBERRY ALMOND BUTTER

1/2 pound margarine
1 pound powdered sugar
1 pound strawberries
1/2 cup finely ground almonds

Cream butter with powdered sugar and work in the pound of hulled strawberries that have been forced through a colander. When well mixed, stir in almonds and pinch of salt, if desired.

For a change-of-pace dessert, strawberries with sour cream custard is a "conversation piece." This recipe will serve 6 and it looks delightful in a glass bowl that has been chilled.

FROZEN STRAWBERRY DESSERT

24 large marshmallows
1 (10-ounce) package frozen
  strawberries (thawed)
1 cup sifted flour
1/2 cup milk
1 envelope Dream Whip
1 stick margarine

Have margarine at room temperature. Cut margarine into flour to make crumbs. Press into bottom of 7x11-inch pan. Bake at 400 degrees until brown. Cool. Melt marshmallows in milk. Add strawberries and let cool. When cool, add prepared Dream Whip. Pour into crust and freeze. Best when eaten partially frozen.

I keep this dessert in the freezer for unexpected guests.

Charlene Stark, Riceville, Iowa

STRAWBERRY ALMOND FRITTERS

Strawberries
1 cup apricot jam
1 cup toasted almonds
1 cup cracker crumbs
2 eggs

Wash, hull, and dry strawberries on paper towel. Force apricot jam through coarse strainer. Finely chop toasted almonds and crush salted crackers until you have a cupful. Beat eggs slightly. Dip each berry in jam and roll in almonds. When all are coated, dip, two at a time, in egg and then crumbs. Chill. Before serving time, heat deep fat to 360 degrees and cook berries until they are golden brown. Serve at once, passing powdered sugar, if desired. These may be fried in skillet also.

Strawberries are not only for royalty, nor do we have to "sew a fine seam" to enjoy them. We are fortunate enough to have these delectable goodies available to us all year long. Whichever recipe you choose, it will add a noble note to your table.

STRAWBERRY GERMAN CREAM
Serves 6-8

1 (10-ounce) box frozen sliced
  strawberries, thawed
1 cup boiling water
1 (3-ounce) package strawberry
  gelatin
1 envelope dessert topping mix

Drain strawberries, reserving syrup. Pour boiling water over gelatin in bowl, stirring until gelatin is dissolved. Add enough cold water to reserved syrup to measure 1 cup; stir into dissolved gelatin. Chill until almost set. Prepare dessert topping mix as package directs. Beat gelatin until foamy. Fold gelatin and strawberries into topping mix. Pour into 1-quart mold. Chill until firm; unmold. Serve with sweetened whipped cream and garnish with strawberries.

Sharon M. Crider, Evansville, Wis.

FROSTY STRAWBERRY SUPREME
Serves 9-12

1 cup all-purpose flour
1/4 cup finely chopped pecans
1/4 cup brown sugar, packed
1/2 cup melted margarine
2 cups egg whites
1 (10-ounce) package frozen
  strawberries, partially thawed
2/3 cup white granulated sugar
2 tablespoons lemon juice
1 cup whipped cream or non-dairy
  whipped topping.

Combine flour, nuts, brown sugar, and melted margarine. Mix well and spread into 13x9-inch pan. Bake at 350 degrees for about 20 to 25 minutes, stirring to crumble. Combine egg whites, sugar, strawberries, and lemon juice in a large deep mixing bowl. Beat with electric mixer at high speed for 15 minutes. Fold in whipped cream or whipped topping. Place one-half the crumbs in bottom of the pan. Pour in strawberry mixture, then top with remaining crumbs. Freeze until firm. Cut into squares to serve. Top each serving with whipped topping, if desired. This is really a "Supreme" dessert.

Note: Use blueberries for a change of pace, adjusting to suit your own taste in regard to sugar.

Shirley Ann Crist, Marion, Ind.

APPLE DUMPLINGS

2 cups flour
2-1/2 teaspoons baking powder
1/2 teaspoon salt
1/2 cup shortening
1/4 cup milk
8 apples
8 tablespoons sugar
4 tablespoons butter
Cinnamon and sugar mixed

Sift flour, salt, and baking powder. Cut in shortening. Add milk and stir. Knead lightly on a floured board. Roll 1/8-inch thick. Divide dough into 8 parts. Peel and core apples. Place one apple on each section of dough. Fill hollow of apple with 1 tablespoon of sugar and 1 teaspoon of butter. Fold dough over apple, pressing edges together. Place in a shallow baking pan. Sprinkle with sugar-cinnamon mixture and dot with remaining butter. Bake at 400 degrees for 30-40 minutes. Serve with cream or half-and-half.

Joy B. Shamway, Freeport, Ill.

GOURMET ORANGE BAKED ALASKA
Serves 6

1 pint orange sherbet
3 large oranges
3 egg whites, stiffly beaten
1/4 teaspoon cream of tartar
1/4 cup plus 2 tablespoons sugar

Scoop sherbet into 6 balls; freeze at least 4 hours until very firm. Cut oranges crosswise in half; cut thin slice from bottom of each half. Cut around edges and membranes; remove fruit and membrane from orange shells. Line bottom of each shell with fruit; refrigerate. Beat egg whites and cream of tartar. Beat in sugar, 1 tablespoon at a time; beat until stiff and glossy. Place orange shells on ungreased baking sheet; fill each with a frozen sherbet ball. Completely cover sherbet ball with meringue, sealing it to the edge of the shell. Bake at 400 degrees for 4-5 minutes, or until meringue is light golden brown. Serve immediately.

Gwen Campbell, Sterling, Va.

BLACK FOREST TRIFLE

1 (9-ounce) package chocolate cake mix
1/4 cup rum or brandy (optional)
1 can cherry pie filling
1 package instant chocolate pudding
1 medium Cool Whip

Bake cake as package directs. Cool and cut in cubes. Prepare pudding as package directs. Arrange one half cake cubes in glass bowl. Sprinkle 1 ounce rum or brandy. Layer one half of pudding, then one half of cherry pie filling; next, one half of Cool Whip. Repeat layering in order given.

Chill at least 3 hours before serving. Looks very pretty in a tall stemmed bowl.

Helen Harlos, Ethel, Miss.

PUMPKIN DESSERT

1-1/3 cups graham cracker crumbs
1/4 cup sugar
1/4 cup soft butter
60 marshmallows
2 cups pumpkin
1 teaspoon cinnamon
1/2 teaspoon ginger
1/2 teaspoon salt
2 packages whipped topping mix, prepared according to package directions
1 cup sweetened whipped cream
Toasted coconut

Mix graham cracker crumbs with sugar and soft butter. Press into a 9x13-inch pan. Bake at 375 degrees for 8 to 10 minutes. Let cool. Melt marshmallows, pumpkin, spices, and salt in a double boiler or other large pan. Fold in whipped topping and spread the mixture over graham cracker crust. Spread the whipped cream over top of pumpkin mixture. Top with toasted coconut. Chill in refrigerator before serving.

Mrs. James Williams, Brainerd, Minn.

OLD-FASHIONED BLUEBERRY BUCKLE
Serves 6

2 cups flour
3 teaspoons baking powder
1/2 cup margarine
1/2 cup sugar
1 egg, beaten
1/2 cup milk
1/2 teaspoon almond flavoring

Topping:
2 cups fresh or frozen blueberries
2 teaspoons lemon juice
1/4 cup sugar
1/3 cup flour
1/2 teaspoon cinnamon
1/4 cup margarine

Sift flour with baking powder. Set aside. In mixing bowl cream margarine and sugar. Add egg; beat until creamy. Combine milk and almond flavoring; add to creamed mixture alternately with flour; beat until smooth. Pour into buttered 9-inch square pan. Sprinkle lemon juice over blueberries and spread over batter. Mix sugar, flour, cinnamon and margarine thoroughly with fingers until crumbly. Spread over blueberries. Bake at 350 degrees for 45-50 minutes, or until it tests done. Serve warm or cold, with cream, if desired.

Foreign &
EXOTIC

ENCHILADAS

1 pound ground beef
1 onion, chopped
2 teaspoons salt
1/4 teaspoon pepper
2 teaspoons chili powder
1 dozen corn tortillas
2 cups sauce (recipe follows)
1-1/2 cups sharp grated cheese

Brown meat and onion; add seasonings. Dip each tortilla in warm oil. On each one, spoon 2 tablespoons sauce, a generous tablespoon of filling and a sprinkling of cheese; roll up and place close together in large pan. Pour remaining sauce and cheese over top. Bake at 350 degrees for 15-20 minutes.

Sauce:
1 (No. 2-1/2) can tomatoes
1 medium onion, chopped
2 teaspoons chili powder
1/8 teaspoon oregano
1 (6-ounce) can tomato paste
1 garlic clove, minced
1/2 teaspoon salt
1/4 teaspoon cayenne pepper

Combine above ingredients. Simmer about 1 hour until slightly thickened.
Jean Baker, Chula Vista, Calif.

JAMAICAN YAM CASSEROLE
Serves 2

1 (1-pound) can yams, drained
1/2 medium banana, thickly sliced
1/4 cup orange juice
1/2 teaspoon salt
1/8 teaspoon pepper
2 tablespoons coarsely chopped pecans
2 tablespoons toasted flaked coconut

Preheat oven to 350 degrees. In a buttered 1-quart casserole, arrange yams and bananas. Pour juice over all. Sprinkle with salt and pepper. Top with pecans and coconut. Bake covered for 30 minutes.

This recipe was given to us by one of our Jamaican friends and has been in the family for over 20 years.
Susan L. Wiener, Spring Hill, Fla.

FRITTURA DIFICHI RUSPOLI— (HOT FRIED FIGS)

8 firm black figs or extra large fresh prunes, peeled
1/2 cup dark rum
1/3 cup all-purpose flour
1/4 cup chopped walnuts
1/2 teaspoon vanilla extract
1/2 cup water (Mix vanilla and water together)
Vegetable oil for frying
Confectioners' sugar

Soak figs in the rum for 1 hour; turn often to completely even out flavor. In a bowl slowly stir the flour into the water and vanilla mixture. Beat until smooth and creamy. Add walnuts and mix well. Put about 3/4 inch of oil into skillet and set on medium high heat. When oil is hot; dip each fig or prune into the prepared batter and drop into the hot oil. Fry until golden brown on each side (about 3 minutes). Sprinkle confectioners' sugar over top and serve hot.
Marie Fusaro, Manasquan, N.J.

GERMAN BLACK BREAD

3 cups white flour
1/4 cup cocoa
2 packages yeast
1 tablespoon caraway seed
2 cups water
1/3 cup black-strap molasses
2 tablespoons butter
1/2 teaspoon honey
1 teaspoon salt
3 - 3-1/2 cups rye flour

Combine the first four ingredients. Heat the next five ingredients until warm (100-120 degrees), stirring to melt the butter. Add to the first mixture; beat on low speed for 30 seconds. Scrape the bowl and beat for 3 minutes on high. Stir in 3 - 3-1/3 cups rye flour to make the dough. Turn out onto a lightly floured surface. Knead until smooth (5 minutes). Cover and let rest 20 minutes; punch down; divide in half and shape into 2 round loaves and place on grease baking sheet or in two greased 8-inch pie plates. Brush loaves with cooking oil.

Slash the tops with a sharp knife. Cover and let rise in warm place until doubled in size (45-60 minutes). Bake at 400 degrees for 25-30 minutes. Cool on a rack.

Leona Teodori, Warren, Mich.

MEDITERRANEAN GREEN AND WHITE CASSEROLE

Serves 6-8

8 ounces spinach noodles
1 tablespoon vegetable oil
1 onion, sliced
1 pound ground beef
2 cups canned tomatoes, with juice
1 (8-ounce) can tomato paste
1/2 teaspoon oregano, crushed
1/2 teaspoon basil
1/4 teaspoon anise seed, crushed
1/8 teaspoon nutmeg
1 clove garlic
1-1/2 cups creamed cottage cheese
1 (8-ounce) package cream cheese
1/2 cup sour cream or plain yogurt
2 tablespoons green pepper, chopped
1-1/2 tablespoons melted butter or margarine
1 cup Italian bread crumbs

Cook noodles until tender; drain; set aside. In skillet with the vegetable oil, cook onion and beef; stir until brown. Put tomatoes, tomato paste, herbs, and garlic into a food processor; process thoroughly. Pour over meat; heat completely. Combine cheese, yogurt, and green pepper. Into a greased 2-quart casserole, spread 1/2 the cooked noodles evenly over the bottom. Cover with cottage cheese mixture; spread remaining noodles on top. Pour melted butter (or margarine) over noodles; spread ground beef sauce mixture evenly over noodles; sprinkle bread crumbs over all. Bake 350 degrees covered, for 30 minutes or until hot and bubbly.

Gwen Campbell, Sterling, VA

L'ORIENT BEAN CASSEROLE

1 stick butter
1/2 cup chopped onions
2 (4-ounce) cans sliced button mushrooms, drained (save liquid)
1/2 cup mushroom liquid

1 (5-ounce) can water chestnuts, drained and thinly sliced
2 packages frozen French cut green beans, thawed
1/3 cup flour
1 teaspoon salt
1/2 teaspoon pepper
2 cups Cheddar cheese, grated
2 teaspoons Tabasco sauce
2 teaspoons soy sauce
1 (No. 300) can French fried onions

In 1/2 cup butter sauté onions, mushrooms, and water chestnuts until tender. Set aside. Melt 1/4 cup butter; blend in flour, salt, and pepper. Gradually add milk and mushroom liquid; stir until thickened and smooth. Add soy sauce, Tabasco sauce, and cheese. Stir until cheese melts. In a buttered baking dish, layer half sautéed vegetables and beans. Pour over half cheese sauce. Repeat for second layer and top with sauce. Bake 350 degrees for 15 minutes. Sprinkle crumbled French fried onions on top. Return to oven, bake an additional 10 minutes.

Mrs. Hobert Howell, Waco, TX

BAVARIAN RED CABBAGE

1-1/3 pound head red cabbage
3 tablespoons butter or bacon drippings
1 large onion, minced
1 large tart apple, peeled and sliced
1 cup hot water
1/3 cup vinegar
2 tablespoons brown sugar
5 whole cloves
1 teaspoon salt

Shred cabbage. Melt butter in pan in which cabbage is to be cooked. Add onion and cook slowly until soft and yellow. Add cabbage, apple, water, vinegar, sugar, cloves, and salt. Toss together. Cover; cook just until cabbage is wilted. Uncover; cook 20 minutes, stirring occasionally.

Marcella Swigert, Monroe City, MO

JAMAICAN BANANA SPICE CAKE

1 cup butter or margarine
1 cup sugar
3 eggs, well beaten
2-1/2 cups flour
1-1/4 teaspoons baking powder
1-1/4 teaspoons baking soda
1 cup dairy sour cream
3 teaspoons vanilla
1 tablespoon rum
1 teaspoon cinnamon (or pumpkin pie spice)
1 cup mashed, ripe bananas (about 3)

Cream together butter and sugar until light and fluffy. Add eggs. Sift flour twice, then resift with baking powder and soda. Add to butter mixture alternately with sour cream. Stir in vanilla, rum, spices, and bananas by hand using a wooden spoon. Pour into a greased 9 x 13 inch pan. Bake in a preheated 350 degree oven for 45 minutes or until done. When cake has cooled, brush with 3 tablespoons rum or wine. Frost with a butter icing.

Agnes Ward, Erie, PA

HUNGARIAN NOODLES AND PEAS

Serves 6

2 cups uncooked fine noodles
1/2 cup chopped onion
3 tablespoons margarine
1 cup sour cream
1/2 cup creamed small curd cottage cheese
1 tablespoon poppy seed
3/4 teaspoon salt
1/8 teaspoon pepper
1 cup cooked peas, drained
2 tablespoons Parmesan grated cheese

Cook noodles according to package directions; drain. In a large saucepan, sauté onions in butter until tender. Combine sour cream, cottage cheese, poppy seed, salt, and pepper; add to onions. Stir in noodles and peas. Heat thoroughly. Sprinkle with Parmesan cheese; serve.

Joy Shamway, Freeport, IL

EAST INDIAN CURRIED BANANAS
Serves 4-6

1/2 cup light brown sugar, firmly packed
1/2 cup dry white wine
1/2 cup orange juice
2 tablespoons lime juice
3 tablespoons melted butter
3/4 teaspoon curry powder
4-6 bananas, peeled

Combine sugar, wine, orange juice, lime juice, butter, and curry powder in a bowl. Place peeled bananas side by side in a square 8x8 inch (or larger) baking dish. Pour sauce over bananas and bake at 300 degrees for 30-35 minutes, basting frequently. Try this with baked ham, roast pork, or poultry instead of a vegetable.

Mildred Sherrer, Bay City, Texas

PORK CANTONESE

1-1/2 pounds boneless pork, cut into cubes
1 tablespoon vegetable oil
1-3/4 cups water
2 tablespoons soy sauce
1 tablespoon beef flavor instant bouillon
2 tablespoons cornstarch
2 cups (8 ounces) sliced fresh mushrooms
1 (8-ounce) can water chestnuts, drained and sliced
1 (6-ounce) package frozen Chinese pea pods, thawed
Hot cooked rice

In large skillet, cook pork in oil over high heat until meat loses its red color and liquid is reduced. Add 1-1/2 cups water, soy sauce, and bouillon. Cover; simmer 30 minutes. Mix remaining water with cornstarch. Blend into meat mixture; stir until thickened. Add vegetables; cover, and cook 8-10 minutes or until hot. Serve immediately with rice.

Lloyd A. Noel, Galesburg, Ill.

CREPE SUZETTES WITH ORANGE SYRUP
Serves 8

1 cup flour
1/2 teaspoon salt
1 teaspoon baking powder
1 tablespoon sugar
1 cup milk
1 egg
1 tablespoon melted butter

Mix and sift flour, salt, baking powder and sugar; add milk, well-beaten egg, and butter; mix well. Drop by small spoonfuls on hot griddle, greased well with oil. Brown both sides; roll while hot. Place in little deep dishes and serve with Orange Syrup poured over them.

Orange syrup:
1 cup orange juice
1 cup powdered sugar

Mix well; beat about three minutes. Serve on cakes that are rolled.

Mrs. K. W. Kenny, Richmond, Va

CAVATINI
Serves 4-6

3 cups uncooked pasta, varied shapes
1 (4-ounce) package sliced pepperoni (cut into quarters)
1-1/2 pounds Italian sausage
1 small can mushrooms
1/2 cup sliced, pitted black olives
3/4 cup diced green pepper
1 medium onion, chopped
1 (15-1/2 ounce) jar spaghetti sauce
1 (6-ounce) can tomato paste
1 (8-ounce) can tomato sauce
2 cups shredded Mozzarella cheese

In a large saucepan cook pastas. Boil until tender; drain. Meanwhile, put remaining ingredients, except mozzarella cheese, in a large bowl and mix well. Add cooked pasta; mix well. Place in a large casserole. Bake covered with foil at 350 degrees for 30 minutes or until bubbly. Remove from oven. Sprinkle with mozzarella. Return to oven until cheese melts.

Ida Bloedow, Madison, W

HUNGARIAN CREAM CAKE

2 cups sifted cake flour
2 teaspoons baking powder
1/2 teaspoon salt
1 cup sugar
2 eggs, well beaten
1-1/4 cups heavy cream
1 teaspoon vanilla

Sift flour once; measure; add baking powder and salt; sift together three times. Gradually, add sugar to eggs and beat well. Add flour, alternately with cream, a small amount at a time. Beat after each addition, until smooth. Add vanilla.

Bake in greased 9x5x3 inch pan, at 350 degrees for 1 hour and 10 minutes. If desired, spread chocolate frosting on top and sides of cake.

Helen J. Cowherd, San Francisco, Calif

HALUPKI
Serves 3-4

1 medium cabbage
1 pound extra lean hamburger
1 cup Minute Rice
Salt and pepper to taste
1 teaspoon garlic powder
1 egg or 2 egg whites (if watching cholesterol)
1/3 cup catsup
Large can V-8 juice
1 bay leaf

In large pot, bring water to a boil. Preboil cabbage for 5 minutes. Combine rest of ingredients, except for V-8 juice and bay leaf. Remove cabbage to a collander to drain and let cool until manageable. With sharp paring knife, remove cabbage core. Pick off partially cooked leaves and lay on paper towels. Place heaping tablespoon of meat/rice mixture in the center of each leaf. Enfold meat/rice mixture in cabbage leaf and secure with a toothpick. Place in large kettle. Cover with V-8 juice and add the bay leaf. Bring to boil and simmer approximately 1 hour.

Joyce Agan, Davidson, N.C.

CHINESE ALMOND COOKIES
Makes 2 dozen

3/4 cup shortening (half butter or
 margarine)
1/2 cup granulated sugar
1-1/2 teaspoons almond extract
2-1/4 cups all-purpose flour
1-1/2 teaspoons baking powder
1/4 teaspoon salt
2/3 cup ground almonds
2 eggs
1 tablespoon water
24 whole blanched almonds

Cream shortening and sugar; add almond extract; beat in 1 egg. Sift together flour, baking powder, and salt; add to creamed mixture. Stir in ground almonds, mixing thoroughly. Shape into 24 balls; place 2 inches apart on

Continued on next page

lightly greased cookie sheet; flatten to 2-1/2 inch diameter. Combine remaining egg and water; brush tops of cookies. Place whole almond on each cookie and bake at 375 degrees for 12-14 minutes until golden brown; cool on rack.
G. Vreheos, Cathedral City, Calif.

EUROPEAN GOULASH WITH POPPY SEED NOODLES
Serves 6

2-1/4 pounds chuck beef, cut into
 1-1/2 inch cubes
2 tablespoons vegetable oil
1-1/2 cups onions, chopped
1 tablespoon flour
1-1/2 tablespoons paprika
1 tablespoon brown sugar
Salt and pepper to taste
1 teaspoon rosemary
1/2 teaspoon thyme
1/4 teaspoon sage
1 clove garlic, minced
1 (16-ounce) can tomatoes
1 (8-ounce) can tomato sauce
1 bay leaf
2 slices crisp cooked bacon,
 crumbled

Brown beef cubes in vegetable oil. Add onion; sauté until tender. Stir in flour and next 10 ingredients; simmer, covered, 2 hours. Serve with poppy seed noodles; sprinkle with crumbled crisp bacon.

Poppy seed noodles:
1 (6-ounce) package broad noodles
2 tablespoons poppy seeds
2 tablespoons butter or margarine

Cook noodles according to package directions; drain. Add poppy seeds and butter; mix well while hot..
Gwen Campbell, Sterling, Va.

MEXICAN SAUCEPAN FUDGE BROWNIES

1/2 cup light corn syrup
1/2 cup margarine
5 (1-ounce) squares semi-sweet
 chocolate
2 tablespoons smooth peanut butter
1/4 cup sugar
1 teaspoon cinnamon
1 teaspoon vanilla
1 tablespoon coffee-flavored liqueur
3 eggs
1 cup unsifted all-purpose flour
1 cup chopped dry roasted peanuts

Grease and flour 8-inch square pan. Set aside. In large saucepan over low heat combine syrup, margarine, chocolate, and peanut butter. Stir steadily until smooth and creamy.

Remove pan from heat; stir in sugar, cinnamon, vanilla, and liqueur. Break in eggs, one at a time, beating after each addition. Beat in flour. Stir in peanuts. Turn into prepared pan.

Bake at 350 degrees for 30 minutes or until toothpick inserted in center comes out clean. Cool in pan 10 minutes. Invert onto rack to finish cooling completely. Spread with glaze (recipe follows); let glaze set for 10 minutes. Cut into 2-inch squares or smaller, if preferred. Sift powdered sugar generously over squares.

Glaze:
3 (1-ounce) squares semi-sweet
 chocolate
1 tablespoon peanut butter
2 tablespoons light corn syrup

In small saucepan melt chocolate and peanut butter on low heat, stirring steadily. Remove from heat; stir in syrup.
Hyacinth Rizzo, Snyder, N.Y.

YORKSHIRE PARKIN (BRITAIN)

2 cups flour
1/2 teaspoon salt
2 teaspoons baking soda
3 tablespoons allspice
3/4 cup oatmeal
1 cup brown sugar, packed
1/2 cup butter
5 tablespoons light corn syrup
1/2 cup milk

Sift flour, salt, soda, and spice. Mix with oatmeal and sugar. Melt butter with syrup and add to dry ingredients, along with milk. Spread into an 8-inch square pan. Bake at 350 degrees for about 50 minutes. Heavy cake bars (squares) are the result. Can be iced or topped with hard sauce, or whipped cream.
Judie Betz, Eureka, Calif.

SPICY FRIED TOFU
Serves 4

1 pound tofu
1/4 teaspoon salt
3 eggs, beaten lightly
1/4 cup flour
2 tablespoons water
Peanut oil
1/4 teaspoon crushed fresh ginger
 root
1 green onion, including top, finely
 chopped
1 tablespoon soy sauce

Cut tofu in half horizontally; sprinkle with salt; let stand 10 minutes. Pat dry; cut tofu in 1x2-inch pieces. In bowl, mix next three ingredients until smooth. Heat 1 tablespoon peanut oil in a wok until hot. Dip tofu pieces, one at a time, in batter; fry three to four at a time in oil until golden brown. (Add more oil, if necessary.) Heat 2 tablespoons oil in wok. Add ginger root and green onion; stir fry 10 seconds. Return tofu to wok with soy sauce; cover; cook 1 minute. Serve immediately.
Alice McNamara, Eucha, Okla.

BAVARIAN POTATO DUMPLINGS
Serves 6-8

2 pounds potatoes, peeled and
  boiled
1/3 cup margarine or butter
1/8 teaspoon salt
1 egg yolk
3/4 - 1 cup sifted flour
1 slice white bread, cut into 1-inch
  cubes
1 tablespoon margarine or butter

Combine potatoes, margarine, and salt; mash until very smooth. Beat in egg and flour, using enough flour to make an easily handled dough. Fry cubes of bread in 1 tablespoon margarine until browned on all sides. Form 2-inch balls of dough. Press a cube of fried bread into the middle of each dumpling and smooth surface. Bring a large kettle of water to boil. Carefully drop potato balls into the boiling water. Bring water back to a boil and lower heat; simmer for 20 minutes. Dumplings will puff up and float to the top of the pot when done. Drain on paper toweling. Serve immediately. Goes great with sauerbraten or pot roast and gravy.
Joy Shamway, Freeport, Ill.

OREILLES DE COCHON
(pig's ears)
Makes 24

1 cup flour
1/2 teaspoon baking powder
1/4 teaspoon salt
1 tablespoon shortening
3 tablespoons milk
1 egg yolk
1 teaspoon vinegar
Fat for frying
Powdered sugar

Mix flour, baking powder, and salt. Cut in shortening. In another bowl, combine milk, egg yolk, and vinegar. Add to flour mixture and stir to blend. Form dough into a soft ball. Place dough on lightly floured board and roll it out paper thin. Cut it in circles using a 2-inch cookie cutter. Drop a few circles at a time into 350 degree deep fat, and twist each one with two forks to form a pig's ear. Drain on brown paper or paper toweling and sprinkle with powdered sugar while still warm.

The literal translation of Oreilles De Cochon is "pig's ears," so named because long ago an unknown Acadian thought the sweet, crunchy pastry looked like a pig's ear.

MARVELOUS MEXICAN SOUP
Serves 8

1 tablespoon vegetable oil
4 cloves garlic
1 onion, diced
1 teaspoon sugar
2 tablespoons chili powder
3 cups tomato purée
2 cups chicken broth
4 tablespoons canned diced green
  chili peppers
2 tablespoons cornstarch
2 cups sour cream or plain yogurt
2 teaspoons salt
2 tablespoons green chili peppers,
  diced (optional)

Sauté garlic and onion in oil in a medium-size soup pan. Add sugar and chili powder. Add tomato purée and broth. Simmer 30 minutes. Mix 4 tablespoons chili peppers with cornstarch in bowl. Add to soup. Simmer 2 minutes. Remove from heat. Put 1-1/2 cups sour cream into a bowl. Stir a ladle of soup into it. Return sour cream mixture to pot. Place over low heat. Stir gently. Taste, and season with salt, if desired. Serve cold. Fold a tablespoon dollop of sour cream or yogurt onto each plate and sprinkle with green chilies, if desired.
Beatrice H. Comas, South Portland, Maine

AMERICAN CHOP SUEY

1/4 pound lean pork, finely cut
1 onion, sliced
2 cups soup stock
1/2 cup uncooked rice
1 bunch celery, cut into strips
1/2 tablespoon salt
1 green pepper, cut into strips
1 cup mushrooms

Cut fat from meat and put in pan and cook pork in the fat together with onion until brown. When brown, add celery, green pepper, mushrooms, uncooked rice, salt, and stock. Cover and cook slowly for 40 minutes. Serve hot with chopped parsley garnish. Coarsely chopped salted almonds are a delicious addition, if desired.
Susan L. Wiener, Spring Hill, Fla.

CHINESE PEPPER STEAK
Serves 6

2 pounds beef round
1/4 cup oil
1 large onion, sliced
1 clove garlic, minced
2 green peppers, thinly sliced
2 cups beef broth
2 tablespoons soy sauce
1/4 teaspoon pepper
Salt to taste, if needed
2 tablespoons cornstarch
1/4 cup cold water
1 (5-ounce) can water chestnuts,
  sliced

Cut beef into slices about 1/4-inch thick by 2 inches long. Brown slices quickly in hot oil, a few at a time, and remove from pan. Cook onion and garlic until onion is wilted. Add peppers, stirring to coat with oil; cover pan and cook over medium heat for 5 minutes. Add broth, soy sauce, and pepper. Stir the cornstarch into the 1/4 cup cold water; then stir into broth/pepper mixture. Add beef slices and water chestnuts. Increase heat; stir for two minutes until thick and hot. Serve with rice.
Eleanor V. Craycraft, Santa Monica, Calif.

ORIENTAL SMOKED CHICKEN

4 or 5 pieces of chicken
2 tea bags or 4 tablespoons of tea
 leaves (not green)
2 tablespoons brown sugar or dry
 rice

In a 9-inch skillet with lid simmer chicken in 2 cups water for 12 minutes; season with salt and pepper, if you like. Remove chicken from pan; discard water; rinse and dry pan. Remove skin, if you like. Line pan with a piece of aluminum foil, fitting it up the sides. Sprinkle it with the tea and brown sugar or rice. Place chicken on rack, such as from a crock pot or pressure cooker, or a cake-cooling rack, over the foil. You can improvise by using canning screw lids, or poached–egg rings, to hold the chicken pieces. Place chicken on rack or rings. Add no liquid! Cover securely and cook over medium heat for 10 minutes. Remove from heat, let *covered* for 7 or 8 minutes. This is important, otherwise the smoke will billow out and set off your smoke alarm as it did mine when the lid was lifted too soon.

If you like, brush chicken with soy sauce. The pieces are a tempting, dark golden brown and have a great "smoked" flavor! Season to taste with salt and pepper, but it's not really necessary. The bottom of the pan will be clean; simply fold up the foil with the tea leaves and discard. The lid's inner side will be smoked, but is easily cleaned.

Spareribs are a delight, but take longer to prepare. Cut ribs into 2-rib pieces, as many as will fit in the pan loosely. Simmer in covered skillet with 2 cups water for 35 minutes, or until almost done. Add more water, if needed. Rinse and dry pan; spread aluminum foil; add tea, and sugar or rice; season with salt and pepper, if desired. Place ribs on rack. Cover; cook on medium heat 10 minutes. Remove and let stand covered for 8 minutes. Spread lightly with soy sauce.

Pork chops are done like spareribs:

Simmer until almost tender then place on rack. Season, if you like. Cook for 8 minutes, let stand covered 6 or 7 minutes.

Fish fillets take only a few minutes. Parboil in 1 cup water for 1 minute, covered, then prepare pan for smoking as above. Place on rack, season if desired, and heat for 4 or 5 minutes. Let stand for 5 minutes, covered. Thick slices of salmon or other fish take longer. Parboil 5 minutes; heat for 6 minutes, let stand covered for 5 minutes.

You can experiment with pieces of duck, turkey, Cornish hen halves, beef ribs, or neck-bones! Once you prepare the chicken you will love the flavor and texture and will want to do other meats, too. Turkey wings are great; be sure to simmer until nearly done first! For variety you can sprinkle a bit of your favorite herbs, spices, onion, or garlic powder over the meat, chicken, or fish before smoking.

Your family will love this method of "smoking!" Even if you are cooking for only one or two, simply follow the directions using a smaller skillet with cover, such as a 7-inch sauté pan.

Note: Do not grease pan for any of the above!

Kathryn M. Wilson, Pontiac, Mich.

PAGACH

2 loaves frozen bread dough
5 pounds potatoes, pared
1 pound cheese (longhorn or
 cheddar), shredded
3/4 stick margarine or butter
1 onion, diced

Thaw bread dough in refrigerator overnight. Sauté onion in butter. Boil potatoes and mash*. Add shredded cheese and beat. Stir in butter and onion. Pat or roll one loaf of bread dough to fit in greased jelly-roll pan. Spread all of the potato and cheese mixture on top. Roll second loaf of bread dough to put on top. Seal all

edges, bake at 350 degrees for 45 minutes. Makes a large quantity; it's simple and delicious!

*Instead of using potatoes you may also fry cabbage with butter and use that as the filling.

Sandy Hershberger, Johnstown, Pa.

MEXICAN GRILLED STEAKS

A hot-pepper-and-lime-juice marinade gives a flavor of Mexico. Decrease the amount of chili pepper, if you can't take the heat. Use with any fish—fatty or lean.

2 good size fish steaks

Mexican Marinade:
1/3 cup fresh lime juice
Zest of 1 lime
3 tablespoons vegetable oil
1 medium fresh jalapeno chili pepper,
 seeded and minced to make about
 1-1/2 tablespoons; or, substitute a
 fresh Serrano pepper or 1 teaspoon crushed red pepper.

Mix marinade until well blended. Marinate fish about 15 minutes, then grill, basting with leftover marinade.

GERMAN KRAUT AND HAM HOCK
Serves 4-6

1 (27-ounce) can sauerkraut, rinsed
 and drained
1-1/2-pound ham hock
1 teaspoon caraway seeds
8 peppercorns, crushed
1 bay leaf
1/2 cup medium-dry white wine
Water

Place sauerkraut and ham hock in 3- or 4-quart cooking pot. Sprinkle with caraway seeds and crushed pepper. Add bay leaf and wine. Add just enough water to cover. Bring to boil; reduce heat; simmer for 1-1/2 hours. Discard bay leaf. Remove meat from bone and place on serving plate. Surround with sauerkraut.

Anna Y. Bodisch, Coplay, Pa

Fantastic
FRUITS

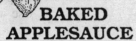

BAKED APPLESAUCE
Serves 6

6 large cooking apples, peeled and cored
2 tablespoons artificially sweetened orange marmalade
1/2 cup orange juice

Preheat oven to 350 degrees. In 3-quart casserole, place apples; dot with marmalade; then pour orange juice over apples. Cover and bake 1 hour or until apples are soft. Stir until apples are chunky.

To cook on range: Prepare ingredients as above but place in 5-quart Dutch oven. Over high heat, cook to boiling. Reduce heat to low; cover; simmer 25 minutes until apples are tender. Stir until apples are chunky. (Exchanges per 1/2-cup serving: 1 fruit)

Nadia Borelko, Dearborn, Mich.

FARM-STYLE FRIED APPLES

1/2 pound bacon
3 large onions, sliced
4 large tart apples
2 tablespoons brown sugar

Fry bacon until crisp; set aside. Peel and slice onions. Core apples (leave skin on); cut cross-wise in 1/4-inch circles. Drain all but 1 table-spoon bacon drippings from pan. Cook onions in reserved bacon drippings 3 minutes; cover with apple slices in an even layer. Sprinkle brown sugar over all; cover. Cook until apples are tender. Serve with crisp bacon slices.

Gwen Campbell, Sterling, Va.

APPLE BROWN BETTY
Serves 6

1/2 cup sugar
2/3 teaspoon cinnamon
1/3 teaspoon salt
3 cups dry stale bread crumbs, fine texture
6 pared, diced apples
5 tablespoons melted butter or margarine

In a cup combine sugar, cinnamon, and salt thoroughly. Cover with layer of apples. Sprinkle with sugar mixtur. Repeat layers, and top with crumbs Drizzle melted butter over crumbs. Bake at 375 degrees for 40 minutes. Uncover pan for last 10 minutes.

APRICOT WHIP

1 envelope orange-flavored gelatin
1/2 cup hot water
1 can apricots, artificially sweetened
1/2 teaspoon lemon juice

Drain canned apricots, reserving juice. Dissolve gelatin in hot water and add 1/2 cup apricot juice and lemon juice. Chill until slightly thickened. Whip with egg beater until fluffy and thick. Chop the drained apricots and fold into mixture. Pour into 4 individual molds. Chill until firm. Unmold on serving dishes. Top with 1 tablespoon prepared whipped topping.

This is perfect for dieters as it only has 115 calories per serving and it's delicious, too!

Susan Wiener, Spring Hill, Fla.

SAUCY POACHED PEARS

3 large pears, pared
12 whole cloves
1/2 cup sugar
1/3 cup orange juice
2 tablespoons lemon juice
1/3 cup white grape juice
1 whole stick cinnamon
1 large orange, peeled and thinly sliced
6 maraschino cherries

Cut pears in half lengthwise; insert 2 cloves in broad end of each pear half. Heat sugar, orange juice, lemon juice, white grape juice, and cinnamon stick to boiling, stirring constantly until sugar is dissolved; place pears in fruit syrup. Simmer uncovered, 10-15 minutes, turning occasionally, until pears are tender. Remove cinnamon stick. Place pears on serving dish; add orange slices and cherries. Pour fruit sauce over pears.

Gwen Campbell, Sterling, Va.

MOCK MARASCHINO CHERRIES

2 pounds Royal Ann Cherries, not too ripe
2 tablespoons salt
1 teaspoon powdered alum
1 quart water
2-1/2 cups sugar
1-1/2 cups water
1 tablespoon red food coloring (optional)
1-1/2 tablespoons fresh lemon juice
1-1/2 tablespoons almond extract

Pit cherries; place them in a glass or ceramic mixing bowl. Dissolve salt and alum in the quart of water; pour over cherries and let them soak overnight. Drain; rinse in cold water until salt taste is completely gone. Drain all water. In a glass or enamel pot, bring sugar, 1-1/2 cups water, and food coloring to a boil. Turn off heat, gently stir in cherries, coating all. Let stand for 24 hours, covered only by a single layer of cheesecloth. Return pot of cherries to boiling; turn off heat; stir in lemon juice and almond extract. Pack hot cherries into clean jars or plastic containers. Store up to 4 months in your refrigerator or freeze in small containers for future use.

Mary Ann Altobell, Virginia, Minn.

EASY FRUIT COBBLER

2/3 stick butter
1 cup sugar
1/4 cup milk
1-1/2 teaspoons baking powder
4 cups fresh peaches or berries of your choice

Melt butter in 8-inch square baking pan. Mix sugar, flour, and baking powder. Add milk. Mix and pour into baking pan with butter. No need to stir. Add fruit evenly over top, and sprinkle with more sugar. Bake at 375 degrees for 25 minutes. (This recipe can be doubled.)

ANYTIME FRUIT COBBLER
Serves 8

1/2 cup butter or margarine
1 cup milk
1 cup self-rising flour
1 cup sugar
4 cups sliced and sweetened fruit or berries

Melt butter or margarine in an 8x12-inch baking dish. Mix in milk, flour, and sugar. Pile fruit on top, but do not stir. Bake at 375 degrees for about 40 minutes or until lightly browned on top. Serve with whipped cream or ice cream.

I have successfully used the following fruits for this recipe: blackberries, blueberries, raspberries, strawberries, peaches, nectarines, and plums.

Delores B. Keller, Macon, Ga.

EASY NO-COOK BLUEBERRY JAM
Makes 5-6 jars

1 quart fresh blueberries
4 cups sugar
2 tablespoons lemon juice
1/2 bottle liquid pectin

Have ready five or six small jelly glasses, about 8-ounce, sterilized, or freezer containers. Remove stems from berries; discard wilted ones; rinse well. Mash with large spoon or potato masher. Mix berries and sugar thoroughly. Mix lemon juice with pectin; add to berries and stir well for 4-5 minutes. Pour into glasses or freezer containers; cover. Let jam stand at room temperature overnight. Store in refrigerator for use up to three weeks, or freeze to use within a year.
Note: A pretty touch for serving can be added by pouring jam into decorated mugs, cream pitchers, juice glasses, etc., instead of jelly glasses for refrigerator storage.

Enjoy blueberries . . . the elite of the berry kingdom!

MELON AMBROSIA
Serves 6

1 cup watermelon balls
1 cup cantaloupe balls
1 cup honeydew balls
1/2 cup lemon or lime juice
Artificial sweetener to equal 2 tablespoons sugar
1/4 cup shredded coconut

Place melon balls in a serving bowl. Sprinkle with juice and artificial sweetener. Top with coconut. Toss well and refrigerate for at least 1 hour. Garnish with mint, if desired.

About 50 calories per serving.

Mrs. Bruce Fowler, Woodruff, S.C.

PEACH COBBLER

6 large or 12 small peaches
6 tablespoons sugar
1 teaspoon lemon juice, fresh
1/2 teaspoon cinnamon
1/4 teaspoon salt
2 cups all-purpose biscuit mix
1/2 cup cold water

Peel peaches; remove pits and cut peaches into slices. Place slices in an 8x8-inch greased baking dish. Sprinkle with sugar, lemon juice, cinnamon, and salt.

Combine biscuit mix and water; form into a ball; place on floured board and knead five times. Roll out into an 8-inch square.

Place pastry over peaches. Press dough gently to sides of dish. Bake in 400-degree oven for 30-40 minutes, until topping is browned. Cool slightly. Serve with Hard Sauce.

Hard Sauce:
1/2 cup soft butter or margarine
1-1/2 cups sifted confectioners' sugar
2 tablespoons brandy *or*
1 teaspoon vanilla

Cream butter or margarine. Gradually beat in sugar and brandy *or* vanilla. Blend until smooth.

Mrs. P.B. Brothers, Richmond, Va.

Meat
DISHES

SALISBURY STEAK WITH ONION GRAVY

1 (10-ounce) can onion soup
1-1/2 pounds ground beef
1/2 cup fine dry breadcrumbs
1 egg, fork beaten
Dash salt
Dash pepper
1 tablespoon all-purpose flour
1/4 cup ketchup
1/4 cup water
1 teaspoon Worcestershire sauce
1/2 teaspoon mustard

In bowl combine 1/3 cup soup with ground beef, crumbs, egg, salt and pepper. Shape into 6 oval patties. In frypan brown patties. Drain off fat. Gradually blend flour into remaining soup, mixing until smooth. Add remaining ingredients, blending well. Add to frypan. Heat to boiling, stirring to loosen up brown bits. Cover; cook 5 minutes, stirring occasionally. Add patties to gravy in frypan. Cover and simmer an additional 15 minutes. These patties freeze very well; place patties and gravy in a "freezer to oven" container for convenience.

Lorraine Caland, Thunder Bay, Ont., Canada

SAUCY SAUSAGE SUPPER
Serves 4

1 (16-ounce) can applesauce (2 cups)
1 (16-ounce) can sauerkraut, drained and snipped (2 cups)
1/3 cup water
2 tablespoons brown sugar, packed
1/2 teaspoon salt
4 small onions, quartered
4 small potatoes, peeled and quartered
1 (12-ounce) Polish sausage, cut diagonally to desired lengths
Snipped parsley

In a 3-quart saucepan, combine applesauce, sauerkraut, water, brown sugar, and salt; add onions and potatoes. Cover and simmer 20 minutes, stirring occasionally. Add sausage; simmer, covered about 20 minutes longer, stirring occasionally. To serve, spoon sauerkraut mixture onto a platter and top with sausage. Sprinkle with parsley.

Agnes Ward, Erie, Pa.

CHOPS WITH AMBER RICE
Serves 6

6 (3/4-inch-thick) pork chops
Salt and pepper to taste
1 cup uncooked rice, rinsed
1-1/2 cups orange juice
1/2 cup water
1/2 teaspoon salt
1 (11-ounce) can cheddar cheese soup

In a skillet brown pork chops on both sides. Season with salt and pepper. Place uncooked rice in a 10x12-inch baking dish. Combine orange juice, water, and the 1/2 teaspoon salt; pour over rice. Arrange browned chops on top. Spread soup over all. Cover and bake in a 350-degree oven for 45 minutes. Uncover and bake 10 minutes longer.

Alice McNamara, Eucha, Okla.

CROCK POT RAVIOLI CASSEROLE
Serves 8

1 (10-ounce) package frozen chopped spinach
1 (8-ounce) package twisty noodles
1 pound ground beef chuck
1/2 pound mild Italian sausage
1 onion, finely chopped
2 tablespoons oil
2 (8-ounce) cans tomato sauce
1 teaspoon salt
1 teaspoon oregano
1/2 cup shredded Parmesan or Romano cheese
1 cup (1/2 pint) sour cream
1 cup (4 ounces) shredded Monterey Jack cheese
3 green onions, chopped

Defrost spinach. Squeeze dry. Cook noodles in boiling, salted water until tender. Drain. Brown meats and onion in oil until crumbly. Add tomato sauce, salt and oregano. Cover. Simmer 30 minutes. Mix in spinach. Spoon half the noodles into a buttered crock pot. Top with half of meat mixture and half the Parmesan cheese. Cover with layers of remaining noodles, meat and Parmesan cheese. Spread with sour cream. Sprinkle with Jack cheese and onions. Cook on high (300 degrees) 1 hour.

Mrs. George Franks, Millerton, Pa.

FRUITED PORK CHOPS

4 pork loin or rib chops, (about 1/2 inch thick)
1 can (8-1/4 ounce) pineapple chunks, drained
1 cup pitted prunes
1/2 cup dried apricots
1/2 cup bottled sweet and spicy French salad dressing

Cook pork over medium heat until brown. Drain. Place pineapple, prunes, and apricots on pork. Pour dressing over fruit and pork. Heat to boiling; reduce heat. Cover and simmer until pork is done-20-25 minutes.
Mrs. Robert T. Shaffer, Middleburg, Pa.

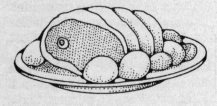

PEPPER PORK CHOPS

6 thick cut pork chops

Pepper Sauce:
1 (8-ounce) can tomato sauce
1 (7-1/4-ounce) jar roasted red peppers, undrained
1 teaspoon oregano
2 garlic cloves, halved
1/2 teaspoon pepper
1/2 cup corn oil
1/3 cup chopped walnuts
1/4 cup grated Parmesan cheese
1/4 cup Marsala wine

Place chops in 13x9x2-inch baking pan. Cook in 350 degree oven until browned on both sides, turning once, . Meanwhile, place all sauce ingredients in blender; whirl until smooth and creamy. Pour sauce over chops and continue baking until chops are tender, about 1 hour.

To serve: Place on platter, garnish with alternating red and green pepper rings.

Hyacinth Rizzo, Snyder, N.Y.

CREOLE PORK CHOPS
Serves 4-6

6 pork chops (1/2-inch thick)
3 tablespoons shortening
6 thin slices lemon
6 thin slices onion
6 teaspoons brown sugar
1/2 cup catsup
1/2 cup water

In a skillet, brown chops in shortening. On each chop place a lemon slice, and an onion slice. Mix together brown sugar, catsup, and water. Pour over chops. Cook covered until tender, about 1 hour.
Mrs. Bruce Fowler, Woodruff, S.C.

LEMONY LAMB CHOPS
Serves 6

6 shoulder lamb chops (cut 3/4 inch thick)
1/3 cup water
1/4 cup lemon juice
1 tablespoon Worcestershire sauce
3/4 teaspoon salt
1/4 teaspoon dried oregano (crushed)
Dash freshly ground black pepper
1 tablespoon cornstarch
2 tablespoons water
1/4 teaspoon grated lemon peel

Trim excess fat from chops. In large skillet, cook trimmings until about 1 tablespoon of fat accumulates; discard trimmings. Slowly brown chops in fat on both sides (about 15 minutes). Combine the 1/3 cup water, lemon juice, Worcestershire sauce, salt, oregano, and pepper; pour over meat. Cover and cook over low heat for 30 minutes or until tender. Remove meat to warm platter.

Pour pan juices into measuring cup; skim off fat. Add water, if necessary, to equal 1 cup liquid; return liquid to skillet. Blend together cornstarch and remaining 2 tablespoons water. Add to skillet, along with lemon peel. Cook and stir until thickened and bubbly. Pass lemon sauce with meat.
Leona Teodori, Warren, Mich.

HERB-GRILLED LAMB CHOPS
Serves 4

4 large loin or 8 rib lamb chops
1 teaspoon thyme
1 teaspoon oregano
1 teaspoon rosemary
3 small bay leaves, crushed
Grated rind and juice of 1 lemon
Pinch of paprika
6 tablespoons oil
Salt and pepper
Butter

Trim chops of excess fat. Mix herbs, lemon rind, and paprika. Rub mixture well into both sides of chops. Arrange chops in large shallow dish; pour lemon juice and oil over them. Season lightly with salt and pepper; place in refrigerator for 3 hours, turning occasionally. When ready to cook, drain chops and place on hot griddle. Sprinkle any leftover dried herbs onto coals. Cook chops 16-20 minutes, turning once or twice.
Mrs. A. Mayer, Richmond, Va.

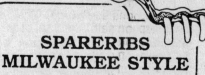

SPARERIBS MILWAUKEE STYLE

4 pounds country style spareribs (trimmed, cut in serving pieces)
1 (12-ounce) can beer
1/2 cup dark corn syrup
1/2 cup finely chopped onion
1/3 cup prepared mustard
1/4 cup corn oil
1 to 2 tablespoons chili powder
2 cloves garlic, minced or pressed

Place ribs in large shallow baking dish. In medium bowl stir together beer, corn syrup, onion, mustard, corn oil, chili powder, and garlic. Pour over ribs. Cover; refrigerate overnight. Remove ribs from marinade. Grill 6 inches from source of heat for about 40 to 45 minutes or until tender, turning and basting frequently, about 40 to 45 minutes or until tender.
Kit Rollins, Cedarburg, Wisc.

LEMON CHICKEN
Serves 4

2 boneless chicken breasts
1 onion, chopped
1/4 cup lemon juice
1 tablespoon margarine
2 egg yolks
1 tablespoon flour
1 cup chicken broth

Cut chicken breasts in half. In skillet, slowly sauté onion in margarine until tender. Add chicken; brown. Add 1 cup chicken broth; cover and simmer 30 minutes. Put egg yolks into bowl along with lemon juice and flour. Mix well. Pour over chicken and stir until thickened (about 10 minutes). Use sauce from chicken to serve over broccoli, if desired.

Peggy Fowler Revels, Woodruff, S.C.

BAKED CHICKEN WITH ORANGE SOY SAUCE
Serves 4

1 (2-1/2 pound) chicken, cut up
   (skin removed)
2 tablespoons soy sauce
1/4 teaspoon salt
1/2 teaspoon celery seed
1/2 teaspoon garlic powder
1/4 teaspoon ground ginger
2/3 cup orange juice

Preheat oven to 400 degrees. Place chicken in 13x9-inch baking pan in a single layer. Top with soy sauce, salt, celery seed, garlic powder, and ginger. Pour orange juice over chicken. Bake 40-45 minutes, until juices run clear when chicken is pierced with a fork. (220 calories per serving)

Norma L. Farrar, Sullivan, Mo.

CHICKEN CACCIATORE

1/4 cup flour
2-1/2 to 3 pounds chicken, cut up
   and skinned
2 tablespoons oil

1 (32-ounce) jar Prego
1 medium onion, sliced
1 medium green pepper, sliced
1 teaspoon Italian seasoning
1 teaspoon garlic powder
 Salt and pepper
1/4 cup red wine
1 (16-ounce) can tomatoes, undrained and cut up
 Hot cooked pasta

Place flour in dish; roll chicken pieces in flour, coating well. In large skillet, brown chicken on all sides in hot oil. Drain excess oil from skillet. Add remaining ingredients, except pasta. Cover; simmer 30-40 minutes or until chicken is fork tender, stirring occasionally. Serve over hot pasta.

Sheila Symonowicz, Loganville, Pa.

HONOLULU CHICKEN

1 broiler/fryer, cut up
1/4 cup flour
1/4 teaspoon salt
Dash of pepper
Oil
1 (10 ounce) jar peach preserves
1/2 cup barbecue sauce
1/2 cup chopped onion
2 tablespoons soy sauce
1 (6 ounce) can water chestnuts,
   drained and chopped
1 green pepper, cut in strips
Hot cooked rice

Coat chicken in seasoned flour; brown in small amount of oil Drain. Mix preserves, barbecue sauce, onion, and soy sauce. Pour chicken; cover. Simmer 40 minutes or until chicken is tender. Add water chestnuts and green pepper the last 10 minutes of cooking time. Serve with rice.

Sandy Greening, Thornton, Colo.

FAST AND EASY CHICKEN KIEV
Serves 4

1 package boneless, thin chicken
   breast fillets
4 tablespoons margarine
1 teaspoon chopped chives
1/2 teaspoon tarragon
1/4 cup flour
1 egg
1/2 cup dry bread crumbs
Hot cooked rice

Preheat oven to 400 degrees. Spread chicken breasts flat on work area and sprinkle with salt and pepper. Place 1 tablespoon margarine on center of each breast; top with 1/4 teaspoon chives and 1/8 teaspoon of tarragon. Fold chicken to enclose margarine completely. Beat egg and 1 tablespoon water in small bowl. Coat chicken rolls with flour; dip in egg, then coat with bread crumbs. Place rolls, seam side up, in 13x9-inch baking pan. Bake 20 minutes. Serve with rice.

Diantha Susan Hibbard, Rochester, N.Y.

MARINATED CHICKEN BREASTS

1 cup sour cream
1 teaspoon Worcestershire sauce
1 teaspoon paprika
1 teaspoon salt
1/4 teaspoon pepper
1 tablespoon lemon juice
1 teaspoon celery salt
1 small garlic clove, crushed
6 split chicken breasts (3 chickens)
Bread crumbs
Butter or margarine

Mix sour cream and next 7 ingredients. Marinate chicken breasts 4 hours or, preferably, overnight. Before baking, roll each piece in fine bread crumbs. Place in baking dish. Dot with plenty of butter or margarine. Bake at 350 degrees for 1 to 1-1/2 hours. May cover when completely baked and turn oven to warm. Will hold 2 hours with no harm to flavor.

Peggy Fowler Revels, Woodruff, S.C.

CHICKEN-IN-A-SHELL
Serves 6

6 baking potatoes
2 tablespoons butter or margarine
1 (10-3/4 ounce) can cream of
  chicken soup
1 cup Parmesan cheese, grated
3 tablespoons fresh parsley,
  chopped
1-1/2 cups cooked chicken, cubed

Bake potatoes until done; cut potatoes in half lengthwise; scoop out insides and reserve, leaving a thin shell. Mash potatoes with butter; add 1/2 cup cheese and remaining ingredients. Spoon into potato shells; sprinkle with remaining cheese. Arrange potatoes in shallow 3-quart baking dish. Bake 375 degrees for 15 minutes.

Gwen Campbell, Sterling, Va.

CHICKEN A LA KING

4 chicken breasts
Salt and pepper
3 heaping tablespoons flour
3 heaping tablespoons butter
2 cups milk
1 small jar diced pimientos
1 small jar sliced mushrooms
3 tablespoons minced parsley
3 tablespoons sherry

Season chicken well; boil until tender; cool and cut into bite-size pieces. Melt butter; add flour and stir until mixed. Add milk and cook until sauce is thick and creamy. Add cut-up chicken, pimientos, mushrooms, parsley, and sherry. Season to taste and serve hot in patty shells or on toast.

Karin Shea Fedders, Dameron, Md.

FISH HASH

2 tablespoons butter
2 cups flaked cooked fish
2-1/2 cups diced boiled potatoes
1/3 cup cream
2 tablespoons minced onion
1 teaspoon lemon juice
1/2 teaspoon salt
1/8 teaspoon pepper

Melt butter in skillet. Combine remaining ingredients and place in skillet; fry slowly until well heated and slightly browned, about 10 minutes. Serve with parsley.
Lucy Dowd, Sequim, Wash.

FISH AU GRATIN
Serves 3-4

1 pound frozen fillet of sole, flounder,
  or haddock
1/3 cup mayonnaise
1/4 cup grated Parmesan cheese
2 tablespoons fine dry bread crumbs

Brush each fillet with mayonnaise. Mix cheese and crumbs. Roll fish in crumb mixture. Place in baking dish. Sprinkle with remaining crumb mixture. Bake in preheated 375 degree oven until fish is lightly browned and flakes easily when tested with fork, about 20 minutes for frozen fish, 15 minutes for thawed or fresh fillets.

HADDOCK-SHRIMP BAKE
Serves 6

1 can shrimp, drained
2 pounds frozen haddock, thawed
1 can shrimp soup
1/4 cup melted margarine
1 teaspoon grated onion
1/2 teaspoon Worcestershire sauce
1/4 teaspoon garlic salt
1-1/4 cups crushed Ritz crackers

Place shrimp and haddock in greased 13 x 9 x 2 inch baking dish. Spread soup over top. Bake in preheated 375 degree oven for 20 minutes. Combine remaining ingredients; sprinkle over fish mixture. Bake for 5 more minutes.

FILLET OF PERCH DIJONNAISE
Serves 2-3

1 (12 oz) package frozen perch fillets
2 tablespoons onion, finely chopped
1 tablespoon butter
1/4 pound sliced mushrooms
2 tablespoons cooking sherry
1 tablespoon Dijon mustard
1 tablespoon freshly chopped parsley
Salt and pepper to taste
1/4 cup dry cracker crumbs
1/3 cup grated Swiss cheese

Preheat oven to 400 degrees. Sauté onion in butter until soft. Add mushrooms and stir over high heat 2 minutes. Stir in sherry, mustard, parsley, and seasonings. Sprinkle half of crumbs in greased 7-1/2 x 11-3/4 inch baking dish. Arrange fish over crumbs in a single layer. Spread mushroom mixture over fish. Sprinkle on remaining crumbs; cover with cheese. Bake 15 minutes. Garnish with sautéed mushrooms.

FLOUNDER BORDELAISE

1 pound fillet of flounder, frozen
2 tablespoons butter
1 clove garlic
1/2 small onion, finely diced
1 cup canned tomatoes, drained and
  chopped
1/2 cup red cooking wine
1 tablespoon minced parsley
Pinch ground thyme
1/2 teaspoon salt
1/4 teaspoon black pepper
1/2 cup fresh bread crumbs

Cut slightly thawed fish into 1-inch slices. Heat butter in large skillet. Sauté onion and garlic for 1 minute. Remove garlic and discard. Add remaining ingredients, except bread crumbs. Simmer, uncovered, until fish flakes, about 5 minutes. Stir in crumbs. Serve with a side dish of rice or thin spaghetti seasoned with butter, Parmesan cheese, and some of the fish sauce.

VEAL PARMESAN

Serves 4

1 pound veal round steak
1/2 cup dry bread crumbs
1/4 cup grated Parmesan cheese
1/2 teaspoon salt
1/4 teaspoon pepper
1/4 teaspoon paprika
1 egg
3 tablespoons water
1 (8-ounce) can tomato sauce
1/3 cup salad oil
1/2 teaspoon oregano

Cut meat into four serving-size pieces; pound until 1/4 inch thick. Stir together bread crumbs, cheese, salt, pepper, and paprika. Beat eggs slightly. Dip meat into egg; dip into crumb mixture, coating both sides. Heat oil in large skillet; brown meat on both sides. Reduce heat; add water. Simmer in covered skillet for 30-40 minutes. Remove from skillet; keep warm. Pour tomato sauce in skillet; stir in oregano. Heat to boiling; pour over meat.

Betty Peel, Milford, Ohio

STUFFED BREAST OF VEAL

Serves 4

1 (4-5 pounds) breast of veal
1 medium-size loaf stale hard Italian bread
1 (3-ounce) box white raisins
2 tablespoons pignoli nuts
2 tablespoons chopped fresh parsley
1 large whole egg
1 cup shredded mozzarella cheese
1 large clove garlic, crushed
1/4 teaspoon salt
1 (3-ounce) container mushrooms, stems and pieces

Make a pocket in veal. Slightly soak bread in water and squeeze dry through a strainer. Mix remaining ingredients with 3/4 of bread (re-serving rest if needed, according to size of pocket). Stuff 3/4 full, allowing for expansion. Sew pocket closed. Season outside of veal with paprika for color.

Place veal in baking pan with cover (or glass baking dish covered with aluminum foil). Add 1 cup water or 1 cup dry wine, plus 1/2 cup water.

Place in 350-degree oven and baste occasionally. Cooking time is approximately 3 hours. Remove cover for last half hour only, to brown.

Cecelia Rooney, Point Pleasant, N.J.

VEAL PARMIGIANA

3/4 teaspoon salt
1/8 teaspoon pepper
1 cup crushed corn flakes
1/2 cup Parmesan cheese
2 eggs, lightly beaten
1/3 cup oil
6 veal cutlets
1 (15-ounce) can Hunt's tomato sauce special
1 teaspoon oregano
1/4 teaspoon garlic salt
6 slices Mozzarella cheese

Combine salt, pepper, corn flake crumbs, and Parmesan cheese. Dip each cutlet into eggs, then crumbs; repeat. In large skillet, heat oil; brown cutlets on each side. Add a few tablespoons of water; cover and cook over low heat for 30 minutes. In saucepan, combine tomato sauce, oregano, and garlic salt. Heat to warm. Place veal in dish; cover with slices of cheese and sauce. Bake in 375 degree oven for about 10 minutes.

Ann Lovett, Humboldt, Tenn.

PORK IN CIDER SAUCE

Serves 4

1 pound boneless pork, cut into bite-size strips
1 tablespoon shortening
2 cups apple juice or cider
1/4 cup grated onion
8 teaspoons cornstarch
2 tablespoons brown sugar
1 teaspoon salt
1/2 teaspoon ground cinnamon
4 tablespoons cider vinegar
2 medium apples, cored and coarsely chopped
2 cups or more hot cooked rice

In a large saucepan or Dutch oven, brown pork strips in shortening. Drain off fat; be sure browned bits are left in the pan for flavor. Add 1 cup only of the cider and the onion. Bring to boil. Reduce heat; cover and simmer about 40 minutes or until meat is tender.

In a bowl, combine cornstarch, brown sugar, salt, and cinnamon. Blend in remaining apple cider and vinegar. Add to pork mixture along with apple. Cook and stir until mixture is thickened and bubbly. Cook and stir 2 minutes more. Add salt and pepper to taste.

Serve over hot rice.

Sherry Busalacchi, Daly City, Calif.

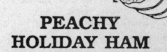

PEACHY HOLIDAY HAM

IMPORTANT: First take off as much gelatin from ham as possible. Use a 3-pound ham, but a 5-pound canned ham works just as well. Place ham in glass casserole dish; set aside.

I saucepan, mix and heat until boiling:

1/2 cup water
1 tablespoon fresh lemon juice
2 tablespoons white granulated sugar
1/2 tablespoon powder from a packet of French's Mi Casa Chili Seasoning Mix, spicy style
3 pinches arrowroot or 6-9 pinches cornstarch
2 tablespoons Worcestershire sauce
1 (16-ounce) can sliced peaches with juice

Pour the above mixture over ham. Place a small piece of aluminum foil over ham so the top does not get tough. The sides are left open. Turn occasionally, once or twice during cooking time. Bake at 350 degrees for 3-5 hours, depending on size of ham. Cook a 3-pound ham for 3-4 hours.

Diane Vaughn, Leominster, Mass.

MARINATED HAM WITH SAUCE VERONIQUE

Serves 8-12

1/4 cup firmly-packed brown sugar
2 tablespoons honey
2 teaspoons Dijon-style mustard
1 (3- to 4-pound) boneless ham
2 cups dry white wine

Combine brown sugar with honey, mustard, and pat over top of ham. With metal skewer or long-tined fork, poke ham in several places. Pour wine over ham. Cover with plastic wrap and refrigerate for 3 to 4 hours, turning ham over several times to marinate.

Roast ham, uncovered, in preheated 325 degree oven for 1-1/2 hours, basting frequently with marinade. Serve with Green Grape Sauce.

Green Grape Sauce
2 cups seedless green grapes
2 tablespoons minced parsley
1 cup chicken stock
1/2 cup dry white wine
3 tablespoons cornstarch
1-1/2 tablespoons lemon juice
1 teaspoon Dijon-style mustard
1/8 teaspoon dried ginger
1/2 cup whipping cream

Cut grapes in half into small bowl. Add parsley and set aside. Combine chicken stock, wine, cornstarch, lemon juice, mustard and ginger in stainless steel or enamel saucepan over medium heat. Bring mixture to a boil, stirring constantly until slightly thickened. Stir in cream. Heat through. Remove sauce from heat. Stir in reserved grape mixture. Makes 3-1/2 cups of sauce.

HAM CROQUETTES

2 cups ground cooked ham
1 tablespoon oil
3 tablespoons margarine
1/4 cup flour
3/4 cup milk
1 teaspoon grated onion

1/2 cup fine dry bread crumbs
1 beaten egg
2 tablespoons water
Oil to deep fry

Melt margarine and add oil; stir in flour. Add milk, all at one time. Cook and stir until bubbly and thick, then cook 2 minutes longer. Stir in meat and onion. Cover and chill thoroughly. Divide into 12 balls and roll each ball in crumbs. Flatten balls somewhat, then dip into a mixture of egg and water; roll in crumbs again. Fry in deep fat for 2 minutes, turning once. Drain well and serve immediately.

Great way to use leftover ham!
Jodie McCoy, Tulsa, Okla.

EASTER-ELEGANT FILLED PORK TENDERLOIN

Serves 5-6

1-1/2 to 2 pounds pork tenderloin
2 tablespoons butter
1 cup onions, thinly sliced
1/4 cup snipped dried apricots
1/4 pound fresh mushrooms, sliced
1/2 cup fresh parsley, chopped
1/2 cup golden apricot nectar
1 cup hot wild rice, cooked according to directions

With sharp knife, cut tenderloin lengthwise, do not cut all the way through. Set aside. In a skillet, sauté onions, apricots, and mushrooms in butter; cook, stirring 3-5 minutes. Add parsley and golden apricot nectar; cook gently 2 minutes longer. Add to hot wild rice; mix thoroughly. Spread center of tenderloin with wild rice mixture. Tie meat securely with string. Brush surface with oil or butter. Set on rack in baking pan. Bake at 350 degrees for 1 hour. Remove string; slice and serve.
Gwen Campbell, Sterling, Va.

NO-HAM BALLS

2 pounds ground beef
1/4 teaspoon onion powder

1/8 teaspoon garlic powder
1/8 teaspoon liquid smoke
1 egg
1/2 cup water
1/4 teaspoon dry mustard
1 tablespoon Morton's quick tender salt
1/2 cup milk
1 cup fine graham cracker crumbs

Mix all ingredients together and shape into small balls. Place balls into a 9x13 inch ungreased baking pan. Bake uncovered in a 350 degree preheated oven for 25-30 minutes; then pour sauce over top of meat balls and return to oven for 15 minutes.

Sauce:
1 teaspoon dry mustard
1 (10-3/4-ounce) can tomato soup
3/4 cup packed brown sugar
1/4 cup vinegar

Mix all ingredients together. These meat balls are great to put in a slow cooker.
Othel Hickman, Ridgeway, Mo.

GOLDEN GLAZED HAM LOAF

Serves 8

1 pound lean ground ham
1 pound ground pork
1 cup soft bread crumbs (2 slices)
1/3 cup chopped onion
1/4 cup milk
1 egg
1/8 teaspoon pepper
1 cup orange marmalade
2 tablespoons lemon juice
1 tablespoon prepared mustard

Preheat oven to 350 degrees. In a large bowl, combine all ingredients, except marmalade, lemon juice, and mustard; mix well. In a shallow baking dish, shape into loaf. Bake 1-1/2 hours. Meanwhile stir together marmalade, lemon juice, and mustard. Use 1/3 to 1/2 cup sauce to glaze loaf during last 30 minutes of baking. Heat remaining glaze and serve with loaf.

Joy B. Shamway, Freeport, Ill.

POT ROAST WITH SOUR-CREAM GRAVY

Serves 6-8

2 tablespoons salad oil
4-5-pound bottom round beef roast
1 medium onion, sliced
1 cup dry red wine
1 cup water
2 tablespoons flour
1/4 cup cold water
1 teaspoon salt
1/4 teaspoon black pepper
1/2 cup sour cream

Heat oil in Dutch oven; brown meat on all sides. Add onion, wine, and water. Cover and simmer gently for 3-4 hours or until tender. Remove meat and keep warm. Drain off all but 1-1/2 cups liquid. Stir flour into cold water until blended; slowly stir into liquid in pan. Add salt and pepper. Cook, stirring over low heat, until thickened. Slowly blend in sour cream. Serve gravy with sliced pot roast.　　Joy Shamway, Freeport, Ill.

ROAST TURKEY WITH BROWN RICE AND SAUSAGE STUFFING

Serves 10-12

1 (10- to 12- pound) turkey
Salt
Pepper
Melted butter or margarine
12 ounces mild bulk sausage
1 large onion, chopped
2 cloves fresh garlic, minced
1 medium green pepper, chopped
3 cups water
1 teaspoon sage
2 cups quick-cooking brown rice

Rinse turkey; pat dry. Rub salt and pepper into neck and body cavities. Secure drumsticks lightly with a string. Insert meat thermometer into center of thigh next to body, but not touching bone.

Roast uncovered on roasting rack in 325-degree oven 20 to 22 minutes per pound, basting occasionally with melted butter. Turkey is done when meat thermometer registers 170 to 175 degrees and thick part of drumstick feels soft when pressed with thumb and forefinger, or drumstick moves easily.

Meanwhile, lightly brown sausage in large saucepan, stirring to crumble. Drain off excess fat. Add onion, garlic and green pepper; sauté lightly. Add water, 1 teaspoon salt, 1/8 teaspoon pepper, sage, and rice.

When turkey is done, remove from oven and let stand 20 to 30 minutes before carving. Bring rice to a boil. Pour into greased 9 x 13- inch glass casserole. Cover with aluminum foil; bake 25 to 30 minutes at 325 degrees or until water is absorbed.

Recipe Provided by California Turkey Industry Board

ROAST LEG OF LAMB WITH APPLE-MINT SAUCE

Serves 6

Leg of lamb
1 teaspoon salt
1-1/2 teaspoons ground ginger
1/8 teaspoon pepper
1/4 cup butter
Flour
1/2 cup beef broth or bouillon
2 tablespoons minced mint or 1/2 cup apple cider or apple juice
1 onion, minced
1 teaspoon sugar

Place lamb on rack in shallow baking pan. In small bowl, mix together salt, 1/2 teaspoon ginger, pepper, and butter. Rub butter mixture generously over lamb. Sprinkle with flour. Bake in preheated 450 degree oven for 15 minutes. Meanwhile cook remaining 1 teaspoon ginger, broth, mint, cider, onion, and sugar over low

heat for a few minutes. Reduce oven temperature to 325 degrees. Cook lamb, basting frequently with sauce, 20 minutes per pound, or until meat thermometer registers 145 degrees for medium-rare, 160 degrees for medium or 170 degrees for well-done.

POT ROAST DINNER

3-5 pounds pot roast
1 package dry onion soup
1 can cream of mushroom soup

Put meat in pan and add the soups. Cover and bake at 350 degrees for 3 hours. Add peeled carrots and potatoes; cover and continue to bake 1 hour or until vegetables are cooked through.

If I'm expecting a house full of guests, I put all the ingredients in the slow cooker the night before or early morning.

S. Armell, Milton, Vt.

DUTCH MEAT LOAF

Serves 6

1 pound ground beef
1 pound bulk pork sausage
1-1/2 cups bread crumbs
1 (8-ounce) can tomato sauce (1 cup)
2 tablespoons brown sugar
3/4 cup water
1 egg
1 teaspoon salt
1/2 cup chopped onion
1 tablespoon vinegar
2 tablespoons prepared mustard

In mixing bowl combine ground beef, sausage, bread crumbs, onion, 1/2 cup tomato sauce, egg, and salt. Shape into loaf in baking pan. Bake 30 minutes at 350 degrees. Drain off excess fat. Combine rest (1/2 cup) of tomato sauce, brown sugar, vinegar, prepared mustard, and water. Bake 45 minutes longer. Baste loaf several times during the baking process.

Sharon M. Crider, Evansville, Wis.

BURIED GOLD MEAT LOAF

1-1/2 pounds ground beef
2 eggs, beaten lightly
2 slices wheat or white bread
    soaked in milk and squeezed dry
1 cup instant mashed potatoes
2 tablespoons Parmesan cheese
2 tablespoons chopped parsley
Salt and pepper to taste
1/8 teaspoon nutmeg
1 cup flour
4 tablespoons vegetable oil
2 cans beef bouillon
3 hard-cooked eggs, shelled

In a bowl combine first 9 ingredients. Flatten mixture on waxed paper; place hard-cooked eggs down the center. Roll up, shaping into a loaf. Roll in flour. In a small roasting pan, brown on all sides. Add the beef bouillon; cook slowly for 1 hour. (Add more bouillon if the loaf becomes dry). Remove loaf from pan; let stand 5-10 minutes. Slice carefully to retain the shape of the egg; arrange on platter. Serve reduced cooking juices separately.
Gwen Campbell, Sterling, Va.

HIGH PROTEIN MEATLESS LOAF
Serves 8

1-1/2 cups crunchy peanut butter
1-1/2 cups cooked beans of your
    choice, lightly mashed
1/2 cup onion, finely chopped
1/4 cup wheat germ or bran
1/2 teaspoon basil
Salt and pepper to taste
1-1/4 cups soft wheat bread crumbs
1-1/2 cups American cheese, grated
1-1/2 cups milk
3 tablespoons fresh parsley,
    chopped
4 eggs, well beaten
2 cups tomato sauce, heated

Combine all ingredients except tomato sauce; mix well. Turn into a greased 9x5x3-inch loaf pan. Bake 350 degrees for 45 minutes. Unmold on serving platter; serve with heated tomato sauce.
Gwen Campbell, Sterling, Va.

REUBEN MEAT LOAF

2 pounds ground beef
2 cups bread crumbs
1 egg
1 tablespoon catsup
1 teaspoon salt
1 (8-ounce) can sauerkraut, rinsed
    and drained
1 cup shredded Swiss cheese
1/4 pound pastrami, chopped
1/4 cup sour cream
1 tablespoon mustard

Combine beef, crumbs, egg, catsup, and salt in bowl; mix well. Combine sauerkraut, cheese, pastrami, sour cream, and mustard. Place one third of meat mixture in loaf pan. Spread with sauerkraut mixture. Repeat meat mixture and sauerkraut mixture, topping with meat mixture. Bake at 350 degrees for 60 minutes.
Julia Milnar, Gilbert, Minn.

GREAT SALMON LOAF

1 (1-pound) can red salmon,
    drained
1/2 cup mayonnaise
1 can celery soup
1 egg
1 cup cracker crumbs
1/2 cup chopped onion
1 tablespoon lemon juice
1 teaspoon salt
Cucumber Sauce (recipe follows)

Mix all ingredients together. Put into buttered baking dish. Bake at 350 degrees for approximately 50 minutes. Serve with Cucumber Sauce.

Cucumber Sauce:
1/2 cup mayonnaise
1 cup sour cream
2 teaspoons lemon juice
1/4 cup chopped cucumber

Combine ingredients and blend well.
Ann Superata, Terryville, Conn.

CHICKEN LOAF

3 cups cooked chicken, cut in
    pieces
1/2 cup chicken broth, without fat
3 slices bread, crumbled
1/2 cup rice, cooked
1-1/2 teaspoons salt
1/4 teaspoon pepper
1/2 cup milk
1 tablespoon onion, minced
1 tablespoon green pepper,
    chopped
1 egg

Heat chicken broth and add chicken, crumbs, rice, salt, pepper, milk, onion, green pepper, and beaten egg. Press firmly into greased loaf pan and bake in 325-degree oven for 1 hour. If gravy is desired, use 3 tablespoons flour with 2 cups of chicken broth.
Suzan L. Wiener, Spring Hill, Fla.

CORNED BEEF LOAF
Serves 6

2 cans corned beef
3 eggs
3/4 cup fresh bread crumbs
3/4 cup milk
1/4 teaspoon poultry seasoning or
    mustard

Grind the contents of two cans corned beef; add to this the beaten eggs, and bread crumbs (which have been soaked a few minutes in the milk); add the poultry seasoning or mustard. Stir the mixture thoroughly, adding more milk, if necessary, to give the right consistency. Put into a deep dish and bake 1 hour in a 325-degree oven.
Lucy Dowd, Sequim, Wash.

COLA ROAST

Serves 8-10

1 (4-5 pounds) bottom round roast
1 teaspoon salt
1/2 teaspoon pepper
1/2 teaspoon garlic powder
3 tablespoons vegetable oil
1-1/2 cups cola-flavored soda
12 ounces chili sauce
2 tablespoons Worcestershire
  sauce
2 tablespoons hot sauce

Combine salt, pepper, and garlic powder; rub over surface of roast. Brown roast on all sides in vegetable oil in a Dutch oven. Drain off drippings. Combine remaining ingredients; pour over roast. Cover and bake at 325 degrees for 3 hours or until tender.

Kit Rollins, Cedarburg, Wis.

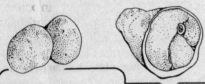

TASTY BEEF ROLLS AND POTATOES

Serves 6-8

4 potatoes
3 slices white bread (remove crusts)
1 teaspoon salt
Prepared mustard
10 carrot sticks
2 cups beef bouillon (or broth)
1-1/2 pounds ground beef
1/2 cup milk
1 egg
1/4 teaspoon black pepper
1/2 cup chopped onion
1/4 cup cooking oil
1 tablespoon flour

Wash and pare potatoes; cut into 1-inch chunks. Set aside. Mix beef, bread soaked in milk, egg, salt, and pepper. Divide into 10 rectangular, or smaller squares if preferred. Spread each rectangle with about 1/8 teaspoon mustard and sprinkle with chopped onions. Place a carrot stick at one end and roll up, pinching seam edge to seal.

In skillet, brown beef rolls in hot oil, turning rolls carefully with spat-ula. Drain off fat and add bouillon; bring to a boil. Add potatoes; cover and simmer on low heat for 30-40 minutes, or until potatoes are tender.

Remove beef rolls and potatoes to hot platter. Dissolve flour in small amount of water and stir into liquid remaining in skillet. Cook until thickened. Pour over beef rolls and serve.

Mrs. J. Sassano, Akron, OH

MOCK CHOPPED LIVER

Serves 4-6

1 pound cooked roast beef
1 large onion, finely chopped
Salt and pepper to taste
Oil for sautéing
2-3 tablespoons mayonnaise,
  optional

Finely mince the roast beef (do not grind). Set aside. Heat enough oil in large skillet to generously coat the bottom. Sauté onions until golden brown. Add minced beef and a bit more oil. Stir quickly over high heat until minced beef colors and becomes slightly crisp. Season generously with salt and pepper and transfer to an attractive serving bowl. If desired, combine mixture with mayonnaise. Serve warm; spread on crackers.

Agnes Ward, Erie, Pa.

CHEESEBURGER PIE

1 package crescent rolls
1 pound hamburger
1/2 small onion, chopped
1/2 teaspoon oregano
1/4 teaspoon basil
Salt and pepper to taste
1 (6-ounce) can tomato paste
1 (8-ounce) package Mozzarella
  cheese

Press crescent rolls into pie crust for 9-inch pan. Brown hamburger, onion, oregano, basil, salt, and pepper to taste. Drain. Add tomato paste; pour into pie shell. Top with cheese. Bake at 425 degrees for 15-20 minutes.

Marcella Swigert, Monroe City, Mo.

BASQUE SKILLET DINNER

Serves 4

1 pound Chorizo or Italian sweet
  sausage, sliced
1/2 cup chopped onion
1 cup diagonally-sliced celery
4 Idaho potatoes, pared and diced
1 (1 pound) can tomatoes
3/4 cup water
1 teaspoon lemon juice
1 beef bouillon cube
1/2 teaspoon salt
1/4 teaspoon pepper
1/4 teaspoon dried leaf thyme

Brown sausage in large skillet over medium heat. Add onion and cook until tender. Stir in remaining ingredients. Cover and simmer 30 minutes, or until potatoes are tender.

SESAME BEEF

1 pound boneless sirloin steak
2 tablespoons sugar
2 tablespoons vegetable oil
2 tablespoons soy sauce
1/4 teaspoon pepper
3 green onions, chopped (with tops)
2 cloves garlic, crushed
1 tablespoon sesame seed
1 tablespoon vegetable oil
3 cups hot cooked rice

Trim fat from steak; cut beef diagonally across grain into 1/8-inch slices. Mix sugar, 2 tablespoons oil, soy sauce, pepper, onions and garlic. Stir in beef until well-coated. Cover and refrigerate 30 minutes. (Or you can marinate several hours.) Cook and stir sesame seed in skillet over medium heat until golden brown. Remove from skillet. Heat 1 tablespoon oil in same skillet until hot. Add beef; cook and stir until light brown, 3-4 minutes. Sprinkle with sesame seed. Serve over rice.

Cheryl Santefort, South Holland, Ill.

Micro- MAGIC

PLAN AHEAD BRUNCH

Serves 9

1 package (12 ounces) frozen hash brown potatoes
6 eggs
1/3 cup whipping or light cream
1 cup (4 ounces) shredded Cheddar cheese
2 tablespoons chopped chives
1/4 teaspoon salt
Dash of pepper
1 cup (4 ounces) diced ham, or Canadian bacon

Place potatoes in 8-inch square baking dish; cover with plastic wrap and microwave on HIGH 6-7 minutes until steaming, stir once. Combine eggs, cream, chives, salt, pepper, cheese, and ham. Add mixture to potatoes, cover with waxed paper, and microwave 12 minutes at MEDIUM (50%) stirring twice. Then finish cooking for 3-4 minutes on HIGH or until set. Let stand 5 minutes, cut into squares.

FRIED RICE

3 tablespoons butter
3 eggs, well beaten
4-5 cups cooked rice
2 tablespoons chopped green onion
1/2 teaspoon salt
1 teaspoon sugar
3/4 tablespoons soy sauce
1 cup cooked, diced ham, chicken, or salami

Melt butter; microwave on HIGH, for 40 seconds. Add eggs; cover; microwave for 1-1/2 minutes. Stir; re-cover and microwave for 1 additional minute. Add remaining ingredients; stir gently to blend and microwave for 3-5 minutes on HIGH.

MICROWAVE POTATOES

Peel and dice 3 or 4 large potatoes. Place in microwave casserole dish; dot with 1/2 stick margarine. Return to microwave and cook 3-5 minutes more, or until potatoes are done. Season with salt, pepper, and parsley flakes.

PEANUT BUTTER PIECES

2 sticks butter
1 pound powdered sugar
1 cup graham cracker crumbs
1 cup peanut butter
1 (12 ounce) package chocolate chips

Place butter in large bowl and microwave on HIGH for 2-3 minutes. When butter is melted, add sugar, crumbs, and peanut butter. Mix until smooth; press into 8x8 dish; microwave on HIGH for 2 minutes. Put chocolate chips in large bowl and microwave 50% for 3-4 minutes; stir several times while cooking.

When melted, spread over peanut butter layer; chill. Cut into squares and store in airtight container.

APRI-ORANGE SAUCE

Makes 2 cups

1/2 cup apricot jam
1 tablespoon cornstarch
1/2 cup orange juice
1/8 teaspoon ground cloves

Combine jam, cornstarch, and orange juice in a 2-cup glass measure; mix well. Microwave on HIGH, uncovered, 2 to 2-1/2 minutes or until mixture boils and thickens; stir once. Stir in cloves.

CORN-ON-THE-COB

Serves 4

4 medium ears of corn (in husk)
8 paper towel sheets

For each ear, hold 2 connected paper towel sheets under running water until soaked, but not dripping. Squeeze gently to remove excess water. Spread paper towel sheets flat on counter. Place corn (in husk) lengthwise in center of 2 connected paper towel sheets. Fold one long side over corn. Fold both ends toward center. Roll up over corn. Place loose edge of packet down on microwave-safe platter. Microwave on HIGH for 9 to 15 minutes, or until tender, rearranging ears once. Let stand for two minutes. Remove and discard paper towels. If desired, place corn in husks on edge of grill to keep warm, turning ears once or twice.

BARBECUED LAMB SHANKS
Serves 4

12 thin lemon slices
4 lamb shanks (about 3-1/2 pounds)
Barbecue sauce
8 paper towel sheets

For each lamb shank, place 2 paper towel sheets, one on top of the other, on the counter. Place three lemon slices diagonally across center of paper towel sheets. Place lamb shank on lemon slices. Fold three corners toward center, covering lamb like an envelope. Roll up over remaining corner. Hold under running water until soaked, but not dripping. Place loose corner down on microwave-safe plate.

Microwave on HIGH for 5 minutes. Rotate plate half turn. Microwave on MEDIUM (50 per cent power) for 5 minutes per pound, rotating plate once. Remove and discard paper towel sheets. Brush lamb shanks with barbecue sauce. Place lamb on hot grill. Grill to desired doneness, 20 to 30 minutes, turning and brushing occasionally with barbecue sauce.

CRAB AND CORN BISQUE
8 servings

2 tablespoons butter or margarine
1 small onion, chopped
1 small red pepper, chopped
1 large celery stalk, chopped
1/4 teaspoon dried thyme leaves
1/8 teaspoon ground red pepper
1 can condensed cream of potato soup, undiluted
2 cups milk
1 (17-ounce) can cream-style corn
1 (12-ounce) package fish and crab blend (surimi)

In 3-quart casserole, melt butter on HIGH one minute; add chopped onion, pepper, celery, thyme and ground red pepper; cover with plastic wrap; turn back one corner to vent. Cook on HIGH for 5 minutes, stirring once. Stir in soup, milk, corn and surimi; cover and vent; microwave on HIGH for 7 minutes or until boiling.

CHEDDAR FISH BUNDLES
Serves 4

1-1/2 cups shredded cheddar cheese'
1-1/2 cups fresh bread crumbs
2 tablespoons mayonnaise
2 teaspoons horseradish
1 pound sole fillets
1 tablespoon margarine, melted

Combine 1 cup cheese, crumbs, mayonnaise, and horseradish; mix lightly. Spoon mixture over fish; roll up; secure with wooden toothpicks. Place fish, seam side down, in baking dish, drizzling with margarine. Microwave on HIGH for 5-6 minutes or until fish flakes easily; turn dish after 3 minutes. Sprinkle with remaining cheese; microwave 1-1/2 to 2 minutes or until melted.

QUICK AND LIGHT FISH PLATTER
Serves 1

2 carrots, cut into 2 inch x 1/8 inch strips
1 stalk celery, cut into 1" slices
1 tablespoon water
Parsley flakes
1 tablespoon butter or margarine
4 to 6 ounces defrosted flounder fillets
2 teaspoons lemon juice
Paprika
1 tablespoon sliced green onion
2 tablespoons almonds, toasted

Place carrot strips around edge of a dinner plate; top with celery, water and parsley; dice 1 teaspoon of butter and place on vegetables. Cover with plastic wrap; turn back one edge to vent. Microwave on HIGH for 2 minutes. Uncover; place fish on center of plate. Top with lemon juice, remaining butter, paprika, and onion. Re-cover with plastic wrap; microwave on HIGH for 2 minutes. Let stand 2 minutes. Sprinkle with toasted almonds.

ITALIAN CHICKEN SUPREME

2 medium carrots, cut in thin strips
1 medium zucchini, cut in thin strips
1 medium onion, thinly sliced
2 whole boneless chicken breasts, skinned and cut in half (about 1 pound)
1 teaspoon Italian seasoning
4 pats butter
Salt and pepper

Divide carrots, zucchini, and onion evenly among the 4 paper towels. Place a pat of butter, salt, and pepper over assembled vegetables. Cover vegetables with boneless chicken breast. Sprinkle with Italian seasoning. Fold towel around chicken and vegetables to completely enclose. Moisten under running water. Place paper towel bundles in a round glass baking dish. Microwave on HIGH for 9-10 minutes, or until chicken is cooked. Remove from microwave and let stand 1 minute before serving.

Makes 4 servings of 1 chicken breast and 1/2 cup vegetables each.

For 2 servings: 6 minutes on HIGH
For 1 serving: 3 minutes , 30 seconds on HIGH
Calories per serving: 167

EGG HAMLET
FOR ONE

1 egg
1 slice of American cheese
1 slice of ham
1 hamburger roll

Break egg into small bowl; blend well. Cover with wax paper; microwave for 1-1/2 to 2 minutes on MEDIUM HIGH (70%), stir once. Assemble sandwich by putting together slice of cheese, ham, cooked egg, and salt and pepper. Wrap sandwich in paper napkin and microwave 30-40 seconds on 70% to heat roll and melt cheese.

POTATO PICK-UPS
Makes 24
(a microwave finger food)

12 small red potatoes
1/2 teaspoon chicken-flavor instant
   bouillon
1/2 cup pimiento-stuffed olives
3 tablespoons mayonnaise
2 tablespoons chopped parsley

Cut each potato in half lengthwise. In 3-quart casserole, cook potatoes, bouillon, and 1/2 cup hot tap water, covered, on HIGH in microwave for 10 to 12 minutes until potatoes are tender, stirring once; drain. Rinse potatoes under cold water; drain; refrigerate about 1 hour or until chilled.

Meanwhile, chop olives. In small bowl, stir olives, mayonnaise, and parsley. Onto cut side of each potato half, spoon a rounded teaspoonful of olive mixture. (35 calories per serving)

Ronnie J. Heroux, Uxbridge, Mass.

POTATO SALAD
Serves 6

1/2 cup low–calorie Italian dressing
2 cups hot cooked, cubed
   potatoes
1/2 cup bias-sliced celery
1/2 cup thinly sliced red onion,
   separated into rings
1/4 cup sliced radishes
2 tablespoons chopped green
   pepper
1/2 teaspoon salt
1/4 teaspoon dried dill weed
2 tablespoons snipped parsley

In a large bowl pour the Italian dressing over the hot cooked potatoes; mix gently to coat. Cover and marinate in the refrigerator for at least 2 hours. Add celery, onion, radishes, green pepper, salt, and dill. Toss gently to combine. Sprinkle with parsley. (46 calories)

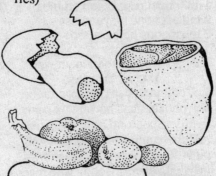

HEARTY GERMAN
POTATO SALAD

3 slices bacon, cut up
1 small onion, chopped
2 tablespoons flour
1 tablespoon sugar
1 teaspoon salt
1/2 teaspoon caraway or celery
   seed
1/8 teaspoon pepper
1/2 cup water
1/4 cup vinegar
2 (16-ounce) cans sliced white
   potatoes, drained
1 package hot dogs, cut into 1/2
   inch pieces

Combine bacon and onion in microwave-safe casserole; cover with paper towel and microwave for 4-5 minutes on HIGH or until bacon is crisp. Stir in flour, sugar, salt, caraway, pepper, water and vinegar until blended. Microwave on HIGH, uncovered, 2-3 minutes; stir twice. Stir in potatoes and hot dogs; mix lightly. Cover with casserole lid. Microwave 6-7 minutes on HIGH or until heated through.

SWEET POTATO
SOUFFLÉ

1 (18-ounce) can sweet potatoes
1/4 cup granulated sugar
1/4 cup dark brown sugar
1/4 cup margarine, melted
2 eggs
3/4 cup evaporated milk
1/2 teaspoon cinnamon
1/2 teaspoon nutmeg
1/4 teaspoon vanilla

Topping:
6 tablespoons margarine, melted
1/2 cup brown sugar
1/2 cup walnuts, chopped
1 cup crushed crackers, Ritz® or
   Townhouse®

Combine potatoes with next 8 ingredients and mix well. Pour into a 2-quart casserole and microwave on 70% for 13-16 minutes. Rotate dish once, if necessary. Combine topping ingredients and spread over potatoes. Microwave on 70% for 2-4 more minutes.

SOUPER CHEESE
POTATOES

4 large potatoes, peeled and cubed
1/4 cup water
1/2 can condensed Cheddar cheese
   soup
1/2 cup sour cream
1/2 cup half-and-half
1 tablespoon snipped chives
1/2 teaspoon garlic salt
1/2 cup (2 ounces) shredded
   Cheddar cheese
Paprika
1 teaspoon parsley
1/8 teaspoon pepper

Combine potatoes and water in a casserole; cover with lid and microwave on HIGH for 12-14 minutes; stir once. Stir in soup, sour cream, half-and-half, chives, and garlic salt. Microwave on HIGH for 4-5 minutes, uncovered; stir once. Sprinkle with cheese and paprika. Let stand, covered, about 5 minutes or until cheese is melted. Sprinkle with paprika, parsley, and pepper.

PARMESAN POTATO SLICES

1 small onion, chopped
1/2 cup chopped celery
2 tablespoons butter or margarine
3 medium unpeeled potatoes, cleaned
1/2 teaspoon garlic salt
Dash pepper
1/4 cup Parmesan cheese, or to taste
1/4 teaspoon poultry seasoning
1/2 teaspoon dried parsley flakes
Paprika

Combine onion, celery, and butter in an 8-inch square baking dish. Cover with waxed paper. Microwave on HIGH 2-1/2 to 3 minutes or until vegetables are just about tender. Thinly slice potatoes into baking dish; mix lightly. Cover and microwave on HIGH 10-12 minutes or until potatoes are tender; stir once. Add garlic salt, pepper, cheese, seasonings; mix lightly. Sprinkle with paprika. Microwave on HIGH for 1-2 minutes, uncovered.

LIME-THYME POTATOES

1/4 cup melted margarine or butter
1 teaspoon grated lime peel
1 tablespoon lime juice
1 teaspoon dried thyme leaves
3 medium baking potatoes
1/4 cup grated Parmesan cheese
Paprika, salt and pepper

In a pie plate combine butter, thyme leaves, lime peel, and juice. Cut each potato lengthwise into eighths; toss in butter mixture. Arrange skin side down on paper-towel-covered plate; sprinkle with cheese, paprika, salt, and pepper. Microwave on HIGH for 13 minutes, covered with waxed paper; rotate dish halfway through.

SESAME-SPRINKLED BRUS-SELS SPROUTS
Serves 4

1 pound brussels sprouts
1 tablespoon water
2 tablespoons butter or margarine
2 teaspoons sesame seed
1 tablespoon soy sauce
1 teaspoon sesame oil
1/8 teaspoon lemon pepper

Combine brussels sprouts and water in a 1-quart casserole; cover; microwave on HIGH for 8-9 minutes or until tender. Drain and set aside. Place butter and sesame seeds in uncovered small glass dish and microwave on HIGH for 3-4 minutes, until toasted; stir twice. Mix in the soy sauce and sesame oil; spoon over the brussels sprouts; sprinkle with lemon pepper. Mix lightly.

PEA PODS ORIENTAL

1 (10-ounce) package frozen pea pods
1 tablespoon oil
1 tablespoon soy sauce

Remove wrapping from box of frozen pea pods. Place box on paper towel in microwave. Microwave on HIGH 3-4 minutes, or until heated through. Place in a bowl; toss lightly with oil and soy sauce. Microwave on HIGH 1-2 more minutes. These are served tender crisp. Do not overcook. Leftovers can be refrigerated and tossed into a salad for another use.

BROCCOLI AND MUSHROOMS

1 pound fresh mushrooms
1 pound fresh broccoli flowerets
1/4 cup hot water
2 cups Italian dressing

In a 3-quart casserole combine broccoli and water; cover and microwave for 1 minute on HIGH. Drain and rinse in cold water. In a bowl or plastic bag combine broccoli, mushrooms, and dressing.

Refrigerate at least 8 hours. If using a bowl stir several times, with a bag just turn bag over several times. Remove vegetables to serving platter with slotted spoon.

CHEESE-STUFFED MUSHROOMS

10 medium large mushrooms
1 tablespoon butter or margarine
1 (3-ounce) package cream cheese
2 tablespoons Parmesan cheese
1/8 teaspoon garlic salt
1/8 teaspoon hot pepper sauce
Paprika

Remove stems from mushrooms by gently twisting them. Place caps, open side up, on microwave-safe plate; set aside. Chop stems; combine stems and butter in a 1-quart casserole. Microwave (HIGH), uncovered, 2-3 minutes or until tender. Add cheeses; mix until softened and creamy. Stir in garlic salt and pepper sauce. Spoon cheese mixture into each cap, mounding mixture. Microwave (HIGH), uncovered, 2-3 minutes or until mushrooms are heated through. Sprinkle with paprika and/or parsley flakes.

PITA CHIPS
Makes 24

1 tablespoon margarine
Dash garlic powder
Dash paprika
1 pocket-bread pita round

Microwave the margarine on HIGH for 30 seconds or until melted. Stir in garlic powder and paprika. Cut pocket bread in half horizontally. Brush inner side with margarine; cut rounds into strips. Place on paper-towel-lined plate. Microwave on HIGH, uncovered, for 1 min. 30 seconds to 1 min. 45 seconds, or until bread is crisp. Serve plain or with favorite dip. (10 calories each)

ULTIMATE NACHOS
Serves 4

Paper towel
24 large tortilla chips
1 cup shredded Monterey Jack,
  Cheddar or Colby cheese
6-7 tablespoons canned refried
  beans
2 tablespoons chopped onions,
  optional
1 medium tomato, chopped
1-2 cups shredded lettuce
1/4 cup sour cream, optional
1/4 cup sliced black olives
1 tablespoon jalapeño pepper,
  fresh or canned, optional
Taco sauce

Place towel on microwave-safe plate; arrange tortilla chips on the paper towel-lined plate. Spread chips with refried beans; top with shredded cheese and chopped onions. Microwave 2-5 minutes at 50% (medium). Before serving, after cheese has melted, top with shredded lettuce, chopped tomato, olives, jalapeño pepper, taco sauce, and small dollops of sour cream.

OUTRAGEOUS SPINACH DIP

1 (10-ounce) box frozen chopped
  spinach
1 (8-ounce) can water chestnuts,
  finely chopped
1-1/2 cups sour cream
1 cup mayonnaise
1 package dried vegetable soup
  mix
2 green onions, finely chopped
1/4 teaspoon garlic powder
1/2 teaspoon seasoning salt

Remove paper from box of spinach; place box on paper towel in microwave oven. Microwave on HIGH for 6 minutes. In mixing bowl combine remaining ingredients; drain and squeeze spinach before adding to cream mixture. Refrigerate for 2 hours before serving. Serving suggestion: Take a round un-sliced loaf of pumpernickel bread and cut a circle in the top and remove. Gently pull bread from inside to be later used to dip. When ready to serve, pour dip into bread.

PUMPERNICKEL SURPRISE MUFFINS

1 cup milk
1/3 cup oil
1 egg
2 tablespoons molasses
3/4 cup whole wheat or white flour
1/2 cup rye flour
1/4 cup packed brown sugar
1/4 cup unsweetened cocoa powder
2 teaspoons baking powder
1 teaspoon caraway seeds
1/2 teaspoon salt
1 (3-ounce) package cream cheese
1/2 teaspoon grated orange rind

Beat together milk, oil, egg, and molasses in 2-cup measure. Combine flours, brown sugar, cocoa, baking powder, caraway seeds, and salt in a bowl. Add milk mixture; stir just until moistened. Cut cream cheese into 12 equal cubes; roll grated orange rind in as you roll into a ball. Line the muffin cups with paper liners; spoon a little batter into each cup, filling 1/4 full. Place a cream cheese ball in the center of each muffin. Top with remaining batter; fill 3/4 full. Microwave, uncovered, on HIGH for 2 to 2-1/2 minutes for 6 muffins.

VEGETABLE CORN MUFFINS
Makes 12 muffins
(Microwave - Diabetes Exchange)

1 cup all-purpose white flour
1/2 cup cornmeal
1 tablespoon sugar
1 tablespoon baking powder
1/2 teaspoon salt
3/4 teaspoon Italian seasoning
1/8 teaspoon garlic powder
2 eggs, beaten
1 tablespoon vegetable oil
1/2 cup corn, drained
1/3 cup skim milk

1/3 cup chopped green pepper
1/4 cup finely chopped onion

Combine all ingredients in mixing bowl. Stir just until blended. Line each muffin or custard cup with 2 paper liners. Fill 1/2 full. Microwave on HIGH as directed below or until top springs back when touched, rotating and rearranging after 1/2 the time.

Cooking time:
1 muffin = 1/4 to 3/4 minutes
2 muffins = 1/2 to 2 minutes
4 muffins = 1 to 2-1/2 minutes
6 muffins = 2 to 4-1/2 minutes

OATMEAL APPLE MUFFINS

1/4 cup water
1/2 cup quick cooking oats
3 tablespoons butter or margarine
2 tablespoons oil
1 egg
1/2 cup packed brown sugar
1/2 cup whole wheat or white flour
1 teaspoon baking powder
1/4 teaspoon salt
1/2 teaspoon cinnamon
1/4 teaspoon nutmeg
3/4 cup chopped apple

Topping:
1 tablespoon butter or margarine
2 tablespoons brown sugar
1 tablespoon flour
1 tablespoon chopped nuts
1/4 teaspoon cinnamon

Microwave water in mixing bowl for 2-3 minutes or until boiling. Stir in oats; let stand 5 minutes. Add butter and oil; stir until butter is melted. Beat in egg and brown sugar; add flour, baking powder, salt, cinnamon, nutmeg; stir until moistened; stir in apple.

Line 12 microwave-safe muffin cups with paper liners; spoon batter into cups, filling 2/3 full. Combine topping ingredients in small bowl; mix with fork until crumbly; spoon mixture evenly onto muffin batter. Microwave on HIGH, uncovered, 2 to 2-1/2 minutes. Repeat with remaining muffins.

Bake
A PIE

APPLE PIE

Makes 8 or 9-inch pie

Pastry for two-crust pie:
5 or 6 apples, pared and sliced
2/3 cup fructose
1/2 teaspoon nutmeg *and/or* 1/2
   teaspoon cinnamon
1/4 cup cornstarch
2 tablespoons lemon juice (if
   desired for extra tartness)

Prepare pastry for 2-crust pie. Spray bottom and sides of pie pan and line with half rolled-out crust. Combine fructose, nutmeg *and/or* cinnamon, cornstarch, and mix well.

Pare and slice apples; add lemon juice, if desired. Stir fructose mixture into apples and arrange in pie crust. Cover with remaining rolled-out crust. Press edges together and flute in attractive manner. Bake at 400 degrees for approximately 45 minutes, or until well browned.

DUTCH APPLE PIE

3 cups sliced apples
3 tablespoons water
1/2 teaspoon cinnamon
1 cup sugar (scant)
3 tablespoons flour
1 9-inch unbaked pie shell

Mix filling ingredients all together; bake in unbaked pie crust for 1 hour in preheated oven of 350 degrees.

Topping:

1/2 cup sugar
1/4 cup Parmesan cheese
1/2 cup flour
3 tablespoons margarine

Mix above until crumbly. Sprinkle evenly over pie. Return pie to oven until topping is light brown. This is a restaurant specialty. The topping gives any one-crust apple pie a unique and delicious flavor.

Mrs. Larry Morris, Lima, Ohio

IMPOSSIBLE FRENCH APPLE PIE

6 cups sliced apples
1-1/4 teaspoons cinnamon
1/4 teaspoon nutmeg
1 cup sugar
3/4 cup milk
1/2 cup Bisquick
2 eggs
2 tablespoons softened butter
Streusel Topping (recipe follows)

Grease pie plate (10x1-1/2-inch). Mix apple and spices; turn into plate. Beat remaining ingredients, except streusel, until smooth, 15 seconds, in blender or 1 minute with mixer. Pour into plate over apples. Sprinkle with streusel. Bake at 350 degrees until knife comes out clean, 55-60 minutes.

Streusel Topping:
1 cup Bisquick
1/2 cup chopped nuts
1/3 cup brown sugar
3 tablespoons margarine

Mix all ingredients together until crumbly.

Sandy Marqueling, Fort Wayne, Ind.

MINCE-APPLE PIE

1 (9-ounce) package instant condensed mincemeat
1/4 cup sugar
2 cups thinly sliced apples
1/4 teaspoon grated lemon peel
1 tablespoon lemon juice
1 teaspoon rum flavoring
Pastry for 9-inch 2-crust pie
Fluffy Hard Sauce (recipe follows)

Prepare mincemeat following package directions, except use 1/4 cup sugar.

Combine mincemeat with apples, lemon peel, lemon juice, and rum flavoring. Line 9-inch pie plate with pastry; pour in mincemeat mixture. Adjust top crust and crimp edges. Cut slits in top of upper crust for escape of steam. Bake at 400 degrees for 40 to 45 minutes. Serve warm with Fluffy Hard Sauce.

Fluffy Hard Sauce:
2 cups sifted confectioners' sugar
1/2 cup butter or margarine
1 egg yolk, beaten
1 teaspoon vanilla
1 egg white, stiffly beaten

Thoroughly cream together sifted confectioners' sugar and butter (or margarine). Stir in beaten egg yolk and 1 teaspoon vanilla. Fold in stiffly beaten egg white. Chill.

Trenda Leigh, Richmond, Va.

HOSPITALITY FRESH PINEAPPLE PIE

9-inch double-crust pastry
3-1/4 cups fresh bite-sized pine-
    apple chunks
2 eggs
3/4 cup sugar
flour
1 teaspoon lemon rind
1/4 teaspoon cardamom
1/4 teaspoon nutmeg
1/2 teaspoon cinnamon

Roll out bottom crust; place in pie pan. Combine pineapple, eggs, sugar, flour, lemon rind, and spices; turn mixture into pie shell. Roll out pastry; cut into lattice strips. Arrange strips over filling; flute the edge; sprinkle strips with small amount of sugar. Bake at 400 degrees for 10 minutes; lower heat to 375 degrees for 40 to 45 minutes. Delicious chilled and served with a dollop of vanilla ice cream or whipped cream.

Gwen Campbell, Sterling, Va

PEACH PIE
Serves 6-8

Pastry for 2-crust 9-inch pie
6 cups peeled and sliced peaches
    (about 2 pounds), or half
    peaches and half nectarines
1/2 cup sugar
3 tablespoons cornstarch
Dash salt
1/2 teaspoon ground nutmeg
1/2 cup sour cream
Milk
Sugar

Roll out half of pastry. Use to line bottom of 9-inch pie plate. Place peaches in pastry-lined pie plate (or alternate layers of peaches and nectarines if nectarines are used).

In small bowl, mix sugar, cornstarch, salt, nutmeg, and sour cream. Pour over peaches. Roll out remaining pastry and make lattice top. Brush pastry with milk and sprinkle with sugar. Bake at 425 degrees for 10 minutes. Reduce heat to 350 degrees. Continue baking 45-50 minutes longer. Cool on rack.

Mrs. L. Mayer, Richmond, Va.

GLAZED PEACH PIE

1 graham cracker Ready-crust pie
    crust
4 cups unsweetened fresh or frozen
    peaches, drained thoroughly
3/4 cup sugar
1/2 teaspoon nutmeg, optional
1/4 cup flour
1/4 teaspoon salt
1 teaspoon lemon juice
1/4 teaspoon almond extract
1/4 cup peach preserves
1 egg yolk, beaten

Brush crust with beaten egg yolk. Bake on cookie sheet for 5 minutes at 375 degrees. Toss together in large bowl peaches, sugar, nutmeg (if desired), flour, salt, lemon juice, and almond extract. Pour into prepared pie shell. With spoon, arrange peaches in concentric circles evenly in pie shell. Bake at 375 degrees for 35 minutes. While baking, melt peach preserves in saucepan. If too thick, add drop of almond extract. Brush peach preserves over baked pie. Allow pie to cool. Serve with ice cream or whipped cream.

Peggy Fowler Revels, Woodruff, SC

PEACH-PRALINE PIE

Unbaked 9-inch pie shell
4 cups sliced peaches
1/2 cup sugar
2 tablespoons tapioca
1/2 cup chopped pecans
1 teaspoon lemon juice
1/4 cup brown sugar, firmly packed
1/2 cup sifted flour
1/4 cup margarine

Combine peaches, sugar, tapioca, and lemon juice in bowl; let stand 15 minutes. Combine flour, brown sugar, and pecans in small bowl; cut in butter with fork or mix with fingers until crumbly. Sprinkle 1/3 of pecan mixture over bottom of pie shell; cover with peach mixture; sprinkle remaining pecan mixture over peaches. Bake in 425 degree oven 10

minutes; reduce heat to 350 degrees and bake 20 minutes longer.

Sharon McClatchey, Muskogee, OK

STRAWBERRY PIE

1/2 cup water
1 envelope unflavored gelatin
1/2 cup sugar
1 (10-ounce) package frozen straw-
    berries
Juice of 1/2 lemon
1 cup heavy cream, whipped
1 baked pie shell

Soak gelatin in cold water, then dissolve over boiling water. Add lemon juice, sugar, and strawberries, partially thawed. Stir with fork. Fold in whipped cream. Pour filling into baked pie shell; refrigerate for two or three hours before serving.

Easy, quick, never-fail, and delicious.

Karin Shea Fedders, Dameron, MD

FRESH STRAWBERRY PIE

2 boxes strawberries
1 cup sugar
3 tablespoons cornstarch
1/4 cup water
1 tablespoon lemon juice
Pinch of salt
1 (9-inch) baked pie crust

Crush 1 cup berries. Add sugar, cornstarch, water and salt, if desired. Cook, stirring constantly, until clear. Remove from heat and add lemon juice. Arrange remaining berries in baked pie crust. Pour cooked mixture over berries and chill. Serve.

During the lazy, hazy strawberry months have you often wished you could have one of these berries in December? Have you frozen one, only to be disappointed, as it was often mushy and fit only for a cold cereal topping? Here is an ideal way to recapture that wonderful taste sensation. . .make this bread and freeze!

STRAWBERRY DAIQUIRI PIE

Serves 6-8

9-inch graham cracker crust, baked and cooled
I pint strawberries, hulled
3/4 cup sugar
1 (1 1/4 oz.) envelope unflavored gelatin
1/3 cup lime juice
1/3 cup light rum
1/2 pint whipping cream, whipped
Whole strawberries for garnish

In blender, combine hulled berries and sugar; process until berries are pureed. Set aside 15 minutes to let mixture soak and blend. In saucepan, stir gelatin into lime juice; let stand 5 minutes to soften. Stir over medium heat until gelatin dissolves. With blender running at medium speed, add gelatin mixture to pureed mixture; process until blended. Strain through fine sieve into bowl. Stir rum into mixture. Refrigerate, stirring often, until mixture begins to mound when spooned on top of itself. Fold in whipped cream. Spoon into crust. Freeze 4 hours. Decorate with whole berries.

lisa Varner, Baton Rouge, LA

CHOCOLATE MOUSSE PIE

Serves 6

1 (6-ounce) package semi-sweet chocolate bits
3 eggs
1 teaspoon vanilla extract
2 tablespoons cold coffee
1 (9-ounce) container frozen whipped topping, thawed
1 (9-inch) prepared graham cracker shell

Melt chocolate over hot (not boiling) water; add one whole slightly-beaten egg and beat well. Separate remaining two eggs and add yolks to chocolate, one at a time, beating well after each addition. Beat egg whites until stiff; carefully fold into chocolate. Then fold in half the topping, the

vanilla, and cold coffee. Turn mixture into pie shell; spoon on remaining topping. Refrigerate for at least two hours or overnight. Freezes well.

Mrs. H. W. Walker, Richmond, VA

CHOCOLATE MOUSSE PIE

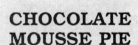

1 (9-inch) pie crust, baked
1 cup chocolate chips
1 egg
2 egg yolks
1 teaspoon rum
2 egg whites
2 cups Cool Whip (divided in half)
1/2 square unsweetened chocolate

Melt chocolate chips over hot, *not boiling* water. Remove from heat and beat in the 1 whole egg and the 2 egg yolks, one at a time. Add rum. Beat 2 egg whites, until stiff peaks form. Fold together 1 cup Cool Whip and the egg yolk mixture and spoon onto the pie crust. Refrigerate until well chilled. Serve topped with the remaining 1 cup Cool Whip and shave the unsweetened chocolate over Cool Whip.

A light, delicious chocolate pie.
Jodie McCoy, Tulsa, Okla.

FRENCH SILK CHOCOLATE PIE

1 baked pie shell
3/4 cup sugar
1/2 cup butter
1 teaspoon vanilla
2 eggs
2 squares unsweetened chocolate

Melt chocolate over hot water and cool. Mix cooled chocolate, butter, and sugar; add one egg and beat 5 minutes; add the other egg and beat 5 minutes more; add vanilla and beat again. Place into a baked shell and serve with whipped cream. Eat heartily!

Agnes Ward, Erie, Pa.

SOUTHERN CHOCOLATE PIE

Serves 8

1 (4-ounce) package German Sweet Chocolate
1/4 cup butter or margarine
1 (13-ounce) can evaporated milk
1 cup sugar
3 eggs
1 teaspoon vanilla
9-inch unbaked pie shell with high rim
1-1/4 cups flaked coconut
1/2 cup chopped pecans

Melt chocolate and butter over low heat. Remove from heat and blend in evaporated milk and sugar. Beat in eggs and vanilla. Pour into pie shell. Top with coconut and nuts. Bake at 375 degrees for 45-50 minutes or until top is puffed. Cool 4 hours.

Lisa Varner, Baton Rouge, La.

GERMAN CHOCOLATE PIE

1 (4-ounce) German Sweet Chocolate bar
1/4 cup butter
1 (13-ounce) can evaporated milk
1-1/2 cups sugar
2 eggs
1 teaspoon vanilla
3 tablespoons cornstarch
Salt to taste
1 unbaked 9-inch pie shell
1/2 cup chopped pecans
1-1/3 cups coconut

Melt chocolate with butter over low heat, stirring until blended. Remove from heat, and gradually blend in milk. Mix sugar, cornstarch, and salt. Beat in eggs and vanilla. Gradually blend in chocolate mixture. Pour into pie shell. Sprinkle with coconut and pecans. Bake at 375 degrees for 45-50 minutes. Cool for 4 hours before serving.

The aroma, as this pie bakes, will fill the house and tickle the taste buds ahead of time.

Linda S. Templin, Steele, Ala.

CHOCOLATE CHIP PIE

1 cup sugar
1/2 cup flour
2 eggs, well beaten
1 stick margarine, melted
1 teaspoon vanilla
1 cup semi-sweet chocolate bits
3/4 cup pecans
1/2 cup coconut
1 unbaked deep dish pie shell

Blend flour, sugar, eggs, melted margarine, and vanilla. Stir in chocolate bits, pecans, and coconut. Pour mixture into unbaked pie shell. Bake at 350 degrees for 30-35 minutes until firm.

Sally George, Poulsbo, Wash.

NUTTY CHOCOLATE PIE

3 eggs
1 cup light or dark corn syrup
1 cup coarsely-chopped walnuts
6 ounces (1 cup) semi-sweet
   chocolate morsels
1/2 cup sugar
2 tablespoons butter or margarine,
   melted
1 teaspoon vanilla extract
1 unbaked (9-inch) pie shell

Preheat oven to 350 degrees. In large bowl, beat eggs until well combined. Add corn syrup, walnuts, semi-sweet morsels, sugar, butter, and vanilla extract. Mix until well blended. Pour evenly into pie shell. Bake at 350 degrees for 50-60 minutes. Cool completely before serving.
Suzanne Dawson, Cypress, Texas

FUDGE PIE

1 stick margarine, melted
1/4 cup cocoa
1/4 cup flour
1 cup sugar
1/4 teaspoon vanilla
2 eggs
1 unbaked pie shell

Mix all ingredients and pour into pie shell. Bake at 350 degrees for 25 minutes.

Mrs. Bruce Fowler, Woodruff, S.C.

HERSHEY BAR PIE

1/2 cup milk
1 (4-ounce) Hershey bar with
   almonds
18 large marshmallows
1/2 pint heavy whipping cream
1 graham cracker crust

In top of double boiler melt Hershey bar, milk, and marshmallows. Whip the cream in bowl until stiff and fold this into chocolate mixture. Pour into crust and place in refrigerator to cool. When cool, place in freezer. Remove at dinner time and pie will be thawed for dessert. Keeps indefinitely in freezer.
Melanie Burnell, Pittsfield, Mass.

GOLDEN APRICOT CREME PIE

1 (8-ounce) package cream cheese
1/4 cup sugar
1 cup heavy cream
1 teaspoon vanilla extract
1/8 teaspoon almond extract
1 (10-1/2 ounce) can apricot halves;
   drain, reserve juice
1 envelope unflavored gelatin
1 ready-made graham cracker pie
   shell
1/2 cup melted currant jelly

Beat cheese and sugar until light and fluffy. Slowly add cream; stir in vanilla and almond extracts. Drain apricot halves; reserve syrup. Soften gelatin in 1/2 cup of reserved apricot syrup; heat syrup mixture to dissolve gelatin. Stir gelatin mixture into cream cheese mixture; pour into pie shell; chill until set. Arrange apricot halves on top of pie in a decorative manner; spoon melted jelly over apricots. Rechill.

Gwen Campbell, Sterling, Va.

BANANA CREAM PIE

Crust:
10 graham crackers, crushed
4 tablespoons sugar
4 tablespoons melted butter

Mix ingredients; pack firmly into 9 inch pie pan. Refrigerate 15 minutes.

Filling:
1 cup cream, whipped
1 tablespoon powdered sugar
1/2 teaspoon vanilla
2 bananas, thinly sliced
Grated coconut
Combine filling ingredients. Just before serving, spoon into shell. sprinkle with coconut.

Monica Turk, Milwaukee, Wis.

BANANA CREAM CHEESE PIE

1 baked pie shell
3 medium bananas
1 (8-ounce) package cream cheese,
   room temperature
1 can sweetened condensed milk
1/2 cup lemon juice
1 tablespoon vanilla

Slice 2 bananas; place them in pie shell. Beat cream cheese until light and fluffy. Add milk gradually and continue beating until mixture is smooth. Stir in lemon juice and vanilla. Pour into pie shell; chill until filling is firm. About 1 hour before serving, slice remaining banana; arrange slices on top of pie filling.

Mrs. Don Shamway, Freeport, IL

CHILLED CANTA-LOPE CREAM PIE
Serves 8

1 9-inch pie shell, baked
2 tablespoons cornstarch
2 tablespoons cold water
1/2 fresh lemon rind, grated
2 tablespoons fresh lemon juice
1/2 cup sugar
2 eggs, separated
1 cup boiling water
1-1/2 teaspoons unflavored gelatin
3 cups cantaloupe, diced
Vanilla ice cream

In a saucepan mix cornstarch with cold water. Stir in lemon rind, lemon juice, sugar, egg yolks, and gelatin; beat together; add boiling water. Cook until thickened; refrigerate until cool. Fold in diced cantaloupe and stiffly beaten egg whites; turn mixture into baked pie shell. Chill pie several hours until set. Cut into wedges, top with vanilla ice cream, and serve.

Gwen Campbell, Sterling, Va.

CREAMY COCONUT PIE

1 (3-ounce) package cream cheese, softened
2 tablespoons sugar
1/2 cup milk
1-1/3 cups Angel Flake coconut
1 (8-ounce) container frozen whipped topping, thawed
1/2 teaspoon almond extract, optional
1 (8-inch) graham cracker crust, prepared

Combine cream cheese, sugar, milk, and coconut in electric blender for 30 seconds. Fold into topping and add extract. Spoon into crust. Freeze until firm, about 4 hours. Sprinkle with additional coconut. Let stand at room temperature, 5 minutes before cutting. Store any leftover pie in freezer.

Suzanne Dawson, Cypress, Texas

PINEAPPLE CREAM PIE

3/4 cup sugar
1/4 cup flour
1/4 teaspoon salt
2 cups milk
3 egg yolks
2 tablespoons butter or margarine
1 cup crushed pineapple
1 teaspoon vanilla

Preheat oven to 325 degrees. Combine sugar, flour, and salt. Add milk gradually, then slightly beaten egg yolks. Add butter. Cook over low heat until thickened. Add pineapple and vanilla. Pour into a 9-inch baked pie crust. Top with meringue; bake 20-25 minutes at 325 degrees.

Ruby Pilcarczyk, Ogden, Utah

RASPBERRY BAVARIAN PIE

1 (10-ounce) package frozen raspberries
1 (3-ounce) package lemon gelatin
1 (3-ounce) package strawberry gelatin
1 (8-ounce) container whipped topping
1 chocolate-flavored pie crust, prepared

Combine raspberries with 1 cup water. Heat to boiling, crushing berries with spoon or wooden pestle to extract juice. Strain and measure juice. Add enough additional hot water to make 3 cups liquid. Pour over gelatin and stir until gelatin dissolves. Chill until thickened. If gelatin mixture becomes too hard, microwave for 10 seconds on full power or until softened. Beat with rotary beater until foamy. Gently fold whipped topping into gelatin mixture. Turn into pie crust. Chill until firm, at least 4 hours.

Peggy Fowler Revels, Woodruff, SC

RHUBARB ORANGE CREAM PIE

1 (9-inch) unbaked pastry shell
3 eggs, separated
1-1/4 cups sugar, divided
1/4 cup butter, softened
3 tablespoons frozen orange juice concentrate, thawed, undiluted
1/4 cup flour
1/4 teaspoon salt
2-1/2 cups rhubarb, cut into 1/2-inch pieces
1/3 cup chopped pecans

Prepare pastry shell; set aside. Beat egg whites until stiff, but not dry. Add 1/4 cup sugar gradually, beating until whites are stiff and glossy; set aside. Beat butter, orange juice concentrate, and egg yolks until well blended. Add remaining cup sugar, flour, and salt. Stir in rhubarb, then gently fold in egg white meringue. Pour into prepared shell. Sprinkle top with nuts. Place pie on bottom rack of oven; bake at 375 degrees for 15 minutes. Reduce temperature to 325 degrees, bake 45 minutes longer.

This is an innovative, delicious rhubarb pie that makes its own meringue topping as it bakes.

Mrs. Robert Combs, Fair Play, Mo.

PECAN-CHEESE PIE
Serves 8-10

1 unbaked (10-inch) pie shell
4 eggs
1 (8-ounce) package cream cheese, room temperature
1/3 cup sugar
2 teaspoons vanilla
1-1/4 cups coarsely chopped pecans
1 cup light corn syrup
1/4 cup sugar
1/4 teaspoon salt

In large bowl, at medium speed, beat together until smooth the cream cheese, 1 egg, 1 teaspoon vanilla, and 1/3 cup sugar. Spread over bottom of pie shell and top with pecans. In a clean large bowl, at medium speed, beat remaining eggs until frothy. Add corn syrup, salt, 1/4 cup sugar, and 1 teaspoon vanilla; beat until well blended. Gently pour mixture over pecans. Bake in a pre-heated 375 degree oven until done, 40 minutes.

This will become one of your favorite pies!!

Joy B. Shamway, Freeport, Ill.

MYSTERY PECAN PIE

1 unbaked pie crust (9-inch)
1 (8-ounce) package cream cheese
1/3 cup sugar
1/4 cup sugar
4 eggs, divided
2 teaspoons vanilla, divided
1/4 teaspoon salt
1-1/4 cups pecan halves
1 cup corn syrup

Beat together the cream cheese, 1/3 cup sugar, 1 egg, 1 teaspoon vanilla, and salt in small bowl; set aside. Beat 3 eggs well; add the 1/4 cup sugar, corn syrup, and 1 teaspoon vanilla; blend well.

Spread cream cheese mixture in bottom of unbaked crust. Sprinkle pecans over cheese layer. Pour corn syrup mixture gently over top of pecans. Bake at 375 degrees for 40 minutes, or until center is firm to touch.

Mrs. W. T. Gore, Aztec, NM

MOCK PECAN PIE

2/3 cup regular oats, uncooked
2/3 cup light corn syrup
2 eggs, beaten
2/3 cup sugar
1 teaspoon vanilla
1/4 teaspoon salt
2/3 cup melted butter or margarine, cooled
1 (8-inch) pie shell, unbaked

Combine oats, corn syrup, eggs, sugar, vanilla and salt, mixing well. Add melted butter and mix thoroughly. Pour into pastry shell and bake 1 hour at 350 degrees. Cool before serving.

Mary Linger, Jacksonville, Fla.

BLENDER PECAN PIE

2 (8-inch) unbaked pie shells
3 eggs
1/2 cup heavy cream

1/2 cup dark corn syrup
1/8 teaspoon salt
1 cup granulated sugar
1 teaspoon vanilla
1 tablespoon sherry
2 tablespoons butter
1-1/2 cups chopped pecans

Put all ingredients into blender, except nuts. Blend 10 seconds or until well mixed. Stir in nuts. Pour into pie shells. Bake at 400 degrees for 30-35 minutes.

Jessie B. Conlon, South Hill, Va.

PECAN CRUNCH PIE

3 egg whites
1 cup sugar
1 teaspoon baking powder
1 teaspoon vanilla flavoring
1 cup crushed graham-cracker crumbs
1 cup chopped pecans

Beat egg whites until stiff. Combine sugar and baking powder; beat into egg whites. Add vanilla. Fold in graham-cracker crumbs, then pecans. Pour into a buttered 9-inch pie plate and bake at 350 degrees for 30 minutes or until done. Cool. Good served with vanilla ice cream or whipped cream.

Marsha Miller, Hilliard, Ohio

PECAN FUDGE PIE

1 (9-inch) unbaked pastry shell
1 (4-ounce) package sweet chocolate
1/4 cup margarine or butter
1 (14-ounce) can condensed milk
2 eggs, slightly beaten
1/4 cup hot water
1 teaspoon vanilla
1/8 teaspoon salt
1/2 cup broken pecans

Preheat oven to 350 degrees. In heavy saucepan over low heat, melt chocolate and margarine. Remove from heat. In large mixing bowl combine remaining ingredients, except pecans. Add chocolate mixture.

Mix well and pour into crust. Top with pecans. Bake 35 to 40 minutes or until top is lightly browned.

Trenda Leigh, Richmond, Va.

PECAN PRALINE PIE

1/3 cup butter or margarine
1/3 cup brown sugar
1/2 cup chopped pecans
1 baked (9-inch) pastry shell
1 (5-ounce) package vanilla pie filling (not instant)
3 cups milk
1 envelope whipped topping

Heat butter, sugar, and nuts in pan until melted; spread on bottom of pie shell. Bake at 450 degrees for 5 minutes. Cool. Prepare pie filling with milk; cool 5 minutes, stirring occasionally. Measure 1 cup of pudding; cover with wax paper and chill. Pour remainder of filling into pie shell and chill. Prepare whipped topping as package directs. Fold 1-1/3 cups topping into reserved, chilled pudding and spread over filling in pie; chill. Garnish with remaining whipped topping and pecans.

Agnes Ward, Erie, Pa.

CRUSTLESS DATE-PECAN PIE
Serves 6

2 eggs
1 cup sugar
Dash salt
1 teaspoon vanilla
1/2 cup soft bread crumbs
1 cup cut-up dates
1 cup coarsely chopped pecans
Vanilla ice cream or whipped cream

Beat eggs lightly in bowl. Add sugar, salt, vanilla, bread crumbs, dates, and pecans. Spoon mixture into buttered 8-inch pie pan and bake at 200 degrees for 40 minutes. Raise temperature to 250 degrees and continue to bake an additional 25 minutes or until top is firm. Cool; cut into wedges and serve with either ice cream or whipped cream.

Agnes Ward, Erie, Pa.

HICKORY NUT PIE

3 eggs, slightly beaten
3/4 cup sugar
1 cup white Karo syrup
1 teaspoon vanilla
2 tablespoons butter or margarine
1 cup hickory nuts, chopped
1 unbaked pie shell

Mix eggs, sugar, syrup, vanilla, and magarine, adding nuts last. Pour into pie shell and bake in 400-degree oven for 10 minutes then reduce heat to 350 degrees and bake 40 additional minutes.

Gladys Mysak, Toledo, IA

CUSTARD PIE

4 eggs, well beaten
6 tablespoons sugar
1 teaspoon vanilla
1/8 teaspoon salt
2 cups milk
1 (9-inch) pie shell
Nutmeg

Beat eggs; add sugar, milk, vanilla, and salt. Pour into unbaked pie shell. Sprinkle top with nutmeg.

Bake in a 425 degree oven for 10 minutes. Reduce heat to 350 degrees and bake 20 minutes longer.

Helen West, Peebles, Ohio

RHUBARB ORANGE CUSTARD PIE

2 cups rhubarb, cut up

Cook until tender in about 1/2 cup water about 5-8 minutes.

1 cup sugar
2 tablespoons cornstarch
3 egg yolks
Juice of one large orange
1 teaspoon grated orange peel
Pinch salt

Mix together sugar, cornstarch, yolks, orange juice, orange peel and salt. Pour this mixture into hot rhu-barb which has been cooked until tender. Cook until it thickens. Pour into a baked pie crust.

Meringue:
3 egg whites
6 tablespoons sugar
1/8 teaspoon cream of tartar
1/2 teaspoon vanilla

Beat egg whites until frothy. Add cream of tartar. When stiff, beat in sugar slowly. Continue beating until sugar is dissolved. Bake in 350-degree oven until lightly browned.
Dorothy M. Radl, Wonewoc, Wis.

EARLY SPRING RHUBARB CUSTARD PIE

Filling:
1 unbaked 9-inch pie shell
4 cups rhubarb, cut into 1/4-inch slices
3/4 cup sugar
2 tablespoons flour
1-1/4 tablespoons fresh lemon juice
1/8 teaspoon salt

Topping:
3 eggs
1 cup whipping cream
2-1/4 tablespoons butter or margarine, melted
1/2 teaspoon nutmeg

In a bowl combine rhubarb, sugar, flour, fresh lemon juice, and salt. Mix well; turn into pie shell; bake 375 degrees for 25 minutes. Meanwhile beat eggs; stir in cream, butter, and nutmeg. Pour over hot rhubarb in pie shell; bake 10 minutes until top is golden. Chill in refrigerator at least 2 hours before serving.
Gwen Campbell, Sterling, Va.

EASY CARAMEL CUSTARD PIE

1 cup instant non-fat dry milk
1/2 cup sugar
1/4 teaspoon salt
1 cup cold water
2 teaspoons vanilla
3 eggs, beaten
1-1/2 cups boiling water
6 tablespoons brown sugar

Dash salt
1/4 teaspoon cinnamon
1 unbaked 9-inch pie shell

Preheat oven to 350 degrees. Sift dry ingredients together; add water and vanilla; mix until smooth. Stir in beaten eggs, then stir in boiling water. Combine brown sugar, cinnamon, and salt; sprinkle over bottom of unbaked pie shell. Pour in custard mixture. Bake 45-50 minutes, or until knife inserted comes out clean. Cool and serve.

Marsha Miller, Hilliard, Ohio

JELLY PIE

1/2 cup butter
1/2 cup plum jelly
1/2 cup evaporated milk
1 teaspoon flour
2 eggs, beaten
1 teaspoon vanilla
1/2 cup sugar
Pinch of salt

Combine butter and sugar; add beaten eggs. Add all other remaining ingredients. Pour into an unbaked 8-inch pie shell. Bake at 350 degrees for 45 minutes. Cool. Cover with a layer of whipped cream; chill. Use any flavor jelly you like. This is an old-fashioned pie and is very good.

Sarah M. Burkett, Centralia, Ill.

MACAROON PIE
Serves 8

16 saltine crackers, finely rolled (about 1/2 cup)
16 pitted dates, finely snipped
1/2 cup chopped pecans
3/4 cup granulated sugar
1/4 teaspoon baking powder
3 egg whites
Heavy cream, whipped

Blend first 4 ingredients. Add baking powder to egg whites and beat until stiff, but not dry. Fold into date mixture and spread in a well buttered 8-inch pie plate. Bake in a preheated 350 degree oven for about 25 minutes. Cool. Serve topped with whipped cream.

Agnes Ward, Erie, Pa.

GARDEN OF EDEN PIE

1 cup Carnation evaporated milk
1 tablespoon lemon juice
1 cup brown sugar
1/4 teaspoon salt
1/4 teaspoon cinnamon
1/8 teaspoon mace
1/2 teaspoon nutmeg
2 cups finely chopped apples
2 cups ground raisins
1 (9-inch) pie pastry shell, unbaked

Mix milk, juice, sugar, salt, and spices. Add fruits; pour into unbaked pie shell and bake in hot oven 450 degrees for 10 minutes to set crust; then reduce temperature to 325 degrees and bake an additional 40 minutes or until filling is set.

Barbara Penland, Goshen, Ind

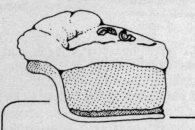

ORANGE COCONUT CHESS PIE

1 stick butter, at room temperature
2 cups sugar
5 eggs
1/2 cup thawed orange juice concentrate
1/3 cup water
1 tablespoon flour
1 tablespoon yellow cornmeal
1/2 cup coconut
2 unbaked 9-inch pie shells

Preheat oven to 350 degrees. Cream butter in large bowl with electric mixer. Gradually add sugar and beat well. Beat in eggs, one at a time. Combine orange juice concentrate and water; blend with butter mixture. Beat in flour and cornmeal. Fold in coconut. Divide mixture evenly between 2 pie crusts. Bake until golden—about 50-60 minutes. Let pie cool before serving.

Jodie McCoy, Tulsa, Okla.

ORANGESICLE PIE

1 (14-ounce) can Eagle Brand Sweetened Condensed Milk (not evaporated)
4 egg yolks
1/2 cup orange juice
1 tablespoon grated orange rind
1 (6-ounce) package graham cracker crumb crust
1 (3-ounce) package cream cheese, softened
1/3 cup confectioners' sugar
1/4 cup sour cream
1/4 teaspoon vanilla extract

Preheat oven to 325 degrees. In large bowl combine sweetened condensed milk, egg yolks, orange juice, and rind; mix well. Pour into crust. (Mixture will be thin). Bake 35 minutes or until knife inserted near center comes out clean. Meanwhile in small mixer bowl, combine remaining ingredients. Beat until smooth and well blended. Spread evenly on top of pie. Bake 10 additional minutes. Cool; chill thoroughly.

Melba Bellefeiulle, Libertyville, Ill.

SHAKER SUGAR PIE

1 unbaked 9-inch pie shell
3/4 cup firmly-packed light brown sugar
1/4 cup flour
2 cups half-and-half
1 teaspoon vanilla extract
Few grains ground nutmeg
1/2 cup butter or margarine, softened

Prick pie shell and bake at 450 degrees for 5 minutes. Set aside. Reduce oven temperature to 350 degrees. Mix brown sugar with flour until blended. Spoon over bottom of partially-baked pie shell. Combine half-and-half, extract, and nutmeg; pour over sugar in pie shell. Dot with butter. Bake at 350 degrees for about 55 minutes, or until crust is lightly browned and filling is set.

A most delicious pie.

Barbara Beauregard-Smith,
Northfield, South Australia

FRENCH COCONUT PIE

3 eggs, beaten well

Add:
1-1/2 cups sugar
1 stick margarine, melted
Pinch of salt
1 cup Angel Flake coconut
1 tablespoon lemon juice

Pour into unbaked pie shell; bake 1 hour at 325 degrees.

Marcella Swigert, Monroe City, Mo.

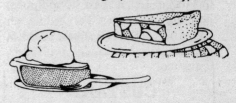

SOUTHERN MOLASSES CRUMB PIE

1 unbaked pie crust

Filling:
1/2 cup molasses
1 egg yolk

Add:
1/2 teaspoon soda dissolved in 3/4 cup boiling water. Mix.

Crumb portion:
3/4 cup flour
2 tablespoons shortening
1/2 teaspoon cinnamon
1/8 teaspoon nutmeg
1/8 teaspoon ginger
1/8 teaspoon cloves
1/2 cup brown sugar, well packed
1/4 teaspoon salt

To make the crumbs combine: flour, sugar, spices, and salt; then work in shortening. Put alternate layers of crumbs and filling into unbaked pie shell. Top with crumbs. Bake in hot oven 450 degrees until edges of crust begin to brown. Reduce heat to 375 degrees and bake until firm (about 20 minutes). Serve plain or with whipped cream.

Claire M. Heroux, Linwood, MA

ICE CREAM PARFAIT PIE

1 (3-ounce) package strawberry
  gelatin
1-1/4 cups hot water
1 pint vanilla ice cream
1 cup sliced strawberries
1 pie shell, baked
Whipped cream, optional

Dissolve gelatin in 1-1/4 cups hot water. Spoon in ice cream and stir until melted. Place in refrigerator until thickened. Let it set 15-25 minutes. Fold in strawberries. Turn filling into baked pie shell. Chill until firm, 30-60 minutes. Serve with whipped cream, if desired.

Beulah Schwallie, Cincinnati, Ohio

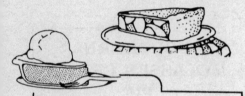

BLACK FOREST PIE

1 (9-inch) unbaked pie shell
3/4 cup sugar
1/3 cup unsweetened cocoa
2 tablespoons flour
1/4 cup margarine
1/3 cup milk
2 eggs, beaten
1 (21-ounce) can cherry pie filling
1 (9-ounce) container frozen whipped
  topping
1 (1-ounce) square unsweetened
  chocolate (coarsely grated)

In saucepan, combine sugar, cocoa, and flour; add margarine and milk. Cook until mixture begins to boil, stirring constantly. Remove from heat. Add small amount of hot mixture to eggs; return mixture to pan. Fold half the can of pie filling into mixture. Pour into crust-lined pan. Bake at 350 degrees for 35-45 minutes or until center is set but still shiny. Cool. Chill one hour. Combine 2 cups topping and grated chocolate; spread over pie. Place remaining pie filling around edge of pie. Cool.

Suzanne Dawson, Cypress, TX

AMISH VANILLA PIE

1/2 cup firmly packed brown sugar
1 tablespoon flour
1/4 cup dark corn syrup
1-1/2 teaspoons vanilla
1 egg, beaten
1 cup water
1 cup flour
1/2 cup firmly packed brown sugar
1/2 teaspoon cream of tartar
1/2 teaspoon baking soda
1/8 teaspoon salt
1/4 cup butter
1 unbaked 9-inch pie shell

Combine first 5 ingredients in 2-quart saucepan. Slowly stir in water. Cook over medium heat until mixture comes to a boil, stirring constantly. Let cool. Combine rest of ingredients (except pie shell) and mix until crumbly. Pour cooled mixture into pie shell and top with crumbs.

Bake at 350 degrees for 40 minutes or until golden brown.

Helen Weissinger, Levittown, Pa.

HAWAIIAN WEDDING PIE

1 (9-inch) baked pie shell
1/2 cup sugar
1/3 cup cornstarch
1-1/2 cups milk
3 beaten egg yolks
1 tablespoon butter or margarine
1-1/2 teaspoons vanilla
1 small can crushed pineapple, well
  drained
1/2-3/4 cup coconut
Whipped cream for topping
Toasted coconut for garnish

Combine sugar, cornstarch, and milk; mix well. Add beaten egg yolks. Cook over medium heat, stirring constantly, until mixture begins to boil and is thickened. Remove from heat. Add butter, vanilla, crushed pineapple, and coconut, thoroughly combining all. Pour mixture into pie shell and chill. When chilled, cover top with whipped cream. Sprinkle with toasted coconut.

Carme Venella, Laurel Springs, NJ

PENNSYLVANIA DUTCH SHOOFLY PIE

2 (8-inch) pastry shells, unbaked
2 cups flour
1 cup sugar
1 teaspoon baking powder
1 stick butter or margarine
1 cup dark molasses
1 teaspoon baking soda
1 cup boiling water
Pinch of salt
1 egg, beaten

Sift together flour, sugar, and baking powder. Cut in butter. In a separate bowl, mix molasses, baking soda, and water. Stir in salt, egg, and 2 cups of the flour-butter mixture. Pour into prepared pie shells and sprinkle with remaining crumbs. Bake at 375 degrees for 45 minutes.

Dorothy Garms, Anaheim, Calif.

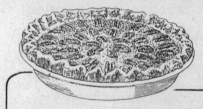

4TH OF JULY PIE

1 pint blueberries
20-25 strawberries, hulled
Whipped cream
1 (3-1/4 ounce) package regular
  vanilla pudding mix
2 cups milk
1 (8-ounce) package cream cheese,
  softened
1/2 teaspoon vanilla
1 8-inch graham–cracker pie crust

Combine pudding mix and 2 cups milk in saucepan. Bring to full boil over medium heat, stirring constantly. Remove from heat. Add cream cheese and stir until smooth. Add vanilla. Let mixture cool for 5 minutes, stirring twice. Pour pudding mixture into pie crust. Refrigerate 3 hours or overnight. Place strawberries in circle on outer edge of pie. Place one in center. Place blueberries over remaining pudding.

Serve chilled, with whipped cream on top.

Chris Bryant, Johnson City, Tenn.

Salad BOWL

BEST PEA SALAD

1 (14-ounce) can small-kernel white corn
1 can small-size peas
1 can French green beans
1 cup diced celery
1/4 cup fresh onion
1 green pepper, chopped
Sliced olives as desired for taste

Dressing:
1 cup sugar
3/4 cup white vinegar
1/2 cup oil
1/2 teaspoon salt
1/4 teaspoon pepper

Boil together dressing ingredients for about 3 minutes—then cool.
Put vegetables in bowl. Pour dressing over vegetables and marinate in refrigerator for about 24 hours before serving.

RASPBERRY TAPIOCA SALAD

5 cups boiling water
Pinch of salt
1 cup tapioca (not Minute) balls
1 (3-ounce) package raspberry gelatin
1 cup sugar
1 cup water
1 (10-ounce) package frozen raspberries
2-3 cups Cool Whip

Cook 1 cup tapioca, pinch of salt and 5 cups boiling water for 20 minutes, stirring often. Take off heat and add one package raspberry gelatin, 1 cup sugar, and 1 cup water. Mix well. Put in bowl and set in refrigerator. Stir often until set. Next day, add frozen raspberries and Cool Whip.
Gen Boyce, Oshkosh, Wisc.

ORANGE-CREAM SALAD
Serves 10

1 (20-ounce) can pineapple chunks, drained
1 (16-ounce) can peach slices, drained
1 (11-ounce) can mandarin orange sections, drained
3 medium bananas, sliced
2 medium apples, cored and chopped
1 (3-1/3 to 3-3/4 ounce) package vanilla instant pudding mix
1-1/2 cups milk
1/2 of a 6-ounce can (1/3 cup) frozen orange juice concentrate, thawed
3/4 cup dairy sour cream
Lettuce

In a large bowl combine pineapple chunks, peaches, orange sections, bananas, and apples; set aside. In small bowl combine dry pudding mix, milk, and orange juice concentrate. Beat with rotary beater 1 to 2 minutes or until well blended. Beat in sour cream. Fold into fruit mixture. Cover and refrigerate several hours. Serve salad on lettuce leaves.
Mrs. A. Mayer, Richmond, Va.

PASTA SALAD

1 pound medium shell macaroni
1/2 pound Provolene cheese
1/4 pound salami
1/2 pound pepperoni
1 can black olives
1 small bottle green olives
1 green pepper
3 stalks celery
1 small onion
1-1/2 teaspoons salt
1 teaspoon pepper
1 teaspoon oregano
3/4 cup oil
1/2 cup cider vinegar
3 tomatoes, chopped

Cook macaroni and drain. Cool. Cut cheese, salami, and pepperoni in bite-size pieces. Slice olives. Dice pepper, celery, and onions. Add salt, pepper, oregano, oil, and vinegar. Combine dressing with other ingredients, except tomatoes; chill overnight Add tomatoes just before serving.
Diantha Susan Hibbard, Rochester, N.Y.

QUICK MACARONI SALAD
Serves 10

1 box macaroni and cheese dinner
1 can tuna, drained
4 eggs, hard cooked
5 tablespoons mayonnaise
1/4 cup chopped pickles

Cook macaroni and cheese dinner as directed on package. Then add and mix all additional ingredients; refrigerate.
Mildred Sherrer, Bay City, Texas

FRUIT COCKTAIL SALAD

1 (5-5/8 ounce) package vanilla flavored Jello instant pudding mix
1-1/3 cups buttermilk
1 (8-ounce) container Cool Whip
1 (30-ounce) can fruit cocktail, well-drained
2 cans mandarin oranges, well-drained
1 cup miniature rainbow-colored marshmallows (optional)

Blend buttermilk into pudding mix using medium speed of mixer. When smooth, blend in Cool Whip. If consistency of mixture seems too thick, add a little more buttermilk. Fold in fruit cocktail and mandarin oranges, reserving half a can of oranges for garnish. Swirl a design on top of salad with a tablespoon. Gently arrange balance of mandarin orange slices in swirled design on top of salad.

Add colored marshmallows to mixture before garnishing, if desired.
Lalla Fellows, Long Beach, Calif.

GOLDEN FRUIT SALAD

2 large Golden Delicious apples, diced
2 large Red Delicious apples, diced
4 large bananas, sliced
2 (20 ounce) cans pineapple chunks, drained (reserve juice)
2 (16 ounce) cans Mandarin oranges, drained
Whole green grapes, optional

Mix Together:
1 cup sugar
4 tablespoons corn starch
Reserved pineapple juice
2 tablespoons lemon juice
2/3 cup orange juice

Stir and boil 1 minute. Pour hot mixture over fruit. Leave uncovered until cool.

Pat Stump, Dunnell, MN

SHORTCUT FROZEN SALAD

1 small package *instant* lemon pudding
1 pint whipped topping, thawed
1/2 cup mayonnaise
2 tablespoons lemon juice
1 (1-pound) can fruit cocktail, drained
1 cup miniature marshmallows
1/4 cup chopped pecans

Prepare pudding according to package directions; blend in whipped topping, mayonnaise, and lemon juice. Fold in remaining ingredients. Turn into a 9x5x3-inch loaf pan and freeze until firm. Slice to serve.

Agnes Ward, Erie, Pa.

GUM DROP FRUIT SALAD

Serves 8

1 (#2 can) pineapple tidbits
1/4 cup sugar
2 tablespoons flour
1/4 teaspoon salt
3 tablespoons lemon juice
1-1/2 teaspoons vinegar
2 cups seedless grapes, halved
2 cups miniature white marshmallows
2/3 cup gumdrops, halved (do not use black drops)
1 (4-ounce) bottle maraschino cherries, drained and halved
1/4 cup chopped pecans
1 cup whipping cream, whipped

Drain pineapple, reserving 1/3 cup of syrup. Combine sugar, flour, and salt. Add reserved pineapple syrup, lemon juice, and vinegar. Cook over medium heat, stirring constantly until thick and boiling. Continue cooking 1 minute. Set aside and cool. Combine pineapple and remaining ingredients, except the whipped cream. Fold the cooked dressing into the whipped cream. Cover and refrigerate for 12-24 hours.

Carmen J. Bickert, Dubuque, IA

BANANA BAVARIAN CREAM

1 (6-ounce) package lemon-flavored gelatin
2 cups hot water
1/4 teaspoon salt
2/3 cup sugar
1/2 cup heavy cream
5 bananas

Dissolve gelatin in hot water. Add salt and sugar. Chill until cold and syrupy. Fold in cream, whipped only until thick and shiny, but not stiff. Crush bananas to pulp with fork, and fold at once into mixture. Chill until slightly thickened. Turn into mold. Chill until firm. Unmold. Serve with Strawberry Sauce. (Recipe below)

Strawberry Sauce:
1/3 cup butter
1 cup powdered sugar
1 egg white
2/3 cup strawberries

Cream butter and sugar, gradually add crushed strawberries and egg whites. Beat well.
Lucille Roehr, Hammond, Ind.

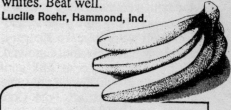

BUNNY SALAD

Serves 6-8

1 (3-ounce) package orange gelatin
1 cup boiling water
1 cup pineapple juice and water
1 teaspoon grated orange rind
1-1/3 cups crushed pineapple, drained
1 cup grated raw carrots

Dissolve gelatin in boiling water. Add pineapple juice/water mixture and orange rind. Chill until slightly thickened. Then fold in pineapple and carrots. Pour into 6-8 individual round molds. Chill until firm. Unmold on crisp lettuce. Add carrot strips to form ears, a large marshmallow for the head, and half a marshmallow for the tail. Serve plain or with mayonnaise, if desired.

Marcella Swigert, Monroe City, Mo.

BANANA YOGURT SALAD

2 large bananas
2 cups yogurt
1/4 cup nuts, chopped
Orange sections
Lettuce

Peel and split bananas; place in serving dishes. Spoon one cup of yogurt onto each banana. Sprinkle with nuts; surround with orange sections and shredded lettuce.
Suzan L. Wiener, Spring Hill, Fla.

APRICOT SALAD
Serves 10-12

2 (16-ounce) cans apricots in syrup, drained. (Reserve juice)
1 (8-ounce) package cream cheese, diced
1 (3-ounce) package lemon gelatin
1 (3-ounce) package lime gelatin
1 (12-ounce) package Cool Whip

Put both gelatins in large bowl and add 2 cups boiling apricot juice, adding enough water to make 2 cups, if not enough juice. Mix until dissolved. Add diced cream cheese. Mix until smooth. Mash apricots slightly and add to gelatin mixture. Fold Cool Whip into mixture.

Pour into 13x9-inch pan. Chill overnight. May be kept in refrigerator for 2 weeks. Spoon serve, or cut into squares. This is a delicious, refreshing, simple-to-prepare salad.
Irene Adney, Eureka Springs, Ark.

BLUEBERRY SALAD

2 (3-ounce) packages grape gelatin
2 cups boiling water
1 (No. 2) can undrained crushed pineapple
1 (16-ounce) can blueberry pie filling
1 cup sour cream
1 (8-ounce) package cream cheese
1/2 cup granulated sugar
1 teaspoon vanilla

In a 9x13-inch pan, mix the gelatin and boiling water until dissolved. Add undrained pineapple and blueberry pie filling. Stir and let set in refrigerator. Mix sour cream with the softened cream cheese, sugar, and vanilla. Do not overbeat. Spread on top of the set gelatin mixture. Chill again in refrigerator. This is a great potluck dish. It can be served as salad or dessert.
Edna Mae Seelos, Niles, Ill.

TASTY APPLE SALAD

1 (20-ounce) can pineapple tidbits, drain and save juice
2 cups miniature marshmallows
1/2 cup sugar
1 tablespoon flour
1 egg, beaten
1-1/2 tablespoons vinegar
1 (8-ounce) container Cool Whip
2 cups chopped apples with skins (Red Delicious)
1-1/2 cups dry roasted peanuts, chopped

Mix pineapple juice, sugar, flour, egg, and vinegar in pan. Cook until thick. Refrigerate overnight. Next day, or 8 hours, mix together apples, nuts, Cool Whip, pineapple, marshmallows and pineapple juice; mix and refrigerate until ready to serve.
Barbara L. Henwood, Glenview, IL

SPICY PEACH SALAD

6 large canned peach halves
1/2 stick whole cinnamon
1 teaspoon whole cloves
1/2 cup white vinegar
1/2 cup sugar

1 (3-ounce) package cream cheese
1/4 cup fresh lime juice
1/4 cup pecans, chopped

Place cinnamon stick and cloves in a small cheesecloth bag; tie firmly; cook with sugar and vinegar for 3 minutes. Remove spice bag; pour over peaches; chill. Fill center of each peach with cream cheese seasoned with lime juice and chopped pecans. To serve: Arrange each peach half on a chilled, crisp lettuce leaf.
Gwen Campbell, Sterling, Va.

PEACH PARTY SALAD
Serves 12

1 (6-ounce) package orange flavored gelatin
2 cups boiling water
1 (15-1/4 ounce) can crushed pineapple, undrained
2 cups canned or fresh sliced peaches, drained
1 egg, beaten
1/4 cup sugar
1-1/2 tablespoons all-purpose flour
1-1/2 tablespoons butter or margarine, softened
1/2 cup whipping cream, whipped
1/2 cup miniature marshmallows
1/2 cup (2 ounces) shredded Cheddar cheese

Dissolve gelatin in boiling water; set aside. Drain pineapple, reserving juice; set pineapple aside. Add enough water to juice to make 1 cup. Add 3/4 cup of juice mixture to gelatin mixture; chill until consistency of unbeaten egg white. Set remaining 1/4 cup of juice mixture aside. Arrange peach slices in a lightly-oiled 12 x 8 x 2 inch dish. Pour gelatin mixture over peaches. Chill until almost firm. Combine egg, sugar, flour, butter, and remaining 1/4 cup juice mixture in a small saucepan. Cook over low heat, stirring constantly until smooth and thickened; cool. Combine pineapple, whipped cream, marshmallows, and cheese; fold in egg mixture. Spread evenly over salad. Cover; chill overnight.
Peggy Fowler Revels, Woodruff, SC

CHERRY FROZEN SALAD

Makes 32-34 small cups

1 (16-ounce) can cherry pie filling
1 large can crushed pineapple, drained
1 can sweetened condensed milk
1 large carton Cool Whip
2 cups miniature marshmallows
1 cup chopped pecans

Mix all together in order given. Spoon into paper cups. Freeze.

This is delicious and can also be used as a dessert.

Mrs. Bruce Fowler, Woodruff, SC

SPRINGTIME SALAD

Serves 6

1 (1-pound) can grapefruit sections
4 green onions, thinly sliced
1/2 cup sliced radishes
1/2 cup cucumber, sliced or greens of your choice

Drain grapefruit. Wash and dry greens (of your choice) and tear into bite-size pieces. Add grapefruit sections, onions, radishes, and cucumber. Toss and serve with a Roquefort dressing, before serving.

Agnes Ward, Erie, Pa.

MOUNTAIN DEW SALAD

1 large package lemon gelatin
1-2/3 cups boiling water
1 cup small marshmallows
1 cup Mountain Dew soda
1 (#303 can) crushed pineapple, drain
1 can lemon pudding or pie filling
1 medium container Cool Whip

Mix gelatin in boiling water with marshmallows until dissolved. Add Mountain Dew and drained pineapple. Chill until set. Mix pudding and Cool Whip. Spread on top of gelatin which has set.

Cheryl Wellman, Quincy, IL

SILHOUETTE SALAD

Serves 4

1 envelope Knox unflavored gelatin
1 cup water, divided
1 (10-1/2 ounce) can condensed cream of chicken soup
1 tablespoon lemon juice
1/8 teaspoon pepper
1 (5-ounce) can boned chicken, diced
1/2 cup diced celery
1/4 cup chopped green pepper
2 tablespoons chopped pimiento
2 teaspoons grated onion

Sprinkle gelatin on 1/2 cup water to soften. Place over low heat and stir until gelatin is dissolved. Remove from heat; stir in soup until well-blended. Add other 1/2 cup water, lemon juice, and pepper. Chill until the consistency of unbeaten egg white. Fold in chicken, onion, green pepper, and pimiento. Turn into a 3-cup mold and chill until firm.

Joy Shamway, Freeport, IL

MOUNTAIN DEW SALAD

1 (6-ounce) package lemon gelatin
1 cup boiling water
1 can cold Mountain Dew beverage
1 (15-ounce) can pineapple chunks or tidbits, drained and juice reserved
1 package lemon pudding (cooked type)
1 cup whipping cream (whipped) or Cool Whip
1 cup colored mini marshmallows

Dissolve gelatin in boiling water; add Mountain Dew and juice drained from pineapple; chill until it begins to thicken. Cook pudding according to package instructions; cool.

Mix gelatin, lemon pudding, and whipped cream, beating together. Add drained pineapple and marshmallows. Pour into a large bowl and chill.

Betty Brennan, Faribault, Minn.

COTTAGE CHEESE DELIGHT

1 quart cottage cheese
1 can crushed pineapple, drained
1 (6-ounce) box orange gelatin
1 small package miniature marshmallows
1 large container Cool Whip

Mix cottage cheese, pineapple, and gelatin powder together. Blend in marshmallows and Cool Whip; chill before serving.

Vivian I. Parks, Mohave Valley, Ariz.

SHAMROCK SALAD

First Layer:
1 (3-ounce) package lime gelatin
1 small can undrained crushed pineapple

Dissolve gelatin in one cup hot water, then cool. Add pineapple. Pour mixture into large mold and chill until set.

Second Layer:
1 (3-ounce) package lemon gelatin
2 (3-ounce) packages cream cheese
10 marshmallows
2 cups whipping cream

Dissolve lemon gelatin in one cup hot water. Mix one package cream cheese with one cup whipping cream. Pour mixture on top of set lime gelatin. Chill until set. Mix remaining cream cheese with one cup whipped cream and the marshmallows cut into small pieces. Turn out mold on lettuce green and top with this mixture. You may decide to serve this creation as a dessert.—Whip 1/2 cup cream; add drained maraschino cherries and drained pineapple slices, arranged, to form an attractive circle on top.

St. Patrick's Day is a special one, not only because it is the beginning of spring, but because of the teasing, elfish nature of this man who makes "everything come up green" on this day. Special foods are your way of contributing to a genial atmosphere for both children and adults. On this day, we are all the same age—Happy St. Patrick's Day!

SLICED CUCUMBERS IN SOUR CREAM
Serves 4

2 cups thinly sliced cucumbers
1/4 cup sliced Spanish onions
1/4 cup seasoned vinegar
1/4 cup sour cream

Pour vinegar over cucumbers and onions, let stand 15 minutes. Drain in a strainer and discard liquid. Combine sour cream with cucumbers. Serve icy cold.

Marcella Swigert, Monroe City, Mo.

CUCUMBER-YOGURT SALAD
Serves 6

5 cups thinly sliced cucumbers (2 large)
3/4 cup thinly sliced red onion (1 small)
1 (8-ounce) carton plain low-fat yogurt
3 tablespoons wine vinegar
1 tablespoon lemon juice
1 tablespoon minced fresh basil
1 clove garlic, crushed
1 teaspoon Dijon mustard
1/8 teaspoon salt
1/8 teaspoon pepper

Combine cucumber and onion in large bowl; cover and chill. Combine yogurt and remaining ingredients in a small bowl; stir to blend. Cover and chill. Pour mixture over vegetables and toss. Serve immediately. (45 calories per serving)

Edna Askins, Greenville, Texas

CELERY SLAW
Serves 6

3 cups celery, thinly sliced
1/2 cup carrots, grated
1 apple, unpeeled, cored, and diced
1/2 cup mayonnaise
2 tablespoons sugar
1/2 teaspoon salt

2 tablespoons vinegar
1/2 cup walnuts, coarsely chopped (optional)

Combine celery, carrots, and apples. Thoroughly blend remaining ingredients and fold into celery mixture. If desired, fold in walnuts or sprinkle over top as a garnish. Chill at least 30 minutes before serving in lettuce-lined bowl. Delightfully crunchy!

Eleanor V. Craycraft, Santa Monica, Calif.

SWEET-SOUR CABBAGE SLAW
Serves 6-8

3 cups finely-shredded cabbage
1 tablespoon grated onion
1/2 teaspoon celery salt
1 tablespoon sugar
1 tablespoon vinegar
1/4 teaspoon salt
1/8 teaspoon cayenne pepper
1/2 cup heavy cream, whipped or sour cream

Combine cabbage, onion, and celery salt. Blend together sugar, vinegar, salt, pepper, and cream. Pour over cabbage and toss.

Grace Lane, Redondo Beach, Calif.

YOGURT COLESLAW
Serves 10-12

1 cup unflavored yogurt
1/4 cup mayonnaise
1/2 teaspoon dry mustard
1 teaspoon seasoned salt
1/2 teaspoon salt
1/2 teaspoon celery salt
1/8 teaspoon pepper
1/4 cup chopped onion
2 tablespoons sugar
8 cups shredded cabbage
1 medium carrot, grated
1/2 cup grated green pepper

Combine yogurt, mayonnaise, dry mustard, seasoned salt, salt, celery salt, pepper, onion, and sugar in a medium bowl. Cover and chill.

Combine cabbage, carrots, and green peppers in large bowl. Pour chilled dressing over vegetables, tossing lightly. Serve immediately.

Joy Shamway, Freeport, IL

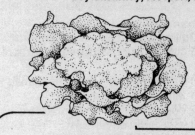

FRUITED COLE SLAW

1 medium head cabbage, shredded
1 medium carrot, grated
1/2 cup crushed pineapple, drained
1 teaspoon salt

Mix salt with cabbage and let stand about half an hour. Squeeze out excess moisture and add carrot and pineapple.

1 cup vinegar
1/2 cup water
1-1/2 cups sugar
1 teaspoon dry mustard
1 teaspoon celery seed

Combine and boil these ingredients 1 minute. Cool. Pour over cabbage, carrot and pineapple mixture; toss to blend. Serve as a chilled salad, if desired. (This slaw can be frozen.)

Trenda Leigh, Richmond, Va.

SPINACH SALAD

2 to 3 packages fresh spinach
1 pound cooked bacon, chopped
1 can water chestnuts, chopped
1 can bean sprouts
2 hard-cooked eggs, chopped

Wash spinach thoroughly and break into bite-size pieces. Add remaining ingredients.

Dressing:
1 cup salad oil (Mazola)
1/4 cup ketchup
1/2 cup vinegar
1/2 cup sugar

Stir dressing into salad and toss well.

Karin Shea Fedders, Dameron, Md.

SPINACH-ORANGE TOSS
Serves 6

1 small onion, thinly sliced
Boiling water
6 cups (8 ounces) fresh spinach, torn
1 (11-ounce) can mandarin oranges, drained
1 cup fresh mushrooms, sliced
3 tablespoons salad oil
1 tablespoon lemon juice
1/4 teaspoon salt
Dash pepper
3/4 cup almonds, slivered

Place onions in bowl and cover with boiling water; allow to stand 10 minutes; drain; and dry on paper towels. Place spinach, which has been torn into pieces, in large salad bowl. Add onions, mandarin orange slices, and mushrooms. Toss lightly with hands; cover with plastic wrap and chill thoroughly.

For dressing, place salad oil, lemon juice, salt and pepper in a screw-top jar and shake well. Chill. Before serving, shake again and pour over spinach-orange mixture. Toss lightly until ingredients are coated. Sprinkle almonds over top and serve immediately. This is a very good side dish with Chinese food.

Eleanor Craycraft, Santa Monica, Calif.

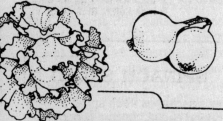

SPINACH SALAD
Serves 6

1/2 pound spinach
1/2 head iceberg lettuce
1 small red onion, thinly sliced and separated into rings
1 slivered hard-cooked egg white (yolk saved for vinaigrette)
Vinaigrette (recipe follows)

Tear spinach and lettuce into bite-size pieces and layer with onion and slivered hard-cooked egg white in a salad bowl. Add vinaigrette and toss well.

Vinaigrette:

In a small bowl mash saved hard-cooked egg yolk; add 1 teaspoon salt, 1/4 teaspoon pepper, 1/4 teaspoon paprika, 1/4 teaspoon dry mustard, 1/4 cup red wine vinegar,

1/2 cup vegetable oil, and 2 tablespoons finely chopped parsley; whisk well.

Mary F. Rutherford, Nebo, N.C.

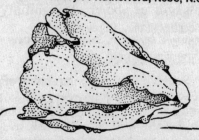

GREEN VEGETABLE SALAD

1 small can English peas, drained
1 can French style green beans, drained
1 can shoe peg corn, drained
1 cup chopped celery
1 cup chopped green pepper
1 cup chopped onion
1 small jar pimientos, chopped

Mix together 1/2 teaspoon salt, 1/2 cup vinegar, 1/2 cup salad oil and 1/3 cup sugar; stir until dissolved. Pour over vegetables; mix well and chill 4-5 hours before serving. Will keep for several days in refrigerator.

Edna Askins, Greenville, Texas

FRESH VEGETABLE SALAD

1 bunch broccoli, broken into flowerettes
1 head cauliflower, broken or sliced
1 bunch celery, sliced
1 box mushrooms, sliced
1 box cherry tomatoes, halved
1 can ripe olives, pitted and drained
1 bag radishes, sliced
3 or 4 carrots, sliced

Toss with one large bottle Italian dressing mixed with one package dry Italian dressing mix. Can prepare several hours ahead of time before serving.

GREEN VEGETABLE SALAD

1 can English peas, drained
1 can French-style green beans, drained
1 can shoe peg corn, drained
1 cup diced celery
1 cup diced green peppers
1 cup chopped green onions or regular onions
1 small can pimientos, diced

Mix together:
1/2 teaspoon salt
1/2 cup sugar
1/2 cup vinegar
1/2 cup salad oil

Stir until sugar is dissolved. Pour over vegetables. Chill overnight. Will keep for several days.

Dovie Lucy, McLoud, Okla.

MUSHROOM SALAD
Serves 4

1 tablespoon butter
1/2 pound mushrooms, cleaned and stems trimmed
3 ounces champagne
1 teaspoon clear Karo syrup
2 tablespoons catsup
2 tablespoons raisins
1 teaspoon pine nuts (pignoli)
Coarsely shredded lettuce

Soak raisins in 1 tablespoon of champagne for 5 minutes. Drain well and set aside. Melt butter in a saucepan. Add mushrooms, and gently sauté for 2 minutes over medium heat, stirring constantly. Add the Karo syrup; mix well a few seconds. To this add champagne, catsup, pignoli, and raisins. Simmer only 1 minute. Pour mixture into a bowl and chill thoroughly. When ready to serve, be sure to serve on a bed of shredded lettuce.

Marie Fusaro, Manasquan, N.J.

EASTER CROWN SALAD

3 (3-ounce) packages cream
   cheese
1/2 teaspoon salt
2 cups grated cucumber, drained
1 cup mayonnaise
1/4 cup minced onion
1/4 cup minced parsley
1 clove garlic
1 tablespoon unflavored gelatin
1/4 cup cold water
1 head lettuce
2 hard-cooked egg yolks, sieved

Mix first 6 ingredients in a bowl that has been rubbed with garlic. Soften gelatin in cold water and dissolve over hot water. Cool to lukewarm and combine with cheese mixture. Beat thoroughly and pack into a deep spring-form pan. Chill until mixture is firm. Remove from mold onto a bed of lettuce and sprinkle sieved egg yolks over top. Garnish with radish roses, if desired.

BEAN AND TOMATO SALAD

1 (15-1/2 ounce) can garbanzo beans
3 tablespoons vegetable oil
1 tablespoon wine vinegar
Salt and pepper
1 pound tomatoes, peeled and sliced
1 medium-size onion, sliced into thin
   rings
2 teaspoons fresh chopped basil or 1
   teaspoon dried basil

Drain beans; rinse under cold water. Beat oil and vinegar together; season with salt and pepper. Add the beans and mix until well coated, being careful not to break up the beans. Arrange tomato and onion slices in a shallow dish; sprinkle with basil, salt, and pepper. Spoon beans on top. Serve chilled.

Diantha Susan Hibbard, Rochester, NY

ZESTY MEXICAN BEAN SALAD

2 medium limes
1/2 of a 12-ounce jar chunky salsa
   (about 3/4 cup)
1/3 cup salad oil
1-1/2 teaspoons chili powder
1 teaspoon salt
1 (16-ounce) can black beans,
   drained
1 (15 to 19-ounce) can red kidney
   beans, drained
1 (15 to 19-ounce) can garbanzo
   beans, drained
2 celery stalks, thinly sliced
1 onion, sliced
1 medium tomato, diced

Squeeze lime juice into bowl; stir in salsa, oil, chili powder, and salt. Add beans, celery, onion and tomato. Toss to mix well. Serve at room temperature or cover and refrigerate, to serve chilled later. Many ingredients may be purchased in the Ethnic Department of your food store.
Edna Mae Seelos, Niles, Ill.

CARROT SALAD
Serves 6

1 pound carrots
1 bunch chives, chopped
1 cup mayonnaise (homemade or
   commercial variety)
2 tablespoons vinegar
Salt and pepper

Peel and finely grate carrots. Combine chives, mayonnaise, and vinegar; season with salt and pepper; blend with a whisk. Pour over carrots and let stand 15 minutes. Serve.
Marcella Swigert, Monroe City, Mo.

RAISIN-CARROT SALAD
Serves 8

1 cup seedless raisins
1-1/2 cups shredded carrots
1/2 cup celery, finely chopped
1/2 cup chopped walnuts
Pinch of salt
Dash cayenne
4 tablespoons mayonnaise

Rinse raisins in hot water; drain; cool and combine with remaining ingredients. Chill and serve on crisp lettuce.

Lucy Dowd, Sequim, Wash.

CARROT-RAISIN SALAD

1/2 cup shredded carrots
1/2 cup seedless (or seeded) raisins
4 tablespoons lemon juice
1/4 cup mayonnaise
6-12 lettuce leaves or 1-1/2 cups
   shredded cabbage

Shred carrots. Soak raisins in lemon juice. Combine ingredients; mix with dressing. Serve in lettuce cups.
Lucy Dowd, Sequim, Wash.

PICNIC SALAD BOWL
Serves 6

1 (No. 2) can asparagus tips
Mustard French Dressing (recipe follows)
3 hard-cooked eggs
1/3 cup deviled ham
Hearts of lettuce
2 strips pimiento
6 wedges Swiss cheese

Marinate asparagus in dressing; chill. Cut eggs lengthwise and remove yolks. Stuff with deviled ham and mashed egg yolks which have been moistened with dressing. Toss lettuce hearts in salad bowl with dressing. Arrange asparagus tips in center (held together with pimiento strips); surround with cheese; border with stuffed egg halves. May substitute cooked green beans for asparagus tips.

Mustard French Dressing:
1 cup olive or salad oil
1/4 cup vinegar
1/2 teaspoon salt
Few grains cayenne
1/4 teaspoon white pepper
2 tablespoons chopped parsley
2 teaspoons prepared mustard

Combine; beat or shake thoroughly before using. Makes 1-1/4 cups dressing.

Sue Hibbard, Rochester, NY

SEAFOOD SALAD

Serves 6-8

1/2 small cabbage (about 1 pound) washed and pulled apart
1 small onion, peeled and sliced
4 tablespoons sweet pickles, finely chopped
1 cup mayonnaise
3 tablespoons sugar
12 fish sticks
12 popcorn shrimp

Combine cabbage, onion, and pickles, and chop until fine, using a hand chopper. Mix mayonnaise and sugar, and add to cabbage salad. Fry fish sticks and shrimp until golden brown; drain on paper towels. Cut six fish sticks and six shrimp into chunks. Mix into cabbage salad. Place in serving bowl. Place remaining fish sticks and shrimp on top.

Merle Brown, Wilson, N.C.

SHRIMPLY GREAT MOLD

Serves 8

1-1/2 tablespoons unflavored gelatin
1/4 cup cold water
1 (10-ounce) can tomato soup
1 (8-ounce) package cream cheese, softened
20 salad shrimp, cooked, peeled and coarsely chopped
1 cup mayonnaise
1 small onion, grated
3/4 cup celery, diced finely
1 tablespoon prepared horseradish

Dissolve gelatin in cold water; set aside. In a saucepan, heat soup; add gelatin mixture; stir until dissolved. Add cream cheese; remove from heat; beat until well blended. Add remaining ingredients. Pour into a well-oiled 1-quart mold; chill until firm. Serve portion on a crisp lettuce leaf; garnish with a lemon twist.

Gwen Campbell, Sterling, Va.

SKILLET HAM SALAD

Serves 4

1/4 cup chopped green onions
1/4 cup chopped green pepper
2 cups diced cooked ham
1 tablespoon fat
3 cups potatoes, cooked and diced
1/4 teaspoon salt
Dash pepper
1/4 cup mayonnaise
1/2 pound sharp, processed American cheese, diced (1-1/2 cups)

Cook onions, green pepper, and meat in hot fat, stirring occasionally until meat is lightly browned. Add potatoes, salt, pepper, and mayonnaise. Heat, mixing lightly. Stir in cheese; heat just until it begins to melt. Garnish with green onions, if desired.

Agnes Ward, Erie, PA

SUPER SUPPER SALAD

Makes 6-1/2 cups

1 (8-ounce) package chicken-flavored rice mix
2 (5-ounce) cans Swanson Mixin' Chicken
1-1/2 cups (about 2 medium) diced tomatoes
1/2 cup chopped fresh parsley
1/2 cup chopped green onion
2 tablespoons vinegar
3/4 cup undiluted evaporated milk
1/2 cup mayonnaise
1/2 teaspoon Italian seasoning

Cook rice mix according to package directions. Cool. Mix rice with chicken, tomatoes, parsley, and onion. Stir vinegar into evaporated milk until milk thickens. Add mayonnaise and Italian seasoning. Stir into rice mixture. Chill thoroughly.

Mrs. Weldon Hill, Queen City, Texas

CRANBERRY TURKEY SALAD

Serves 4-6

1 can whole cranberry sauce
2 cups cooked diced turkey
1 cup finely diced celery
1/2 cup chopped walnuts
1/4 cup mayonnaise
2 tablespoons lemon juice
Lettuce leaves

Combine all ingredients except lettuce leaves and mix well. Arrange salad on lettuce leaf. Garnish with additional reserved walnut pieces, if desired.

Mrs. Robert T. Shaffer, Middlebury, Pa.

CHUNKY CHICKEN SALAD

1 cup raw carrot, shredded
1/2 cup Miracle Whip, thinned slightly with cream
1 cup chicken, cooked and diced
1/4 cup minced onion
1 cup diced celery
1 tablespoon pickle relish
1 small can shoestring potatoes or 2 cups sesame sticks

Combine vegetables with dressing and relish. Add chicken and potato sticks or sesame sticks just before serving.

Bulah Lashua, Muncie, IN

POPCORN SALAD

Serves 6-8

6 cups popped popcorn
1/2 cup green onion, sliced
1 cup celery, diced
3/4 - 1 cup mayonnaise
3/4 cup chopped cooked bacon (reserve some for top)
1 cup grated cheese (reserve some for top)
1/2 cup sliced water chestnuts

In bowl, combine popcorn, sliced onion, diced celery, mayonnaise, bacon, cheese, and water chestnuts. Chill. Top with reserved bacon and grated cheese. Best when used within 3-4 hours.

Pat Stump, Dunnell, MN

DILLY DELI SALAD
Serves 6

1 cup (8 ounces) Wish Bone Creamy Italian Dressing
4 cups thinly-sliced, cooked potatoes *or* 3 cans (1 pound each) sliced, potatoes, drained
Cold cuts: Use any of the following, cut into 1/2-inch cubes to equal 3/4 pound. Choose from salami, ham, turkey, corned beef, roast beef, bologna, or your favorite cold cuts.
Cheeses: Shredded to equal 1/2 pound—American, Cheddar, Swiss, Muenster, brick, or your favorite cheeses
1 medium tomato, coarsely-chopped and drained
1/2 cup chopped dill pickles

In large bowl, combine all ingredients. Pack into a spring-form pan and chill for 4 hours or overnight. Garnish, if desired with additional pickles.

Agnes Ward, Erie, PA

RICE SALAD MILANO
Serves 6

3 cups hot cooked rice
1/4 cup vegetable oil
2 tablespoons lemon juice
1 clove garlic, minced
1/2 teaspoon salt (optional)
1/2 teaspoon *each* rosemary and oregano leaves, crumbled
1/2 teaspoon ground black pepper
1 small zucchini, thinly sliced
1 medium tomato, seeded and chopped
3 tablespoons grated Parmesan cheese

Spoon rice into large mixing bowl. Blend oil, juice, garlic, and seasonings. Stir into rice. Cover; let cool. Add remaining ingredients. Serve at room temperature or chill. ❖Recipe provided by the Rice Council.

QUICK MACARONI SALAD
Serves 10

1 box macaroni and cheese dinner
1 can tuna, drained
4 eggs, hard cooked
5 tablespoons mayonnaise
1/4 cup chopped pickles

Cook macaroni and cheese dinner as directed on package. Then add and mix all additional ingredients; refrigerate.

Mildred Sherrer, Bay City, Texas

EGG-RICE SALAD
Serves 6

2 cups cold quick-cook rice, cooked
4 hard-cooked eggs, finely chopped or grated
1 cup diced celery
2/3 cup chopped sweet pickle
1 tablespoon chopped green pepper
1 tablespoon red pepper (optional); may use pimiento for color
1 cup diced or shredded Cheddar cheese
3/4 cup mayonnaise
2 tablespoons sweet pickle juice

Combine all ingredients; mix thoroughly.

Dorothy Selock, Shelbyville, Ill.

ORIENTAL SALAD

1 cup peas, drained
1 cup white corn, drained
1 cup bean sprouts
1 (8-ounce) can water chestnuts
1 large green pepper, chopped
1 cup celery, chopped
1/2 cup vinegar
1 cup sugar
1/2 cup oil
1/4 cup water

Place peas, corn, bean sprouts, water chestnuts, green pepper, and celery in bowl. Combine vinegar, sugar, oil, and water; pour over vegetables. Chill several hours or overnight.

This is a great dish with turkey or pork.

Carol Thomas, Hagerstown, Ind.

SPAGHETTI SALAD

1 pound spaghetti
2 tablespoons (McCormicks) salad seasoning
1 (12-ounce) bottle Kraft Zesty Italian Dressing
1 chopped cucumber
1 chopped onion
1 chopped green pepper
1 or 2 stalks celery
2 or 3 tomatoes, chopped, seeds removed

Cook spaghetti and rinse. Place spaghetti in a large bowl and sprinkle with salad seasoning. Pour Italian dressing over spaghetti. Add remaining ingredients; mix well. This makes a large bowl of salad. Recipe may be halved. Will keep for days in the refrigerator. This salad is delicious. Every time I serve it, I am asked for the recipe. Great for church dinners.

Mrs. H. Allen, Mt. Juliet, Tenn

INCREDIBLE MACARONI SALAD

1 (7-1/4 ounce) package macaroni and cheese dinner
1 (10-ounce) package frozen peas
1 medium tomato, chopped
3/4 cup salad dressing or mayonnaise
1/2 cup celery, sliced
1/4 cup onion, chopped
1/2 teaspoon salt
Dash pepper
6 hard-cooked eggs

Prepare macaroni and cheese as directed on package. Add peas, tomato, salad dressing, celery, onion, and seasonings. Chop 5 eggs and add to mixture. Mix lightly. Chill. Stir in additional dressing before serving, if desired. Garnish with remaining egg.

Have several packages of macaroni and cheese dinners on hand, as you will want to make this dish again. Truly different from your ordinary macaroni salad!

Mrs. George Franks, Millerton, PA

Salad
DRESSINGS

CREAMY BLUE CHEESE DRESSING
Makes 2 cups

6 ounces crumbled blue cheese
1 cup real mayonnaise
3/4 cup buttermilk
1/4 teaspoon onion powder
1/4 teaspoon garlic powder

Combine all ingredients; mix until well blended and creamy. Serve over tossed green salad.

Agnes Ward, Erie, PA

MASON JAR DRESSING

1 can condensed tomato soup
3/4 cup herb salad vinegar
1 teaspoon salt
1/2 teaspoon paprika
1/2 teaspoon pepper
1 teaspoon onion juice
1 tablespoon mustard
1-1/2 cups oil, (salad or olive)
1/2 cup sugar

Combine dry ingredients separately. Combine liquid ingredients separately. Moisten dry ingredients with a little of the liquid, then pour all together into a quart fruit jar and *shake*.

Worcestershire sauce or a little liquid from dill pickles may be added for additional zest.

Always shake well before using.

Agnes Ward, Erie, PA

GARLIC DRESSING

3 cups Miracle Whip
1-1/2 cups salad oil 1/2 cup vinegar (scant) white or wine
2-1/2 tablespoons sugar
1-1/2 teaspoons salt
1-1/2 teaspoons Accent
1 or more cloves garlic
1/3 cup onion
Parsley

Mix all together in blender. Store in covered container in refrigerator. Add blue cheese, if desired. Shake well before serving.

Rosie O'Connell, Greensburg, Pa.

THOUSAND ISLAND DRESSING

3 large dill pickles
3 medium onions
3 large green peppers, seeded
1 small can pimientos
5 hard-cooked eggs
1 quart mayonnaise
1 bottle chili sauce

Grind ingredients together and drain well. Clean grinder and grind 5 hard-cooked eggs. Combine all ingredients with 1 quart mayonnaise and one bottle chili sauce. Store in refrigerator until ready to serve.

Frances Tucker, Fulton, Mo.

RANCH SALAD DRESSING
Makes 2-1/4 cups

2 cups plain lowfat yogurt
1/4 cup mayonnaise
1/2 teaspoon garlic powder
1/4 teaspoon monosodium glutamate
1 teaspoon dried minced onion
1/4 teaspoon pepper
1/4 teaspoon paprika
1/2 teaspoon onion powder
1 teaspoon dried parsley flakes
1/4 teaspoon dried dill weed
1/2 teaspoon celery salt

Mix all ingredients together. Refrigerate for 1 hour to blend flavors. Use as dip for raw vegetables or salad dressing.

Lorean Pulley, Riesel, TX

CREAMY SALAD DRESSING
Makes 1 pint

1/4 cup sugar
3/4 teaspoon dry mustard
1/2 teaspoon salt
2 tablespoons flour
2 egg yolks or 1 whole egg
1/2 cup vinegar
1/3 cup hot water
1/2 cup cream, whipped

Mix dry ingredients in saucepan. Add beaten egg; stir to blend well. Add vinegar and hot water. Cook on low heat; stir until mixture is thickened. Remove from heat; cool. Fold in whipped cream. Store in covered jar; refrigerate.

Lucy Dowd, Sequim, Wash.

Sandwich
TASTIES

CONEY ISLAND HOT DOGS
Serves 10

1 package onion soup mix
1 cup hot water
1/2 pound ground beef
2 tablespoons shortening
1 teaspoon chili powder
3/4 cup catsup
1 pound cooked hot dogs or franks
Hot dog buns

Soak onion soup mix in hot water for about 15 minutes. Strain out onion pieces and save liquid. Brown onion pieces and ground beef in shortening in large skillet. Add seasonings, catsup, and liquid drained from onions. Simmer together about 30 minutes. Serve on hot dogs in buns.

Sharon M. Crider, Evansville, Wisc.

BAKED STUFFED POCKET

1/2 cup cottage cheese, un-creamed
1/2 small tomato, chopped
1/2 small onion, chopped
1/4 green pepper, chopped
1 teaspoon dill weed
1 ounce mozzarella cheese

Mix all ingredients well, except the mozzarella cheese and stuff into whole wheat mini-pita bread. Top cottage cheese mixture with slice of mozzarella and close pita pocket. Wrap in foil and bake at 350 degrees for 15 minutes. Make sure cheese is melted and serve immediately.

Susan L. Wiener, Spring Hill, Fla.

MUSHROOM BURGER

1 pound ground beef
1 teaspoon salt
1/3 cup chopped onion
1/2 cup chopped fresh mushrooms
Dash tabasco

Mix all ingredients thoroughly. Form into four patties and broil until desired doneness. Serve on heated hamburger buns and garnish with fresh mushroom caps and cherry tomatoes.

Susan L. Weiner, Spring Hill, Fla.

HOT TUNA BURGER BASH

2 (6-1/2-ounce) cans drained tuna (2 cups)
1/3 cup cracker crumbs (or bread crumbs)
1/4 cup minced onion
1/8 teaspoon pepper
1/3 cup milk
1 egg
2 tablespoons mayonnaise

In a mixing bowl combine tuna, cracker crumbs, onion, pepper, milk, egg, and mayonnaise. Mix until well blended. Form into 4-6 patties; chill 30 minutes. Fry and brown on both sides. Great served on hamburger buns with cole slaw, or as an entrée served with fresh mixed veggies.

Gwen Campbell, Sterling, Va.

FRANK AND BACON TWIRLS
Serves 6

8 frankfurters
8 ounces Cheddar cheese
1 tablespoon prepared mustard
2 teaspoons grated onion
1/8 teaspoon Worcestershire sauce
8 slices bacon
8 frankfurter rolls

Slice the frankfurters in half lengthwise. In a small bowl, mash the cheese with a fork, then blend in mustard, onion, and Worcestershire sauce. Spread generously between frankfurter halves. Roll one strip of bacon around each of the frankfurters. Grill over hot coals, turning often until bacon is browned to taste. Serve in toasted frankfurter rolls and wrap in aluminum foil.

Marcella Swigert, Monroe City, Mo.

ENGLISH MUFFIN SNACKWICHES

1 can chopped ripe olives
1/2 cup chopped green onions
1-1/2 cups grated cheddar cheese
1/2 cup mayonnaise
1/2 teaspoon curry powder
1/2 teaspoon chili powder
6 split English muffins

Mix all ingredients and spread on muffins. Broil until bubbly. Quarter and serve. Variations: May add shrimp, crab, or tuna to the spread.

Sue Thomas, Case Grande, Ariz.

CHOW MEIN BURGERS
Serves 8

1 pound ground beef
1/2 cup chopped onion
1 (1-pound) can chop suey vegetables, drained
3 tablespoons soy sauce
2 tablespoons cornstarch
8 hamburger buns, toasted
Chow mein noodles

Combine ground beef and onions in skillet; cook until brown. Drain off excess fat. Add vegetables. Mix 1/3 cup water, soy sauce, and cornstarch; stir into beef mixture. Cook, stirring constantly until thickened. Spoon onto bottom halves of buns. Sprinkle with chow mein noodles. Cover with bun tops.

Sharon M. Crider, Evansville, Wisc.

HAM AND CHEESE MELT-AWAYS

1 pound chipped ham
1 pound sliced Swiss cheese
1 cup soft margarine
2 tablespoons yellow mustard
1-1/2 teaspoons poppy or celery
  seeds
1 tablespoon Worcestershire sauce
12 hamburger buns

Chop or cut fine the chipped ham and cheese. Cream butter until fluffy; add mustard, seeds, and Worcestershire sauce; mix well. Add ham and cheese; mix very well. Mix all this by hand with wooden spoon or fork. Then spoon mixture onto hamburger buns. Wrap in foil. Sandwiches may be frozen, refrigerated, or baked at once in 275-degree oven for about 30 minutes.
Really a great sandwich!!
Marjorie Baxla, Greenfield, Ohio

PIZZA BURGERS

1 pound ground beef
1/2 cup chopped onion
1 (15-ounce) jar pizza sauce
1 (4-ounce) can sliced mushrooms,
  drained

1 teaspoon oregano
1-1/2 cups shredded mozzarella
  cheese
8 hamburger buns, sliced

Brown meat and onion; drain. Stir in sauce, mushrooms, and oregano. Refrigerate several hours. Heat oven to 400 degrees. Stir cheese into meat mixture and spoon onto sliced buns. Sprinkle each Pizza Burger with mozzarella cheese before placing in oven to bake. Bake at 400 degrees for 10 minutes on cookie sheet.

Sandy Marqueling, Fort Wayne, Ind

SUPER TUNA MELT

1 can chunk light tuna (packed in
  vegetable oil or water)
1/2 small onion, chopped
1 hard-cooked egg, chopped
1/2 teaspoon sweet pickle relish
1 or 2 tablespoons mayonnaise
  according to your taste
1/4 teaspoon celery seed
Dash of salt
Dash of pepper
Velveeta cheese slices
Spicy brown mustard
Hamburger buns

Combine tuna with first 7 ingredients. Mix well. Spread bottom of hamburger buns lightly with the mustard. Divide the Velveeta slices in half; place halves on top of mustard. Spread tuna mixture on top of cheese. Wrap hamburger buns with aluminum foil and bake in oven or toaster oven for approximately 10 minutes or until cheese is melted. Very tasty!

Cheryl Whitehouse, Robbinsville, N.Y.

GEMINI FRANKBURGERS
Makes 6

1 (10-3/4-ounce) can Campbell's
  tomato soup
1-1/2 pounds ground beef
1 teaspoon salt
1-1/2 teaspoons chili powder
6 frankfurter buns, split and toasted
6 frankfurters, split lengthwise
1/2 cup chopped onion
2 tablespoons butter or margarine

1 tablespoon brown sugar
1/2-1 teaspoon vinegar

Mix 1/3 cup soup, beef, salt, 1 teaspoon chili powder; spread evenly on buns (cover edges). Firmly press frankfurters into meat. Place on broiler pan. Bake 12-15 minutes at 450 degrees. Cook onion and remaining chili powder in butter; add rest of soup and ingredients; heat. Serve over burgers.

This is good and especially great for teens after a game or a special Sunday-night supper.

Mrs. Melvin Habiger, Spearville, Kan.

FILLED HAMBURGERS
Serves 4

1 pound lean, ground beef
1 egg
1/4 cup fine dry bread crumbs
1 small minced onion
Salt and pepper to taste
2 teaspoons Worcestershire sauce
1 (8-ounce) can tomato sauce
1/2 teaspoon garlic powder

In a large bowl place all ingredients in order. Mix well. Divide meat mixture into 8 equal portions; shape each portion into a patty 1/4 to 1/2-inch thick.

Stir together:
1 cup (4 ounces) shredded sharp
  Cheddar cheese
1/4 cup shredded Swiss cheese
2 tablespoons catsup
1/2 teaspoon margarine, softened
1/2 teaspoon prepared mustard
1 tablespoon finely chopped green
  onion, top included

Spread even amounts of filling over 4 of the patties to within 1/4 inch of edges. Dampen edge of each patty with a little water. Top with remaining patties and pinch edges of meat together to completely enclose the cheese mixture. Heat a large skillet and cook hamburgers by cooking over medium-high heat to desired doneness. Meanwhile, have ready 4 hamburger rolls on a bed of lettuce and set each hamburger on a roll and serve hot.

Marie Fusaro, Manasquan, NJ

Sauces &

TOPPINGS

THICK SPAGHETTI SAUCE

4 medium onions, diced
1/2 cup salad oil
4 medium garlic cloves, minced
16 pounds tomatoes, peeled and diced
1 (12-ounce) can tomato paste
1/4 cup sugar
1/4 cup chopped parsley or 2 tablespoons parsley flakes
2 tablespoons oregano leaves
2 tablespoons salt
2 tablespoons basil
3/4 teaspoon cracked pepper
2 bay leaves

In 12-quart pan, over medium heat, add all ingredients. Heat to boiling; reduce heat to medium; partially cover and cook 2 hours. *Discard bay leaves.* Makes 10 pints. One pint is enough to serve over one 8-ounce package of spaghetti. Will freeze up to 1 year.
NOTE: Green peppers, mushrooms, and meat may be added.
Betty Ireton, Kingston, OH

TOMATO MUSTARD SAUCE

Makes 1-1/2 cups

2 tablespoons butter
1/4 cup minced celery
2 tablespoons minced onion

2 tablespoons flour
2 tablespoons prepared mustard
1 teaspoon salt
1/8 teaspoon pepper
1-3/4 cups (No. 2 can) canned tomatoes, strained

Melt butter. Add celery and onion; cook until tender. Stir in flour and mix until smooth. Add mustard, salt, and pepper. Gradually, add tomatoes and cook over low heat until mixture boils and becomes thickened. Fine for hamburgers and frankfurters.
Marcella Swigert, Monroe City, Mo.

CONEY ISLAND SAUCE

1/3 pound ground beef
1 (11-1/4 ounce) can tomato paste
1 tablespoon yellow mustard
1/4 cup water

Brown beef, but do not drain. Add remaining ingredients and stir to blend. Heat well. Enough to spoon over 8 hot dogs.
Kit Rollins, Cedarburg, WI

TARTAR SAUCE

3/4 cup (stiff) mayonnaise
2 tablespoons chopped chives
2 tablespoons chow chow
1/2 tablespoon minced parsley
1/2 tablespoon lemon juice

Combine ingredients in order. Chill and serve with all types seafood or fish.
Lucy Dowd, Sequim, Wash.

CHEESE SAUCE

1/2 onion, minced
2 tablespoons oil (peanut)
1 tablespoon flour
1/4 teaspoon dry mustard
1-1/2 cups buttermilk
1 cup shredded Cheddar cheese

Sauté onion in oil for 5 minutes. Add flour and mustard; stir. Add buttermilk, stirring constantly to thicken. Set aside; add cheese. Let stand until cheese melts into sauce.
Helen Trehey, Eureka, Calif.

CHILI SAUCE

6 quarts ripe tomatoes
8 large onions, chopped
1 hot red pepper, chopped
3 sweet green peppers, chopped
1/4 cup pickling salt
1/2 cup white sugar
1 tablespoon mustard seed
1 tablespoon celery seed
1 tablespoon cinnamon
1 teaspoon allspice
1/2 teaspoon ground cloves
1 teaspoon chili powder
2-1/2 cups 4% white vinegar

Simmer all ingredients together in large enamel kettle very slowly for several hours until sauce is quite thick. This can be canned in sterile jars, but today's quicker way is to freeze it in small meal-size containers. It is excellent with baked beans.

BARBECUE SAUCE

1/3 cup vinegar
1/4 cup ketchup
2 tablespoons salad oil
2 tablespoons soy sauce
1 tablespoon Worcestershire sauce
1 teaspoon mustard
1 teaspoon salt

Mix all ingredients together and allow mixture to come to a boil. This is a basic barbecue sauce to be used with all types of meats.

Jean Hugh, Pittsburgh, Pa.

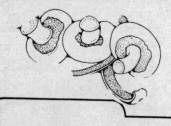

BARBECUE SAUCE

1/4 cup soy sauce
1/2 cup soybean sauce
1/2 teaspoon garlic salt
2 teaspoons sugar
1 teaspoon lemon juice
2 tablespoons cooking sherry
Dash of salt and pepper

Mix all ingredients together. Pour over 2 or 3 pieces of chicken. Refrigerate chicken in a covered dish for a few hours. Cook chicken on the barbecue grill.

M. Piccinni, Ozone Park, N.Y.

BARBECUE SAUCE

1 cup ketchup
1 chopped onion
1/2 clove garlic, finely cut
2 teaspoons chopped green chili peppers
1/2 small bay leaf
1/4 teaspoon pepper
1/3 cup lime juice
1/2 teaspoon salt
1/2 cup water
1 teaspoon dry mustard

Combine all ingredients in a 2-quart saucepan. Cover and heat to boiling; reduce heat and simmer for 40 minutes. Strain, forcing pulp through into the sauce.

MUSHROOM SAUCE

Makes 1-1/2 cups

1/2 pound fresh mushrooms, sliced
3 tablespoons melted margarine, divided
1 tablespoon all-purpose flour
3/4 cup half-and-half
1 teaspoon soy sauce

Sauté mushrooms in 2 tablespoons margarine; set aside. Combine flour and remaining margarine; place over low heat, stirring until smooth. Gradually add half-and-half; cook, stirring constantly, until smooth and thickened. Stir in soy sauce and mushrooms. Serve hot with toast or steak.

Barbara Beauregard-Smith, Northfield, S.A., Australia

MUSHROOM SAUCE

Makes 2-1/2 to 3 cups sauce

1/2 pound mushrooms, washed and thinly sliced
1 teaspoon chopped onion
1/2 teaspoon chopped parsley
6 tablespoons butter
4-5 tablespoons flour
1 cup stock or bouillon
1/4 cup sour cream
Salt to taste
1/2 teaspoon lemon juice
Butter for sautéing

Melt butter (about 2 tablespoons) and sauté onion and parsley. Add mushrooms and allow to cook for about 5 minutes. In another pan melt remaining butter; blend in flour, mixing well. Gradually add the stock and mix thoroughly. Blend in sour cream; then add salt. Pour sour cream-stock mixture into pan with mushrooms, stirring constantly, and allow to simmer gently for 15 minutes. Remove from heat and add lemon juice.

Agnes Ward, Erie, Pa.

LOW-CALORIE HOLLANDAISE SAUCE

Makes 1-1/2 cups

1 cup skim milk
2 tablespoons lemon juice
Dash red pepper
3 drops imitation butter flavoring
4 egg yolks
1/4 teaspoon salt
1-1/2 teaspoons cornstarch

Heat milk in saucepan until bubbles form around edge. Combine egg yolks, salt, red pepper, lemon juice, flavoring, and cornstarch in electric blender; cover and swirl until smooth. Slowly, add hot milk to mixture with blender on medium speed. Pour mixture into the saucepan in which milk was heated. Heat over medium heat until it reaches boiling, stirring often. Serve over Eggs Benedict or hot cooked vegetables of your choice. (45 calories per tablespoon)

Ruby Pate Bodkin, Jacksonville, Fla.

HERB AND HONEY SAUCE FOR CHICKEN

3/4 cup onion, finely chopped
1 clove garlic, minced
1/4 cup salad oil (or olive oil)
1/2 cup wine vinegar
2 tablespoons Worcestershire sauce
1 teaspoon dry mustard
1 teaspoon salt
1/4 teaspoon rosemary
1 (12-ounce) can pear nectar
1/4 cup honey
1 teaspoon prepared horseradish
1/2 teaspoon thyme
1/4 teaspoon pepper

Cook onions and garlic in hot oil until tender, but not brown. Add all remaining ingredients. Simmer uncovered for 5 minutes. Let cool, then pour over chicken and let it marinate for 3 hours minimum. When broiling chicken, use as a basting sauce. Heat leftover sauce and serve separately with chicken.

Sue Thomas, Casa Grande, Ariz.

CRAN-RASPBERRY CHOCOLATE SAUCE

7 ounces semi sweet chocolate
1 cup whipping cream
1/4 cup cran-raspberry juice concentrate, thawed, undiluted

In double boiler over medium heat, combine chocolate, whipping cream, and cran-raspberry juice concentrate until well blended and heated through. Serve hot or warm.

INSTANT HOT FUDGE SAUCE
Makes 1-1/2 cups

2 (4-ounce) bars semi sweet chocolate
3 tablespoons cream
1 to 4 tablespoons water

Melt chocolate bars over boiling water. Stir in cream, a tablespoon at a time. Stir until smooth and glossy. Remove from heat. Thin to desired consistency with 1 to 4 tablespoons water.

LEMON SAUCE
Makes 3/4 cup

Grated peel and juice of 1/2 lemon
   (about 1-1/2 tablespoons juice)
1 tablespoon butter
1/4 cup sugar
1 tablespoon flour
1/2 cup boiling water

Grate peel and squeeze lemon; set aside. In a small saucepan melt butter over low heat. In a custard cup thoroughly combine sugar and flour; add to melted butter. Over low heat whisk in water until smooth; stir in lemon juice and peel. Stir over low heat until boiling; set aside to cool. Serve slightly warm. Keeps several days in refrigerator.

Dorothy E. Cornell, Elkton, Md.

PINE-COT SAUCE
Makes 2 cups

1 cup dried apricots
3/4 cup water
1/2 cup sugar
1 (8-1/2-ounce) can crushed pineapple, undrained

Place apricots and water in heavy saucepan and cook, covered, over very low heat until fruit is pulpy and falls apart when stirred. Add sugar and stir until dissolved. Add crushed pineapple with juice and bring mixture to a boil. Remove from heat. Chill. Stores well in refrigerator.

PEACH PRESERVES
Makes 6-1/2 pints

3-1/2 cups sugar
2 cups water
5 cups sliced, peeled, hard-ripe peaches
1/2 teaspoon ginger

Combine sugar and water; cook until sugar dissolves. Add peaches and cook rapidly until fruit becomes clear. Stir occasionally. Cover and let stand 12-18 hours in a cool place. Drain fruit and pack into hot jars, leaving 1/4-inch head space. Adjust caps. Process half-pints or pints, 20 minutes at 180-185 degree hot water bath.

Joy Shamway, Freeport, IL

PEAR CONSERVE

8 cups pears, sliced thin
6 cups sugar
1 small can crushed pineapple
1-1/2 cups chopped nuts
1/2 cup cherries (canned or bottled)

Peel pears and slice thin, measuring after preparation. Combine with sugar and let stand overnight. Add pineapple and simmer until pears are soft. If syrup is not as heavy as desired, remove fruit; boil down to desired consistency or add a little pectin, perhaps a teaspoon if preferred, to thicken quickly.

Add cherries and nuts to mixture. Bring to a rolling boil and put into sterilized canning jars. Seal with rings and lids that have been sterilized.

Good on breads, muffins, poultry, and meats.

Deborah Hooker, San Bernardino, CA

BLUEBERRY-PEACH CONSERVE

1 medium-size navel orange
1 lemon
2-1/2 pounds firm ripe peaches, peeled and sliced
1 pint fresh blueberries
1/3 cup granulated sugar
1/2 cup grape juice
1 tablespoon plus 1 teaspoon Sweet 'N Low® granulated sugar substitute

Peel orange and lemon; finely chop rind. Remove pits from pulp and chop pulp. Place fruit, their juices and rind in large pot. Add peaches and blueberries; sprinkle with sugar and let stand 30 minutes. Add grape juice and Sweet 'N Low. Over medium heat, bring to a boil; boil, stirring frequently, 35 to 45 minutes or until fruit is thick and translucent.

Spoon into hot sterilized jars, allowing 1/4 inch headspace (or follow jar manufacturer's instructions if different). Wipe rims with clean cloth dipped in hot water. Close according to jar manufacturer's instructions and process in boiling-water bath 15 minutes. Makes four 8-ounce jars.

Calories: 15 per tablespoon

CHIMICHURRI (ARGENTINE PARSLEY SAUCE)
Makes 1 cup

1/4 cup red wine vinegar
1/3 cup olive oil
1/2 cup minced onion
1/4 cup minced parsley
1 large clove garlic, minced
1 teaspoon oregano
1 teaspoon pepper
Cayenne to taste
Salt to taste

Combine all ingredients in a bowl. Let stand at room temperature, cover, for 2 hours. Serve sauce over broiled meats, steaks, sausages, etc. This is very delicious!
Agnes Ward, Erie, Pa.

CELERY GARLIC SAUCE FOR BROILED FISH

1 cup butter or margarine
1/3 cup finely chopped celery
2 tablespoons finely chopped onion
2 cloves garlic, crushed
3 tablespoons finely chopped parsley
Salt and Pepper

Melt butter in saucepan. Sauté celery, onion, and garlic until tender and onion is transparent. Add remaining ingredients; simmer 10-15 minutes. Brush fish with half of sauce. Broil. Turn fish. Brush with other half of sauce. Fish is done when it flakes easily with a fork.
Kit Rollins, Cedarburg, Wis.

STRAWBERRY-RASPBERRY SAUCE
Makes 2 cups

2 cups fresh strawberries, hulled
1 (10-ounce) package frozen raspberries, thawed and drained

Combine strawberries and raspberries and purée.

BUTTERSCOTCH MARSHMALLOW SAUCE
Makes 2 cups

1 cup firmly packed light brown sugar
2 tablespoons light corn syrup
2 tablespoons unsalted butter
1/2 cup heavy cream
1/4 teaspoon salt
1 teaspoon vanilla
1 cup miniature marshmallows

In heavy saucepan combine brown sugar, corn syrup, butter, cream and salt. Bring mixture to a boil, stirring until sugar is dissolved and boil, undisturbed, until it registers 235 degrees on a candy thermometer. Stir in vanilla and let mixture cool for 10 minutes. Stir in the marshmallows and serve sauce warm over vanilla or chocolate ice cream. Sauce keeps, covered, in refrigerator up to 1 week. Reheat sauce before serving.

CHERRY SAUCE

1-1/2 pounds fresh sweet cherries, stems and pits removed
1/2 cup white grape juice
1 tablespoon lemon juice
1 whole cinnamon stick
1 teaspoon Sweet 'N Low granulated sugar substitute

In medium-size saucepan over medium heat, combine all ingredients; cook, stirring frequently, 35 to 40 minutes or until slightly thickened. Cool and pack in freezer containers or sterilized jelly jars. Seal and cool completely; freeze. Makes two 8-ounce freezer containers or jars.

Serve over ice milk, fresh fruit, angel food cake or sponge cake.
Calories: 75 per 1/4 cup.

PRALINE SAUCE

1 cup firmly packed dark brown sugar
1/2 cup chopped pecans
3 tablespoons boiling water
2 teaspoons butter
Ice cream (flavor of your choice)

Combine sugar, nuts, boiling water, and butter in small saucepan and bring to a rolling boil. Remove from heat and cool. Cover and refrigerate.

CHOCOLATE PEANUT BUTTER SAUCE
Makes 3/4 cup

1/2 cup water
1/3 cup sugar
1 (1-ounce) square unsweetened chocolate
1 tablespoon light corn syrup
1/8 teaspoon salt
1/4 cup smooth or chunky peanut butter
1/4 teaspoon vanilla
Vanilla ice cream

Combine water, sugar, chocolate, corn syrup, and salt in medium saucepan. Bring to a boil over medium heat, stirring constantly until sugar dissolves and chocolate melts. Reduce heat to low and simmer 3 minutes. Remove from heat and whisk in peanut butter and vanilla. Serve warm over vanilla ice cream.

BLENDER CARAMEL SAUCE
Makes 1-1/4 cups

3/4 cup brown sugar
2 tablespoons soft butter or margarine
1/4 teaspoon salt
1/2 cup hot evaporated milk

Put all ingredients into blender container. Cover and process at *mix* until sugar is dissolved.

PANCAKE SYRUP

2 cups sugar
3-1/3 cups Grandma's molasses
3 cups water
2 tablespoons cornstarch

Combine all ingredients together in saucepan. Bring to a boil and cook for about 2 minutes, or until slightly thickened. Inexpensive to make; ready-made syrup costs much more!!

Bernice Magnant, New Bedford, MA

MANGO-PEACH CHUTNEY

1-1/2 cups cider vinegar (5% acetic acid)
1/2 cup water
1/2 cup brown sugar, packed to measure
3 tablespoons Sweet 'N Low granulated sugar substitute, or to taste
2-1/2 pounds peaches, peeled, pitted and diced (about 5 cups)
3 mangoes (about 2-1/2 pounds), peeled and cubed (about 3-1/2 cups)
1/2 cup golden raisins
1 tablespoon lime juice
1-1/2 teaspoons ground cinnamon
1-1/2 teaspoons grated lime rind
1-1/2 teaspoons dry mustard powder
1 teaspoon salt
1/2 teaspoon ground ginger
1/4 teaspoon garlic powder

In large heavy saucepan over high heat, bring vinegar, water, brown sugar and Sweet 'N Low to a boil. Reduce heat to low; add remaining ingredients and cook, stirring, 1 to 1-1/4 hours or until mixture is thick and has texture of preserves. Taste for sweetness; add more Sweet 'N Low, if desired.

Spoon into hot sterilized jars, allowing 1/4 inch headspace (or follow jar manufacturer's instructions if different). Wipe rims with clean cloth dipped in hot water. Close according to jar manufacturer's instructions and process in boiling-water bath 20 minutes. Make 3 pints or 6 half pints.

Calories: 20 per tablespoon

SPICED PLUM SPREAD

3-1/2 pounds ripe red plums, pitted and quartered
1/2 cup unsweetened apple juice
1/4 cup honey
2 tablespoons plus 2 teaspoons Sweet 'N Low granulated sugar substitute
1 teaspoon bottled lemon juice
2 whole cinnamon sticks
8 whole cloves

In medium-size saucepan over medium heat, combine all ingredients. Cook, stirring frequently, 40 to 45 minutes or until thickened. Remove cinnamon sticks and cloves. Spoon into hot sterilized jars, allowing 1/4 inch headspace (or follow jar manufacturer's instructions if different). Wipe rims with clean cloth dipped in hot water. Close according to jar manufacturer's instructions and process in boiling-water bath 15 minutes. Makes three 8-ounce jars.

Calories: 30 per tablespoon

CHEESY CORN SPREAD
Makes 3-1/2 cups)

1 (12-ounce) package (3 cups) shredded sharp Cheddar cheese
1/2 cup dairy sour cream
1/2 cup mayonnaise or salad dressing
1/4 cup finely chopped onion
1/2 teaspoon salt
1 (12-ounce) can "Green Giant Mexicorn," drained (golden sweet corn with sweet peppers)

Bring cheese to room temperature. In large bowl, crumble cheese with fork or blend with mixer to form small bits. Mix in remaining ingredients, except corn, until well blended. Stir in corn. Cover; chill several hours or overnight. Can be stored in refrigerator up to 1 week. Serve with raw vegetables or crackers.

Agnes Ward, Erie, Pa.

CHEESE & HERB BUTTER

1/4 cup butter
1/4 teaspoon basil
1/4 teaspoon oregano
1/4 teaspoon marjoram
1/4 teaspoon thyme
Dash of Worcestershire sauce
Dash of Tabasco sauce
1 tablespoon grated Parmesan cheese

Melt butter; remove from heat and stir in remaining ingredients. Serve sauce with meat and vegetables, fish, or bread.

Stella Trulove, Somerville, Texas

ONION AND HERB BUTTER

1/4 cup butter
1 teaspoon onion powder
1 teaspoon basil
1 teaspoon chervil
1/2 teaspoon oregano

Melt butter; add onion powder. Remove from heat and stir in remaining herbs.

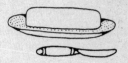

TARRAGON VINEGAR

2 cups white, cider or wine vinegar
1 teaspoon crushed dried tarragon

Bring vinegar to a boil. Add tarragon. Pour into heat-safe container, close tightly. No need to refrigerate. Let stand a few days and strain before using.

Agnes Buxton, Oklahoma City, Okla.

SWEET MUSTARD

1/4 cup mustard seed
6 tablespoons dry mustard
1 tablespoon turmeric
1-1/4 cups boiling water
1/2 cup dry white wine
1/4 cup vinegar
1 tablespoon peanut oil
1/4 cup sugar
1/2 cup finely chopped onion
2 teaspoons finely minced garlic
1/4 teaspoon allspice
1/4 teaspoon cinnamon
1/4 teaspoon ground cloves
3 tablespoons cornstarch

Combine mustard seeds, mustard, turmeric, and water in a small bowl. Let stand one hour. Meanwhile, combine vinegar, wine, oil, sugar, onion, garlic, allspice, cinnamon, and cloves in a saucepan. Bring to a boil and simmer five minutes. Pour mixture into a blender with cornstarch and blend for two minutes. Spoon and scrape the mixture back into a double boiler and cook for five minutes or until thick, stirring constantly.

HOT HONEY MUSTARD

3/4 cup cider vinegar
3/4 cup dry mustard
1/2 cup honey
2 eggs

Combine mustard and vinegar in small bowl. Blend well; cover and let stand overnight. Next day combine the mustard mixture, honey, and eggs in a small saucepan. Cook over low heat, stirring constantly, until thickened, about seven minutes. Cool. Refrigerate, covered, up to several weeks. This is great brushed on ham steak, just before broiling, or spoon thickly over brie that has had the rind removed. Sprinkle with almonds and heat at 400 degrees until the cheese is soft. Serve with French bread.

ALL-PURPOSE HERB BLEND
Makes 1/4 cup

1 tablespoon onion powder
1 teaspoon black pepper
1 tablespoon dried oregano
1 tablespoon parsley flakes
1-1/2 teaspoons tarragon
1-1/2 teaspoons basil

Blend all ingredients well. Store in tightly covered jar. Serve with poultry, meats, roasts, salads and vegetables.

SENSATIONAL SEASONING

1 (26-ounce) box of salt
1-1/2 ounce ground black pepper
2 ounces pure garlic powder
1 ounce chili powder
1 ounce MSG (or Accent)
2 ounces ground red pepper

Combine above ingredients and mix well. Store in airtight container. Use the seasoning as you would salt. Great on eggs, hamburger, and vegetables.

Sharon McClatchey, Muskogee, Okla

MUSHROOM GRAVY
(Low fat and low salt)

3 tablespoons arrowroot (thickener)
1 large chopped onion
1 pound sliced mushrooms
4 cups water
1 package no-oil salad dressing mix (preferably one with garlic and cheese)
2 tablespoons low-sodium soy sauce

Make a paste by stirring some of the cold water into the thickener until a creamy consistency is reached. Sauté onion in water in a non-stick pan and add the mushrooms. Stir until browned or beginning to cook. Cover with remaining water; add the salad dressing mix and soy sauce. When very hot, stir in the thickener. Continue to stir until smooth. Allow to

boil lightly. Remove from heat and cover.

Susan L. Wiener, Spring Hill, FL

CALICO RELISH
Makes 2-1/2 quarts

2 cups sliced cauliflower flowerets
2 carrots, cut into julienne strips
1 green pepper, cut into strips
10-12 green beans
1 zucchini, sliced
1 small jar stuffed olives
3/4 cup wine vinegar
1/4 cup olive oil
1 tablespoon sugar
1 teaspoon salt
1/2 teaspoon oregano
1/4 teaspoon pepper
1/4 cup water
Cherry tomatoes (optional)

In large pan, combine all ingredients except tomatoes. Bring to a boil and simmer covered, 5 minutes. Cool and let marinate at least 24 hours. Store in refrigerator. Cherry tomatoes may be added just before serving.

Marcella Swigert, Monroe City, MO

UNCOOKED RELISH

1 pint sweet red peppers, chopped
1 pint sweet green peppers, chopped
1 quart cabbage, chopped
1 pint white onions, chopped
2 teaspoons celery seed
4 cups sugar
1 quart cider vinegar
1 or 2 hot peppers (optional)
5 tablespoons salt

Put each vegetable through food chopper, using coarse blade. If vegetables are covered with liquid, drain off and discard liquid. Measure each vegetable after chopping. Mix vegetables with salt and let stand overnight. Next morning, drain off and discard all liquid. Add spices, sugar, and vinegar to drained vegetables and mix well. Pack into sterilized jars and seal at once. This relish is very good on hot dogs or hamburgers.

Helen Taugher, Nicholson, PA

Soups &
STEWS

GREEN PEPPER STEW
serves 4

1 onion, chopped
4 tablespoons shortening
2 cups water
2 green peppers, chopped
2 tomatoes, chopped
1 teaspoon salt
1/2 teaspoon black pepper
4 medium- sized potatoes,diced
2 tablespoons flour

Brown onion in shortening. Add water, peppers, tomatoes, salt and pepper. Cook for 20 minutes. Add potatoes and cook until potatoes are soft but not mushy. Mix flour with small amount of water. Add just enough to vegetables to thicken.

Elizabeth S. Lawson, Delbartow, W.V.

DELICIOUS TOMATO SOUP
Makes 9 cups

2 teaspoons olive oil
2 cloves garlic, crushed
2 teaspoons chopped fresh ginger
6 cups chicken broth
1 (28-ounce) can whole tomatoes, chopped
4 green onions, including 1 inch of tops, chopped

In a 2-1/2-quart saucepan, heat oil, then sauté garlic and ginger until lightly browned. Add broth and tomatoes with their juice. Simmer for 20 minutes. Serve and sprinkle with green onions.

Betsy P. Race, Euclid, Ohio

VEGETABLE BEEF SOUP
Serves 6

1 pound ground beef
1-1/2 cups cold water
1 medium onion, chopped
3 medium carrots, diced
3 medium potatoes, cubed
2 cups tomatoes or tomato juice
1/3 cup uncooked noodles
Salt and pepper to taste

Simmer beef and water 15 minutes. Add remaining ingredients. Simmer until vegetables are tender.

Mrs. Bruce Fowler, Woodruff, S.C.

MEXICAN ABONDIGAS SOUP
Serves 8

5 cups water
1 onion, chopped
1 (7-ounce) can chili salsa
1 can stewed tomatoes
1 teaspoon coriander
1 pound lean ground beef
1/2 teaspoon garlic powder
1/4 teaspoon oregano
Salt and pepper to taste

Cook onion in salted water for 10 minutes. Add 2/3 can chili salsa. Add tomatoes and coriander; simmer for 30 minutes. Mix remaining ingredients into ground beef and form into small balls. Add meatballs to broth and bring to boil. Simmer 30 minutes.

When the Irish fled their country and its famines, we were glad they brought this taste to our shores.

QUICKIE CORN CHOWDER

1/4 cup butter
1 large onion, diced
1 large can cream-style corn
2 (7-ounce) cans tuna fish
3 cups milk
1 teaspoon seasoned salt
1/2 teaspoon salt
1/4 teaspoon pepper

Melt butter; sauté onions until lightly browned. Add remaining ingredients. Heat and serve.

Serve this with crusty rolls and a salad for a quick, nutritious meal.

Rosie O'Connell, Greensburg, PA

BEEF CHOWDER
Serves 8-10

1-1/2 pounds ground beef
1/2 cup chopped celery
1/2 cup chopped onions
1/3 cup chopped green pepper
2 (10-1/2 ounce) cans condensed cream of celery soup
2 (16-ounce) cans tomatoes, cut up
1 (17-ounce) can whole kernel corn
1/4 cup snipped parsley

Cook beef, celery, onions, and green pepper until meat is browned; drain. Add remaining ingredients and 1/2 teaspoon salt. Simmer, covered, for 20 minutes. Stir often. Add salt to taste.

Leean Franson, West Caldwell, N.J.

GRANDMA'S VEGETABLE SOUP

4 pounds boneless stew meat, cubed
1 soup bone
3-1/3 cups tomatoes, chopped
3 onions, sliced
4 stalks celery, diced
1 bay leaf
Salt and pepper to taste
3 turnips, diced
3 potatoes, diced
1 small head cabbage, shredded
1/2 cup diced carrots
1 cup green peas (frozen)

Place beef, soup bone, tomatoes, onions, celery, bay leaf, and seasonings in large, heavy kettle. Cover with water and simmer for 2 hours; add water, if needed. Add diced turnips, potatoes, cabbage, and carrots; let simmer for another hour. Add green peas and cook until done. Taste; adjust seasonings. Serve with warm French bread.

Nothing tastes better than a bowl of homemade soup on a blustery winter day. At the first hint of cool weather, there is something in the air that seems to make us think about putting on a pot of soup. Bubbling soup on the stove is a good way to begin the season. These cooler days offer us the opportunity to enjoy the outdoors, hiking in the fall, skiing after the snow piles up, or eagle watching along a lake or stream. If you are looking for a main course that is both nutritious and simple to make on these active days, these soups, simmering without much attention and a meal in themselves, will surely fill the bill.

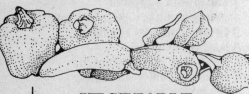

VEGETABLE LOVER'S CHILI

Serves 4

1 tablespoon vegetable oil
1 medium onion, chopped
1 rib celery, chopped
1 carrot, sliced finely
1 clove garlic, minced
2 tablespoons chili powder
1/2 teaspoon ground cumin
1/4 teaspoon oregano
1/4 teaspoon salt
1/2 teaspoon hot sauce
1 cup water
1 cup lentils, rinsed and sorted
1 (16-ounce) can crushed tomatoes
1 (10-ounce) can white kidney beans (cannellini)

Garnish:

1 tomato, chopped
1 green onion, chopped

In 2-quart saucepan, heat oil. Add onion, celery, carrot, and garlic; cook until tender, about 10 minutes. In a bowl, combine chili, cumin, oregano, salt, and hot sauce. Stir into mixture in saucepan, add water, cover, and bring to a boil. Stir in lentils; bring to a boil. Cover; simmer 15 minutes. Stir in crushed tomatoes and white kidney beans. Cover; simmer 10 minutes. Serve chili topped with the chopped tomato and green onion.

Gwen Campbell, Sterling, VA

HURRY UP VEGETABLE SOUP

Serves 6

2/3 cup celery
1/2 cup onion, chopped
1 clove garlic, minced
3-1/2 cups water
1 cup frozen carrots
1 cup frozen okra, chopped
1 cup frozed cauliflower
1 cup frozen broccoli
1 cup canned tomatoes, chopped
2 cups tomato juice or V-8 juice
1 cup tomato sauce
1/2 teaspoon seasoned salt
Black pepper, to taste
1-1/2 teasopoons Worcestershire sauce
4 beef-flavored bouillon cubes

In large pot, cook celery, onion, and garlic in water until tender. Add okra, cauliflower, broccoli, carrots; bring to a boil, and cook 7 minutes. Add remaining ingredients. Simmer 15 minutes.

ZUCCHINI SOUP
Makes 4 quarts

1 pound sweet Italian sausage
2 cups chopped celery
4 cups chopped or thinly sliced zucchini
1 cup chopped onion
2 quarts canned tomatoes (may use juice of fresh tomatoes)
3 teaspoons salt
1 teaspoon Italian seasoning
1 teaspoon oregano
1 tablespoon sugar
1/2 teaspoon basil
1 clove garlic
2 chopped green peppers

Slice and brown sausage in large pot. Drain off fat. Add rest of ingredients and cook 30 minutes. May have to add some water. Freeze leftovers.

Marjorie W. Baxla, Greenfield, Ohio

PEA SOUP

2 cups dried green split peas
1 ham bone with meat left on
1 large onion, diced
3 stalks celery with leaves, chopped
Bay leaf
1 cup sliced carrots
1 cup cream

Soak split peas in 3 quarts cold water overnight. When ready to cook, add remaining ingredients; heat to boiling. Cover and simmer for approximately 4 hours, or until peas are tender. Season to taste with salt and pepper (always remove bay leaf).

Before serving, add 1 cup cream; stir in well, and heat thoroughly. Serve with hot bread and a fresh fruit for dessert.

These colder days also bring more colds and flu symptoms. If you really want a soup that cures illness, how about chicken? Scientific evidence has recently proved that chicken soup has some therapeutic value for the sniffles and sneezes. It helps cure upper respiratory infections and also adds potassium, which is lost through fevers of a cold or flu.

QUICK POTATO SOUP

1 medium potato, peeled and cubed
1 medium onion, peeled and chopped
2 cups milk
1 teaspoon chicken flavor bouillon granules, or one cube
1 tablespoon sugar
1 cup dried potato flakes
Pinch white pepper
2 slices bacon, diced
1/4 cup smoked ham or diced, boiled ham
2 quarts of water (more or less)

In saucepan, fry bacon until partially cooked, *not* crisp. Drain off most fat; add chopped onions. Cook until transparent. Add water, ham, chicken flavor bouillon, to hot bacon. Simmer until all is tender, about 15 minutes. Add sugar, pepper, and half of dried potato flakes, stirring well until all is mixed. Simmer an additional 10 minutes. Add rest of potato flakes, stirring well, then all milk. Simmer another short time until soup is well thickened. Add diced potato; cook until soft.

Note: If a thinner soup is wanted, add additional milk. Skim milk powder, or canned milk works well, as long as it is added slowly and never boiled, only simmered.

If a brighter soup is wanted, add cubed red pepper, or a few canned or frozen sweet peas at the same time as the potato flakes. When checking for taste, a bit of salt can be added, but as the ham, bacon, and chicken bouillon are cooked, salt may not be needed.

George B. McCroskey, Oregon, OH

POTATO SOUP
Serves 4-6

2 (10-1/2 ounce) cans of chicken consommé
1 soup can water
2 cups diced potatoes
2 scallions, chopped
1 soup can milk
1 teaspoon Worcestershire sauce
1/2 cup sour cream

Combine consommé, water, potatoes, and scallions in a large saucepan; bring to a boil. Reduce heat; simmer until potatoes are tender, about 12 minutes. Blend smooth in a blender; return to saucepan. Stir in milk and Worcestershire sauce; heat. Stir in sour cream. Can be eaten hot or well chilled.

Joy Shamway, Freeport, Ill.

IRISH CREAM OF POTATO SOUP
Serves 6

4 stalks celery and leaves
2 medium onions
1 medium carrot
1-1/2 cups water
2 chicken bouillon cubes
1-1/2 cups cooked, mashed potatoes
1 tablespoon butter
2 cups half-and-half

Chop celery, onions and carrot; add water and simmer 30 minutes. Strain through sieve (large tea strainer will work). Stir bouillon cubes into strained vegetable-water. While hot, pour over potatoes, stirring until dissolved. Rub through strainer to make sure no lumps remain. Add butter and half-and-half; heat. Sprinkle paprika and parsley flakes on top.

If you have never tried bisques, you do not know what you have missed. The definition of a bisque is a thick, rich creamy soup with shellfish as its base. Bisques always have been popular in the southern states, most of which border a waterway, But today, all regions enjoy their own variety of this thick soup. We will wager that the official definition does not match the taste of this hearty soup which is served both as a first course at dinner or as lunch, all by itself.

EASY POTATO-CHEESE SOUP
Serves 6

1 package au gratin potatoes
1 (#303) can chicken broth
3 cups water
1/4 cup carrots, finely diced
1/4 cup celery, finely diced
1 small can Pet milk
Chopped parsley

Combine contents of potato package, including cheese sauce mix, broth, water, carrots, and celery in a 3-1/2 quart saucepan. Bring to a boil, stirring occasionally. Reduce heat and simmer, covered, for 15 minutes or until potatoes are tender. Remove from heat; add milk. Garnish with parsley.

Agnes Ward, Erie, Pa.

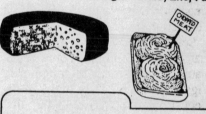

HAMBURGER SOUP

1 pound hamburger
1 cup chopped onion
1 cup celery
1 cup diced potatoes
1 quart tomatoes
2 large carrots, grated medium
1 tablespoon salt
1 bay leaf
1/4 teaspoon basil
1/4 teaspoon thyme
1/4 teaspoon fresh ground pepper
2 tablespoons beef bouillon
6 cups water
2 small cans whole kernel corn
1 small can yellow wax beans
1 cup frozen peas

Fry hamburger with onion until done. Add everything else except corn, beans, and peas. Simmer 30 minutes. Add last 3 ingredients and simmer another 5 minutes. A really great "hurry up" meal, tastes like it took hours to prepare.

Linda Taylor, New Lenox, IL

CHICKEN SOUP

1 large chicken, cut up
2 eggs
Juice of 2 lemons
2 teaspoons salt
8 cups water

Boil chicken* and salt in water about 2 hours. Remove chicken from broth; skin and debone; dice.

Beat eggs until light. Slowly add lemon juice; add 1 cup warm broth very slowly. Add to remaining broth with diced chicken and continue to heat through.

*For a different taste add finely chopped carrots, celery, and onion to the chicken when originally cooking.

A wonderfully-flavored and hearty soup such as this one needs only warm bread with butter, a tossed salad, and a dessert to make a filling meal.

Soups date back to prehistoric man when he combined bones, meat, water, and hot rocks in animal skin bags to produce a tasty brew. In ancient Roman cookbooks, the first known printed cookbooks contained recipes for soup. Both Queen Elizabeth I and Queen Victoria drank a cup of mutton broth to begin each day. The first soup "restorative" (later to be known as restaurant, and serve other foods) was established in Paris in 1750.

George Washington deserves credit for increasing the popularity of soup in our country. He requested that his personal cook, with few provisions, create a warm meal for his troops at Valley Forge. But it was our European ancestors who brought with them their favorite soups, and over the years, these soups have been adapted and blended to use local ingredients to suit a variety of tastes.

CHILI-BEEF SOUP
Serves 6

1/2 pound ground beef
1/2 cup chopped onion
1/2 cup chopped celery

1 (16-ounce) can-stewed tomatoes
1 (10-1/2 ounce) can condensed beef broth
1 soup-can water
1 teaspoon chili powder
1/2 teaspoon salt
1/2 teaspoon Worcestershire sauce
1 cup cooked peas

Brown meat in large, heavy Dutch oven or kettle. Drain off fat. Add onion and celery; cook until vegetables are done. Stir in tomatoes, beef broth, water, chili powder, salt, and Worcestershire sauce. Cover and cook until all is tender, about 15 minutes. Stir in peas; heat through.

HOT DEER CHILI
Serves 4-6

2 pounds coarsely ground venison
3 tablespoons chili powder
1 teaspoon black pepper
1 medium onion, chopped
1 bell pepper, chopped
1/2 teaspoon chopped jalapeño pepper
1 small can tomatoes (already seasoned with peppers, or regular tomatoes if others are unavailable)
1 (20-ounce) can tomato juice
1/2 teaspoon garlic salt
1/4 teaspoon salt
1 tablespoon oil
1/2 cup water

Sauté onion, bell pepper, and jalapeño pepper in oil in large skillet or pan until onion is clear; add meat and cook until meat loses its redness; add chili powder and black pepper. Mix well and cook 2 minutes, then allow it to set for 3 minutes. Add tomatoes, tomato juice, and salts. Heat to boiling, then simmer for 1 to 1-1/2 hours. Add water, as needed.

Note: You may use beef instead of venison.

AMERICAN CHILI
Serves 8

2 pounds stewing beef, cut in 1/2-inch cubes

2 tablespoons cooking oil
2 cups chopped onions
2 cloves garlic, minced
1 (1-pound) can tomatoes, cut up
1 beef bouillon cube
2 tablespoons chili powder
1-1/2 teaspoons salt
1 teaspoon dried oregano leaves
1 teaspoon ground cumin
2 (15-ounce) cans pinto or kidney beans

Brown meat in hot oil in Dutch oven. Add onion, garlic, tomatoes, bouillon cube, chili powder, salt, oregano, and cumin. Cover and simmer 1-3/4 hours. Add undrained beans; simmer 15 minutes.

Barbara Beauregard-Smith, SouthAust.

QUICK & EASY CHILI CON CARNE
Serves 5

1 pound ground beef
1 cup onion, chopped
1 (1-pound) can kidney beans
1 (8-ounce) can tomato sauce
1 teaspoon salt
2 teaspoons chili powder
1 bay leaf

Stir and sauté ground beef and onions together until beef is well done. Add kidney beans, tomato sauce, salt, chili powder, and bay leaf. Cover and cook slowly for 1 hour.

Suzan L. Wiener, Spring Hill, Fla.

BEEF STEW WITH DUMPLINGS
Serves 6

2 (24-ounce) cans beef stew
1 cup water
2 cups Basic Campers' Mix
1 cup milk

Combine canned stew and water. Bring to a boil. Combine Basic Campers' Mix and milk. Spoon onto hot stew. Cook, uncovered, over low coals for 10 minutes; cover and cook 10 minutes longer.

HEARTY POLISH STEW

1/4 cup butter or margarine, divided
1 pound stewing beef, cut in 1-inch cubes
1 large onion, chopped (1 cup)
1 medium apple, cored, unpeeled, chopped (1 cup)
1 clove garlic, minced
1 pound sauerkraut, drained, rinsed well
1 can (14 1/2 oz) tomatoes, drained, chopped
1 1/2 cups beef broth
7 small Idaho® potatoes, unpared, cut in chunks
1/2 pound Polish sausage (Kielbasa), cut in 3/4 inch slices
3/4 tsp caraway seeds
1/4 tsp pepper

In a Dutch oven or large, heavy kettle melt 2 tbsps butter; brown meat quickly over high heat. Reduce heat to medium. Add remaining 2 tbsps butter; cook onion, apple and garlic until tender. Stir in sauerkraut and tomatoes. Gradually stir in broth, scraping up bits from bottom of pan. Add potatoes, sausage, caraway seeds and pepper. Cover. Simmer 1 hour 10 minutes or until meat is tender.

OYSTER STEW

Serves 4

1 quart milk
1/4 cup butter
1 teaspoon Worcestershire sauce
1 teaspoon salt
2 tablespoons flour mixed with 2 tablespoons water
1 pint oysters (with liquid)
Cayenne pepper

Put all ingredients, except oysters and cayenne pepper in a kettle. Cover; cook and stir well. Add oysters. Cook on low, until oysters curl. Sprinkle with cayenne pepper; serve hot with crackers.

Lucy Dowd, Sequim, Wash.

COUNTRY FISH STEW

Serves 3

1 pound frozen fillets of perch, haddock, or other choice
2 teaspoons cooking oil
2 teaspoons cornstarch
1/4 cup cold water
1-1/2 teaspoons instant minced onion or 2 tablespoons fresh grated
1/2 teaspoon salt
1/4 teaspoon black pepper
1/4 teaspoon ground nutmeg
1 cup half-and-half
1 (8-1/2 ounce) can whole kernel corn, undrained
Chopped parsley for garnish

Thaw fish if frozen; cut into 1-inch pieces. In 3-quart saucepan, heat oil. Dissolve cornstarch in cold water; add seasonings. Stir into heated oil. Gradually add half-and-half, stirring constantly. Add fish and corn. Cook over medium heat, stirring often, for 8-10 minutes, or until fish flakes easily when tested with a fork. Garnish with chopped parsley.

FISH CHOWDER

1-1/2 pounds cod or haddock
2 cups diced potatoes
1 cup diced carrots
1 quart water
1/2 pound salt pork, diced
1 onion, chopped
2 tablespoons flour
1 pint milk
Salt and pepper

Cut fish into small pieces; remove bones and skin. Cook fish, potatoes, and carrots in water for 15 minutes. Fry the salt pork until crisp; remove from drippings; cook onion in drippings for a few minutes. Add flour and stir until well blended. Add milk.

Stir this mixture into fish and vegetables with the seasonings, and simmer 10 minutes longer, stirring frequently.

CORN CHOWDER

Serves 5

1/2 pound bacon
1 medium onion, chopped
2 medium potatoes, peeled and chopped
2 cups half-and-half
1 (17-ounce) can cream style corn
1/2 teaspoon salt
Pepper
1/2 cup milk

Fry bacon in a heavy Dutch oven until crisp; remove, reserving 2 tablespoons drippings in Dutch oven. Crumble bacon; set aside.

In reserved drippings, sauté onion until tender; add potatoes and water. Cover and simmer 15-20 minutes or until potatoes are tender. Stir in half-and-half and milk, corn and seasonings. Cook over medium heat, stirring frequently, until thoroughly heated.

Sprinkle each bowl with bacon.

CORN CHOWDER

Serves 4-6

1 tablespoon butter
3 slices bacon
1 large onion, chopped
4 large potatoes, peeled and diced
3 cups milk
1 cup creamed corn, fresh or canned
2 cups corn kernels
1 teaspoon salt
1 teaspoon finely chopped parsley

Heat butter in a large heavy pan. Add bacon and onion; cook until tender. Add potatoes and cook over medium heat for 5 minutes. Stir in 2 cups milk. Bring just to a boil. Cover and simmer until potatoes are tender. Gently stir in the creamed corn, whole kernels, and remaining milk. Heat through; season and sprinkle with parsley. Serve with croutons and sliced cooked sausage.

Patsy Saulnier, Nova Scotia, Canada

CAULIFLOWER-HAM CHOWDER

2 cups diced potatoes
3/4 cup diced celery
1 (13-3/4-ounce) can chicken broth
1/4 cup water
2 tablespoons butter
1/8 teaspoon white pepper
2 cups sliced cauliflower
1/2 cup diced onions
1 cup cream
1-1/2 cups milk
3 tablespoons cornstarch
2 cups diced cooked ham

In large saucepan cook cauliflower, potatoes, onions, and celery covered in chicken broth until almost tender (about 10 minutes). *Do not drain.* Add butter to melt. In mixing bowl, gradually stir in milk and cream. Blend water, cornstarch, and pepper; stir into milk mixture. Pour over vegetables. Cook and stir until thickened and bubbly. Stir in ham. Simmer over low heat for 10 minutes. Season to taste. Garnish with parsley.

Donna Holter, West Middlesex, Pa.

CLAM CHOWDER
Serves 6-8

1 cup potatoes, diced
1 small onion, diced
1 tablespoon butter
2 tablespoons flour
3 cups whole milk
Pinch of pepper
1/2 teaspoon salt, or to taste
1 (8-ounce) can minced clams

Simmer potatoes and onion together in small amount of water until tender. Melt butter in small pan, then blend in flour making a smooth paste. Drain juice from clams and blend into butter and flour mixture. Add to cooked potatoes and onions; stir in milk and clams. Heat to serving temperature, *but do not boil.* Season to taste and serve.

Trenda Leigh, Richmond, Va.

CHEESE VEGETABLE CHOWDER
Serves 8-10

2 cups chopped cabbage
1 cup celery slices
1 cup thin carrot slices
1 (16-ounce) can cream-style corn
1 teaspoon salt
1/4 teaspoon thyme
2-1/2 cups (10 ounces) shredded American process cheese
1 cup onion slices
1 cup peas
1/2 cup (1 stick) butter
3 cups milk, reconstituted
1/8 teaspoon pepper

Sauté cabbage, onion, celery, peas, and carrots in butter in saucepan 8-10 minutes, stirring frequently. Add corn, milk, and seasonings; heat over low heat for 15 minutes, stirring occasionally. Add cheese; stir until melted. Makes approximately 2 quarts.

Donna Holter, West Middlesex, Pa.

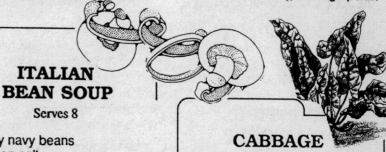

ITALIAN BEAN SOUP
Serves 8

1 cup dry navy beans
1 teaspoon salt
1 (8-ounce) can tomato sauce
1 cup chopped onion
1 cup chopped carrots
1/2 cup chopped green pepper
2 cloves garlic, minced
2 beef bouillon cubes
1-1/2 teaspoon each crushed dried basil and oregano, or 3 teaspoons Italian seasoning mix
1/2 cup macaroni

Rinse beans; add 8 cups water. Soak overnight. Do not drain. Stir in 1 teaspoon salt and remaining ingredients, except macaroni. Cover and simmer 1-1/2 hours. Stir in macaroni and cook, uncovered, until macaroni is done, about 15 minutes.

Our neighbors to the south certainly knew how to cure any ills with this savory broth.

FRENCH MARKET BEAN SOUP

1-1/2 cups mixed beans
2 or 3 smoked ham hocks
1 pound smoked sausage, thinly sliced
1 large onion, chopped
Juice of 1 lemon
1 (16-ounce) can tomatoes
2 cloves garlic, chopped
1 (4-ounce) can green chilies, chopped
1 (8-ounce) can tomato sauce
Salt and pepper to taste

Rinse and drain beans; cover with water; soak overnight. Cook in same water with ham hocks and onion until tender, about 3 hours. Remove meat from bones and return meat to mixture. Add remaining ingredients. Simmer 30-60 minutes. Soup should be thick, but add small amount of water, if desired.

Sharon McClatchey, Muskogee, Okla.

CABBAGE AND TOMATO SOUP
Serves 8-10

1 small head of cabbage
2 cans tomato soup
1 (16-ounce) can tomatoes, cut into quarters
1 large onion, sliced thin
2 tablespoons freshly-squeezed lemon juice
1/2 cup firmly-packed brown sugar
1/2 pound chuck steak, cubed
1/2 cup ground gingersnaps

Place cabbage in stock pot. Cover with hot water. Simmer over medium-low heat for 30 minutes; stirring occasionally. Add remaining ingredients. Simmer uncovered 1-1/2 hours, stirring occasionally.

Diantha Susan Hibbard, Rochester, NY

TOMATO SOUP ALA HERBS
Serves 8

An attractive, hearty soup using herbs to make it appear more elegant.

1 medium onion, chopped
1 clove garlic, minced
2 tablespoons butter or margarine
4 cups water
2 pounds ripe tomatoes, peeled and chopped
2 carrots, thinly sliced
4 red potatoes, unpeeled, and cubed
2 stalks celery, chopped
1 chicken bouillon cube
1/2 teaspoon fresh or 1/4 teaspoon dried of the following herbs: thyme, basil, and rosemary
Salt and pepper to taste

In large kettle or Dutch oven, sauté onion and garlic in margarine or butter. Stir in water, tomatoes, carrots, potatoes, celery, bouillon cube and spices. Bring to boil; reduce heat and simmer, covered, about 45 minutes or until vegetables are well-done.

CREAMY RUTABAGA SOUP
Serves 6

3 cups cubed rutabaga
2 chicken bouillon cubes dissolved in 1-1/2 cups boiling water
1 small onion, chopped
2 tablespoons margarine
1/4 teaspoon celery salt
1/2 teaspoon salt
Dash of pepper
1 teaspoon sugar
1-1/2 cups milk
1 cup light cream
Nutmeg

Sauté onion in margarine; add rutabaga, bouillon cubes, and water. Cook until very soft. Press through sieve (or use blender). Add remaining ingredients, except cream and nutmeg. Add cream; heat through but do not boil. Serve hot, sprinkled with nutmeg, bacon bits, or toasted croutons.

Margaret Hamfeldt, Louisville, KY

CREAM OF PEANUT SOUP
Serves 6

1/2 cup butter or margarine, melted
1 cup celery, thinly sliced
1 medium onion, minced
2 tablespoons flour
2 quarts chicken broth
1 cup creamy peanut butter
1 cup light cream or evaporated milk
1/4 cup fresh snipped parsley
1/4 cup coarsely chopped peanuts

In 3- or 4-quart saucepan, melt butter. Add celery and onion. Cook until lightly browned, stirring constantly. Stir in flour. Blend well. Gradually stir in chicken broth. Bring to a boil. Stir in peanut butter. Simmer 15 minutes. Just before serving, reheat over very low heat. Stir in cream. Garnish with snipped parsley and chopped peanuts.

SOME LIKE IT HOT VICHYSSOISE

1/4 cup butter
1 large onion, sliced (1 cup)
8 small Idaho® potatoes, pared, halved
3 medium carrots, sliced
1 quart water
1 tsp ground ginger
3/4 tsp salt
1/8 tsp pepper
2 cups milk
1 tbsp soy sauce
2 tbsps chopped scallion

In large saucepot or heavy kettle melt butter; saute onion until tender. Add potatoes, carrots, water, ginger, salt and pepper. Bring to a boil. Reduce heat. Simmer 30 minutes or until vegetables are tender. Remove 4 potato halves; dice and set aside. Puree remaining vegetables and cooking liquid in blender or food processor. Return to saucepot. Stir in milk, soy sauce and cubed potatoes; heat. Sprinkle soup with scallions before serving.

BOUNTIFUL BEAN SOUP
Serves 6

1 pound dry navy beans
2 quarts cold water
1 meaty ham bone
1 bay leaf
1/2 teaspoon salt
6 whole black peppercorns
Vinegar to taste

Rinse 1 pound beans. Add 2 quarts cold water. Bring to a boil and simmer 2 minutes. Remove from heat. Cover; let stand 1 hour. Do not drain. Add remaining ingredients. Cover; simmer 3 hours. Remove ham bone. Mash beans slightly, using potato masher. Cut ham off bone. Add ham to soup. Cook 30 minutes more. Season to taste. This is a wonderful nutritious soup; prepare in a slow cooker or slow pot.

Dyndee Kannenberg, Brown Deer, Wis.

CREAMY PIMIENTO SOUP
Serves 7

2 tablespoons butter or margarine
3 tablespoons flour
1/4 teaspoon salt
1/8 teaspoon pepper
1 teaspoon onion, grated
3 cups milk
4 cups chicken broth
3/4 cup pimientos
Chopped parsley, for garnish

In a saucepan melt butter; add flour, seasonings, and onion. Place milk, broth, and pimientos into food processor; pulse 5 times; add to flour/butter mixture. Cook, stirring constantly, until thickened. Sprinkle chopped parsley on individual servings.

Gwen Campbell, Sterling, Va.

SPONGE SOUP

Serves 16-20

12 eggs
1-1/2 pounds ground beef
14 tablespoons flour (heaping)
14 tablespoons grated Parmesan
  cheese (heaping)
1 tablespoon salt
1 tablespoon baking powder

Beat eggs until frothy. Then mix in the ground beef, flour, grated Parmesan cheese, salt, and baking powder. Knead ingredients together. Spread in a 9x12-inch cake pan, and bake 25-30 minutes at 350 degrees. Remove from oven, let cool, and cut into 1/2-inch cubes. Place the cubes in a beef broth and reheat. The mixture also can be made ahead and frozen until the day before serving.

END-OF-THE-GARDEN SOUP

1-1/2 pounds beef soup meat
3 quarts water
1-1/2 cups green beans
1-1/2 cups potatoes
2 cups carrots
1 cup turnips
1 cup sweet corn
1 onion
1 clove garlic
Salt and pepper to taste

Wash all vegetables and chop. Combine vegetables, meat, and water; boil slowly for about 4 hours. Serve with crackers.

Very good for those cool fall evenings.

Winnie Dettmer, Canfield, Ohio

SHERRIED WILD RICE SOUP

Serves 4

2 (10-ounce) packages frozen
  white and wild rice combination
2 tablespoons butter or margarine
1 tablespoon onion, minced
1 tablespoon celery, minced
1 tablespoon carrot, minced
1/4 cup flour
4 cups chicken broth
1 cup light cream
3 tablespoons dry sherry
2 tablespoons chives, minced

Prepare rice according to package directions. In a saucepan, melt butter; sauté vegetables until tender. Blend in flour; cook 2 minutes; blend well. Stir in the prepared rice; simmer 5 minutes. Blend in cream, broth, and sherry. To serve, garnish each individual serving with minced chives.

Gwen Campbell, Sterling, Va.

SHRIMP BISQUE

Serves 4

1 cup celery, finely chopped
1 cup diced potatoes
1/2 cup onion, diced
1 cup water
Salt and pepper to taste
2 cups half-and-half
2 tablespoons all-purpose flour
1/2 pound fresh, boiled shrimp (or 8-
  ounce package frozen)
2 tablespoons butter

In heavy saucepan combine celery, potatoes, onion, water, and seasonings. Bring to boil; reduce heat and simmer, covered, until potatoes are done, about 15 minutes.

Blend half-and-half and flour together; stir into potato mixture. Add shrimp and butter. Cook, stirring constantly, until thickened.

Chowders are well known in the northeast part of our country because of the origination. This inviting dish takes its name from the French word, chaudiére, a large kettle used by French settlers to cook soups and stews. These settlers often contributed part of their daily catch to a community kettle, adding potatoes and corn.

BASQUE BREAD SOUP

Serves 4

2 large cloves garlic, lightly crushed
1/4 cup olive oil
4 cups water
2/3 cup fine stale bread crumbs,
  toasted
1 teaspoon salt
2 eggs, slightly beaten
Salt and pepper to taste

In a small heavy skillet, sauté garlic in oil over moderately high heat until golden brown. Remove and discard the garlic; keep oil warm. In a saucepan, bring water to a boil and stir in the toasted bread crumbs, oil, and salt. Remove the pan from the heat; whisk in the eggs. Season with salt and pepper. Ladle into heated bowls.

ROCKY MOUNTAIN SOUP

Serves 8

3 cups water
1-1/4 cups dried pinto beans
3 slices bacon, chopped
2 cloves garlic, minced
1/2 cup chopped onion
1 (1-pound) can tomatoes, cut up
2/3 cup uncooked brown rice
1 teaspoon salt
1/2 teaspoon paprika
1/4 teaspoon pepper

Rinse beans. In a large kettle or Dutch oven, combine beans and 3 cups water. Bring to boiling. Reduce heat; simmer 2 minutes. Let stand one hour. Drain. Add 5-1/2 cups fresh water to beans. Simmer, covered, 1 hour. While beans are simmering, cook bacon until almost crisp. Add onion and garlic. Cook until vegetables are tender, but not brown, stirring occasionally. Stir bacon mixture, tomatoes, rice, salt, pepper, and paprika into bean mixture. Bring to boiling. Cover and simmer for 45 minutes to 1 hour or until rice and beans are tender. Stir occasionally.

Joy Shamway, Freeport, Ill.

Vegetable
DELIGHTS

GREEN VEGGIE BAKE
Serves 6-8

2 tablespoons butter or margarine
1/2 cup chopped onion
1 teaspoon salt
1/4 teaspoon pepper
4 ounces sour cream
1 to 1-1/2 tablespoons cornstarch
1 cup broccoli
1 cup green beans
1 cup peas
1 cup American or cheddar cheese, grated
2 tablespoons butter or margarine, melted
1 cup Ritz (salad) crackers

Cook onion in 2 tablespoons butter until tender. Add cornstarch, salt, pepper, and sour cream; mix well. Stir in green vegetables. Put in casserole dish, top with grated cheese. Combine remaining 2 tablespoons butter and cracker crumbs; place on top of cheese. Bake at 350 degrees for 30 minutes. This recipe was created for those "timid" green–vegetable eaters. Also great for leftovers.

Beth Zellars, Franklin, Ind.

SAVORY SOUTHERN FRIED CORN

4-6 ears fresh corn
5 slices bacon
3 tablespoons green pepper, minced
1/2 cup sweet milk
1 teaspoon salt
1/4 teaspoon pepper
Dash sugar

Cut corn kernels from cob; set aside. Cut bacon in half; fry in skillet until crisp; drain. Discard all but 4 tablespoons bacon drippings; reserve fried bacon strips for garnish later. Add corn and green pepper. Cook without stirring, until bottom is golden brown. Add milk and seasonings; stir until combined. Cover and cook over low heat 10 minutes longer. Arrange bacon over top when served.

Gwen Campbell, sterling, Va.

SUNSHINE SWEET POTATO BALLS
Makes 18-20 balls

1/4 cup butter, melted
1/4 cup milk
2 tablespoons sugar
1/2 teaspoon salt
1/4 teaspoon pepper
4 cups cooked, mashed sweet potatoes
18-20 miniature marshmallows
3 cups coarsely crushed cornflakes

Beat butter, milk, sugar, salt, and pepper into mashed sweet potatoes. Form 2-inch balls with a center of a marshmallow. Roll in cornflakes. Place in greased 9-1/2x12-3/4-inch baking pan. Bake in moderate oven of 375 degrees for 25-35 minutes. May be frozen first, then baked without defrosting for 45 minutes at 375 degrees.

Audrey L. Reynolds, Lumberport, W.V.

RED CABBAGE

1 head red cabbage
4 tablespoons margarine
1/2 jar grape jelly
1 chopped onion
1 apple, sliced
1/2 teaspoon salt

Shred cabbage and put in a colander; pour boiling water over cabbage two times and allow to thoroughly drain. Melt margarine in a large skillet. Place cabbage, apples, and onions in the skillet. Add grape jelly and salt; simmer to desired tenderness.

This vegetable is different and very good.

SOUPER SCALLOPED POTATOES
Serves 4-6

1 (10-3/4 ounce) can condensed cream of mushroom *or* celery soup
1/2 cup milk
1/2 cup minced onion
1/2 teaspoon salt
1/4 teaspoon pepper
1 quart thinly sliced raw potatoes

Combine soup, milk, onion, salt and pepper, and mix well. Place half of potatoes in a 1-1/2–quart casserole. Cover with half of the soup mixture. Repeat layers. Bake covered in a 375–degree oven for 1 hour. Uncover and bake 15 additional minutes.

Melba Bellefeuilee, Libertyville, Ill.

HERBED ROASTED CORN

Prepare fresh corn for roasting by husking, removing silk and trimming ends. Place ears back into husks. Soak in ice water for 1 hour. When ready to roast, shake off excess water and spread on the following herb butter:

Combine 3/4 cup soft butter with 2 teaspoons chopped chives and 1/2 teaspoon garlic salt.

Arrange on rack and broil 7 minutes on one side; turn with tongs and broil on other side until done, about 30 minutes.

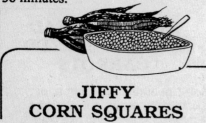

JIFFY CORN SQUARES

1 small box Jiffy cornbread mix
2 eggs
1 small carton sour cream
1 stick margarine
1 can whole kernel corn, drained
1 can cream style corn

Combine above ingredients. Pour into greased 9x9-inch baking dish. Bake for 30 minutes at 350 degrees.
Betty Slavin, Omaha, Neb.

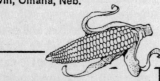

EGGS WITH CORN
Serves 4

2 ears corn
4 tablespoons butter or margarine
Salt and pepper to taste
8 eggs, beaten
Chopped chives

Boil corn in salted water 3-4 minutes. Drain and remove kernels with a sharp knife. Melt butter in small skillet; add corn, salt, and pepper. Stir for a few minutes while corn absorbs some of the butter. Pour eggs into the skillet; stir over moderate heat until scrambled. Serve sprinkled with chopped chives.

BACK-HOME SCALLOPED CORN

4 slices bacon, chopped
1-1/4 cups crushed saltine crackers
1 medium onion, chopped
2 eggs, beaten
1 pound can cream-style corn
1 (4-ounce) can pimientos, drained and chopped
1 cup milk
1 cup grated cheddar cheese
1/4 teaspoon salt
1/4 teaspoon pepper

Fry bacon until crisp; remove from skillet. Combine 2 tablespoons bacon fat with 1/4 cup cracker crumbs; set aside. Cook onion in remaining bacon fat until tender. Add remaining crumbs; mix and brown lightly. Combine onion crumb mixture with eggs, corn, pimientos, milk, cheese, bacon, salt, and pepper. Pour into greased shallow 1-1/2-quart casserole. Top with reserved crumbs. Bake in a moderate oven, 350 degrees for about 45 minutes.

Great casserole to take to church suppers!

Sarah Burkett, Centralia, Ill.

CORN OYSTERS
Serves 6

1/2 cup sifted flour
3/4 teaspoon salt
1/2 teaspoon baking powder
1/4 cup milk
1 egg, slightly beaten
2 cups fresh corn kernels
1/3 cup cooking oil

Sift flour with salt and baking powder into a bowl. Slowly add milk and beat until smooth. Beat in egg and mix in corn. Heat oil in a large, heavy skillet over moderate heat for 1 minute. Drop batter by tablespoonsful into skillet and fry, a few "oysters" at a time, 3-4 minutes until browned on both sides. Drain on paper toweling and set, uncovered, in a 250-degree oven to keep warm while you fry the rest.

CORN STICKS
Serves 6

2 cups fresh corn kernels, cooked and drained
1 cup sifted flour
1 teaspoon baking powder
1/2 teaspoon salt
1/4 teaspoon pepper
2 beaten egg whites
2 beaten egg yolks
1/2 cup milk
Oil for deep frying

In a bowl combine flour, baking powder, salt, and pepper. In another bowl combine egg yolks, corn, and milk; add flour mixture; fold in egg whites. With a tablespoon drop batter into hot oil. Cook, turning once, until golden. Drain on absorbent paper. Keep warm. Repeat until all batter is used.

CORN PIE
Serves 6

1 9-inch pie shell
4 eggs, lightly beaten
1-1/4 cups milk or light cream
1-1/4 teaspoons salt
1 tablespoon grated yellow onion
1-1/2 cups fresh corn kernels

Preheat oven to 425 degrees. Prepare pastry and fit into a 9-inch pie pan, making a high fluted edge. Prick bottom and all sides of pastry with a fork; cover with waxed paper, and fill with uncooked rice or dried beans. Bake 5-7 minutes until crust is firm but not brown. Remove rice or beans and waxed paper. Stir together all filling ingredients and pour into pie shell. Bake 10 minutes at 425 degrees; reduce heat to 350 degrees and bake 30 minutes longer or until center is almost firm. Cool about 10 minutes before cutting.

CUCUMBERS SUPREME

2 medium cucumbers
1 large onion, sliced and separated
   into rings
1 cup Seven Seas Buttermilk
   Recipe Dressing
Green—onion tops for color

Peel and slice cucumbers. Peel, slice, and separate onions into rings. Mix and add Seven Seas Dressing. Garnish with green onion tops. Cucumbers could not be any tastier!! Also a very quick side dish to add to any meal.

Mrs. C. O. Shepardson, Apple Valley, Calif.

CABBAGE AU GRATIN

1-1/2 pounds cabbage
2 tablespoons butter
6 tablespoons flour
2 cups milk
1/4 pound grated cheese

Cut up cabbage and cook in salted water until tender. Make a white sauce with the butter, flour, and milk. Fill a greased baking dish with alternate layers of cabbage and white sauce. Cover top with cheese; bake in 350 degree oven for 20 minutes.

Joy Shamway, Freeport, IL

CRUNCHY CABBAGE

Serves 6-8

8 cups thinly sliced green cabbage
Boiling water
1 (10-3/4 ounce) can cream of
   celery soup
1/2 cup mayonnaise
1/2 cup milk
1/2 teaspoon salt
2 cups corn flakes
2 tablespoons butter or margarine,
   melted
1/2 pound shredded Cheddar
   cheese

Cook cabbage in boiling water 3-4 minutes. Drain. Combine next four ingredients in saucepan. Heat, just until hot. Toss corn flakes in the bottom of a 1-1/2 quart casserole, reserving some for top. Alternate layers of cabbage and sauce, ending with sauce layer. Top with remaining corn flakes and cheese. Bake at 375 degrees for 15 minutes. Serve hot.

Lori Gerich, Hayward, Wis.

FRENCH SKILLET CABBAGE

4-6 cups shredded cabbage
1 green pepper, shredded
2 large onions, sliced (not chopped)
2 cups diced-sliced celery
2 tomatoes, chopped
6-8 slices bacon
1/4-1/3 cup bacon drippings

Fry bacon; remove from skillet and crumble; reserve drippings. Combine all vegetables in large skillet with bacon drippings. Cover; cook over medium heat for 7-10 minutes or until vegetables are still crisp-cooked. Add bacon just before serving. Do not substitute for bacon or the drippings.

Alice Dick, Montpelier, Ohio

MARINATED CARROTS

Serves 8

1 bag large carrots
2 cloves garlic, sliced
1/2 teaspoon salt
1/2 teaspoon pepper
1/4 cup olive oil
2 tablespoons wine vinegar
1 teaspoon oregano

Scrape carrots; cut into thick slices. Boil in water 10 minutes, or until tender, taking care not to overcook. Drain well; place in bowl with garlic, salt, pepper, oil, vinegar, and oregano. Stir; mix well. Let stand in marinade twelve hours before serving.

Helen Robiolo, Union City, NJ

GLAZED CARROTS

Serves 6

2 cups sliced carrots
1 cup undiluted frozen orange juice
1/2 cup sugar
2 tablespoons cornstarch
Dash of nutmeg

Cook and drain carrots. Mix remaining ingredients; cook until thick. Pour sauce over carrots and let stand a short time. Serve hot.

Juanita Cecil, Mooresville, Ind.

FREEZE AHEAD GOLDEN GLAZED CARROTS

1-1/2 pounds baby carrots or 1-1/2
   pounds carrots, cut into strips
2 tablespoons all-purpose flour
1/4 cup light brown sugar
1/2 teaspoon salt
1/4 teaspoon thyme
1 tablespoon cider vinegar
1 tablespoon lemon juice
1/2 cup orange juice
Grated peel of one orange
2 tablespoons butter

Put carrots in saucepan. Pour boiling water over them and boil exactly 5 minutes. Drain thoroughly. Blend together flour, sugar, salt, and thyme. Add vinegar, juices, and orange rind. Bring to a boil while stirring, and continue stirring until creamy. Add butter and cook for 5 minutes over very low heat. Line a casserole with foil, leaving enough around the edges to cover. Add the blanched carrots to foil-lined casserole; pour sauce over them. Freeze uncovered. When frozen, cover completely with the foil. Remove package from casserole and put back into freezer. To serve, unwrap carrots, put back into same casserole. Bake, covered in a 350-degree oven for 40 minutes. Uncover for the last 15 minutes of baking. This is a very nice way to use the first baby carrots from the garden, and then when you serve them it brings back the "taste of summer."

Lillian Smith, Montreal, Que, Canada

SCALLOPED CARROTS

5 cups raw carrots, sliced or diced
1 onion, sliced
1/2 cup butter
1/2 pound Velveeta cheese
12 Ritz crackers

Cook carrots until done; drain. Sauté onion in butter. In baking dish, layer carrots and cheese. Pour onions and butter over top. Break up Ritz crackers and sprinkle over top. Bake at 350 degrees for 30-40 minutes.

Evelyn Eckhart, Alexandria, Minn.

GREEN BEAN AND CARROT COMBO
Serves 6-8

1 pound can green beans, drained
1 pound can sliced carrots, drained
1/2 teaspoon sugar
1/4 teaspoon salt
1/4 teaspoon onion powder
1 can cream of celery soup
1/4 cup milk

Combine all ingredients; mix well. Place in greased casserole and bake for 25-30 minutes at 350 degrees.

Sharon Crider, Evansville, Wis.

GLAZED CARROTS WITH BACON 'N ONION
Serves 4

1 pound carrots, scraped and sliced diagonally
3 slices bacon
1 small onion, chopped
3 tablespoons brown sugar
1/8 teaspoon pepper

Cook carrots, covered, in small amount of boiling water for 15 minutes or until crisp tender; drain. Cook bacon in skillet until crisp; crumble. Reserve 1 tablespoon drippings in skillet. Sauté onion in drippings. Add brown sugar, pepper, and carrots. Cook until heated; sprinkle with crumbled bacon.

Edna Askins, Greenville, Texas

COLORFUL CARROT RING
Serves 4

1/2 cup soft bread crumbs
3 eggs
1 small onion
1/4 cup parsley
1 tablespoon butter or margarine, melted
1/4 teaspoon cinnamon
1/4 teaspoon salt
1/8 teaspoon pepper
2-1/2 cups carrots, cooked
1 tablespoon brown sugar or maple syrup

Place all ingredients in food processor; process 1 minute or until carrots are cut very fine. Turn into an 8-inch ring mold; set in a shallow pan of water; bake at 375 degrees for 30 minutes or until set and firm. Unmold on serving plate; fill center with tiny peas.

Gwen Campbell, Sterling, Va.

POTATOES AND MUSHROOMS

8-10 small, new potatoes
1/4 cup butter, melted
2 tablespoons green onions or chives, chopped
1/2 pound mushrooms, chopped
1 cup meat stock
2 egg yolks
1 teaspoon lemon juice
Salt and pepper

Cook potatoes in jackets until tender. Drain and dry. Place in a casserole, adding butter and chopped onion. Beat egg yolks and add lemon juice, mushrooms, and meat stock. Season with salt and pepper. Pour over potatoes in casserole. Bake uncovered in preheated 350 degree oven for 30-40 minutes.

Betty Perkins, Hot Springs, AR

SWISS POTATOES

1-1/2 cups large baking potatoes, thinly sliced
1 teaspoon salt
1 teaspoon minced dried onion
2 eggs, beaten
1-1/2 cups milk, scalded
1/4 pound Swiss cheese, grated

Mix together all above ingredients, saving some grated cheese to sprinkle on top. Place into medium-sized, lightly-buttered casserole. Sprinkle top with reserved cheese. Place in preheated 350 degree oven and bake for 1 hour.

Recipe can be doubled easily.

Agnes Ward, Erie, Pa.

POTATO CELERY SUPREME
Serves 4

4-6 medium potatoes, cut into small pieces
Salt and pepper to taste
1/3 stick margarine
1 can cream of celery soup
1/2 cup water

Put cut potatoes into greased casserole; add salt and pepper, margarine, soup, and water. Stir lightly. Bake covered in a 350 degree oven for 1-1/2 hours.

Edna Askins, Greenville, Texas

COUNTRY-FRIED POTATOES

2 tablespoons butter or margarine
2 tablespoons bacon drippings (or shortening)
6 cooked, pared, thickly sliced potatoes
1 medium onion, chopped
Salt and pepper to taste

Melt butter and drippings or shortening in heavy skillet. Add sliced potatoes and chopped onions to hot skillet. Season with salt and pepper. Cook over low fire until bottom crust is brown; turn, and brown other side.

OVEN BARBECUED POTATOES

Serves 6

2 cups (8 ounces) Cheddar cheese, grated and divided
1 (10-3/4 ounce) can cream of mushroom soup
1/3 cup milk
1/4 cup barbecue sauce
1/4 teaspoon salt
1/4 teaspoon oregano
1/8 teaspoon pepper
4 medium potatoes, unpeeled and thinly sliced
1/2 teaspoon paprika

In large bowl combine 1-1/2 cups cheese, soup, milk, barbecue sauce, oregano, salt and pepper; blend thoroughly. Add potato slices; toss until well coated. Spoon mixture into a greased 9-inch square pan; cover with foil and bake at 350 degrees for 45 minutes. Remove foil; bake about 30 minutes longer or until tender. Remove from oven. Sprinkle remaining cheese and paprika on top. Let stand 5-10 minutes before serving.

Agnes Ward, Erie, PA

POTATO-CHEESE LOGS

2 medium potatoes, diced
2 tablespoons cream
2 tablespoons butter
1 egg, beaten lightly
1/2 teaspoon salt
1/8 teaspoon pepper
Dash cayenne pepper
1 clove garlic, crushed
3 tablespoons Parmesan or Romano cheese, grated
1 tablespoon parsley, minced
1/2 cup fine bread crumbs or cornflake crumbs

Boil potatoes until soft; drain and mash with cream and butter and whip until fluffy. Beat in egg, salt, pepper, cayenne, and garlic. Fold in cheese and parsley. Wet hands and shape into rolls, 2 inches long by 1 inch in diameter. *Roll in crumbs. Bake at 400 degrees for 15-20 minutes.

*To freeze, place on baking sheet immediately after rolling in crumbs and before baking. Place in freezer until firm; then pack in container and return to freezer. When needed, place frozen logs on lightly greased baking sheet and bake uncovered for 30 minutes at 400 degrees, turning once.

Eleanor V. Craycraft, Santa Monica, Calif.

BAKED CREAMED POTATOES

2 tablespoons butter or margarine
2 tablespoons flour
1 teaspoon salt
1/8 teaspoon white pepper
1-1/2 cups milk
1/2 teaspoon celery salt
1/4 cup chopped parsley
3-1/2 cups diced cooked potatoes (4 to 5 medium potatoes)
1 cup soft bread crumbs
2 tablespoons butter or margarine, melted

Preheat oven to 375 degrees. Butter a 1-1/2-quart casserole. Melt 2 tablespoons butter in a large saucepan. Sprinkle in flour, salt, and pepper; let it bubble up. Remove from heat and add milk all at once and stir to blend. Return to heat and stir until boiling, thickened, and smooth. Remove from heat and stir in celery salt, parsley, and potatoes. Pour into prepared casserole.

Combine bread crumbs and melted butter; sprinkle over all. Bake at 375 degrees for about 20 minutes or until hot and well-browned. These can be prepared ahead and then heated.

Lillian Smith, Montreal, Quebec, Canada

POTATOES RIO GRANDE

Serves 4

1-1/3 pounds (4 mid-size) potatoes, cut into 3/4 inch cubes
2 teaspoons vegetable oil
1 medium green (or red) bell pepper, seeded and cut into strips
1 (4-ounce) can diced green chiles
1 large clove garlic, pressed
1 (16-ounce) can stewed tomatoes
1/4 teaspoon pepper
Salt to taste
1/2 cup shredded Cheddar cheese
2 tablespoons chopped parsley

Continued on next page

Cook potatoes, covered, in 2-3 inches boiling water in 3-quart saucepan until not quite tender (about 12 minutes). Meanwhile, heat oil in large skillet. Add green pepper; toss over high heat, 5 minutes. Add chiles and garlic; cook and stir, 2 minutes. Stir in tomatoes and pepper. Cook to reduce liquid by half. Drain potatoes; add to skillet. Gently cook; stir to heat through. Stir in salt. Sprinkle cheese over potato mixture; cover to melt cheese. Sprinkle with parsley.

Judie Betz, Lomita, CA

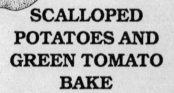

SCALLOPED POTATOES AND GREEN TOMATO BAKE

8 medium-size unpeeled potatoes, thinly sliced
3 large green tomatoes, thinly sliced
1 medium-size onion, diced
1 cup flour
1 pound Cheddar cheese, grated
1/4 pound bacon, browned and crumbled
Salt and pepper to taste
1/2 cup milk

Butter a large baking dish. Put a layer of potatoes on the bottom. Cover with a layer of green tomatoes. Sprinkle on a little bit of onion, flour, Cheddar cheese, bacon, salt, and pepper. Continue layering until dish is full; end with layer of cheese. Pour milk over the top; bake at 350 degrees for 1 hour or until potatoes are cooked and bubbling brown on top.

Gwen Campbell, Sterling, VA

FRIED GREEN TOMATOES

6 green tomatoes
3 tablespoons flour
1-1/4 teaspoons salt
Pepper to taste
4 tablespoons bacon fat
1 cup evaporated milk
1-1/4 teaspoons sugar

Wash tomatoes, but do not peel. Cut in half crosswise. Mix flour, salt, sugar, and pepper. Roll tomatoes, one at a time, in flour mixture. Brown on both sides in hot bacon fat. Remove to serving dish and keep warm. Add evaporated milk to same frying pan. Boil slowly, stirring constantly until thickened (about 2 minutes). Pour over tomatoes before serving.

Joy Shamway, Freeport, Ill.

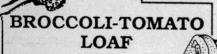

BROCCOLI-TOMATO LOAF

2 cups broccoli, cooked
2 eggs
1 cup canned tomatoes
1 cup onion
1/2 cup celery
3 tablespoons butter or margarine
1/4 teaspoon salt
1/8 teaspoon pepper
1/4 teaspoon sugar
1 cup coarse cracker crumbs
Quick Cheese Sauce (recipe follows)

In a food processor or blender, chop and mix first 9 ingredients; stir in crumbs. Bake in a greased loaf pan at 350 degrees for 40 minutes. Serve with Quick Cheese Sauce.

Quick Cheese Sauce:

1/3 cup milk
1 cup Cheddar cheese, cubed
2 tablespoons flour
1/8 teaspoon salt
1/2 teaspoon Worcestershire sauce

In a saucepan over low heat, blend all ingredients until hot, thickened, and cheese has thoroughly melted.
Gwen Campbell, Sterling, Va.

GOLDEN MERINGUE TOMATOES

4 large tomatoes
2-1/2 tablespoons butter, softened
4 eggs, separated
Salt and pepper to taste
1/3 cup grated Romano cheese
2 tablespoons chopped parsley or chives

Stand tomatoes upright; cut a slice from the top of each tomato. Scoop out pulp; finely chop and mix with softened butter, egg yolks, salt, and pepper. Add half the cheese and half the herbs. Put the mixture into tomato shells. Place tomatoes in an ovenproof dish; cook 12 minutes in 350 degree oven. Beat egg whites until stiff; fold in remaining cheese and herbs. Remove tomatoes from oven; top each with the meringue. Bake also at 350 degrees for about 6 minutes, or until meringue is set, puffed, and golden.

Mrs. Gwen Campbell, Sterling, VA

GARDEN SALAD STUFFED TOMATOES

6 firm red tomatoes
1/2 teaspoon salt
1/8 teaspoon pepper
1/4 cup peas, cooked
1/4 cup lima beans, cooked
1/4 cup carrots, raw julienne strips
1/4 cup asparagus tips
1/4 cup zucchini, grated
2 hard-cooked eggs, chopped

Cut a slice from the stem end of each tomato; scoop out pulp; set aside; discard seeds. Sprinkle shells with salt and pepper; invert on rack to drain for 15 minutes. Combine all vegetables and tomato pulp with enough mayonnaise to form a firm mixture; fill tomato shells. Top each shell with chopped hard-cooked eggs.

Gwen Campbell, Sterling, VA

FRIED TOMATOES
Serves 4

6 or 8 firm (or green) tomatoes
1 egg
1 tablespoon water
Fine bread or cereal crumbs
Salt and pepper to taste

Wash the tomatoes; remove the stem end, and slice into 1/2-inch slices. Beat the egg slightly; mix water in; dip tomato slices in this mixture and then roll in crumbs seasoned with salt and pepper. Set aside.

Heat oil in heavy skillet and place tomato slices in hot oil. Brown on one side; turn carefully, and then reduce heat so tomatoes can cook thoroughly before browning.

Lift from skillet onto heated platter and serve immediately.

If you are from the country (or wish you were), and aren't counting calories, you'll pour hot, creamy gravy over the top.

TOMATO-CUCUMBER MARINADE
Serves 6

2 medium tomatoes, sliced
2 cups cucumber, peeled and thinly-sliced
1/2 medium onion, thinly-sliced and separated into rings
1/2 cup salad oil
1/4 cup white wine vinegar
1 teaspoon salt
1 teaspoon basil
1 teaspoon tarragon
1/8 teaspoon pepper
Shredded lettuce

Alternate layers of tomato, cucumber, and onion in shallow glass dish. Combine other ingredients except lettuce; beat well with electric mixer. Pour over layered vegetables; chill covered, for 5-6 hours. Drain, reserving marinade. Arrange marinated vegetables on shredded lettuce. Pass reserved marinade for individual servings of dressing.

Diantha Hibbard, Rochester, NY

HAM, EGG, AND VEGETABLE BAKE

Serves 6

2 medium potatoes, peeled, cooked, and thinly sliced
1/4 cup cooked, minced ham
3 hard-cooked eggs, sliced
1 small head cauliflower, cooked and liquid reserved
1 tablespoon flour
1 tablespoon butter
Salt and pepper to taste
1/4 cup grated cheese

Grease a baking pan. Spread a layer of potato slices over bottom. Sprinkle with minced ham. Spread egg slices over ham. Cover with crumbled cauliflower and one more layer of potatoes. In a small saucepan soften the butter and stir in flour. Mix cauliflower liquid and skim milk to make one cup. Add gradually, stirring constantly. Cook over low heat until sauce thickens slightly. Season to taste and pour over mixture in baking pan. Sprinkle with grated cheese and bake in 350–degree oven for 30 minutes. (145 calories per serving)

Judy Codenys, LaGrange, Texas

SUMMER VEGETABLE MEDLEY

Serves 6

2-3 medium zucchini, washed and coin-sliced
1 cup fresh mushrooms, washed and sliced
1/4 cup chopped onion
1/4 cup chopped green pepper
3 tablespoons butter or margarine
2 tomatoes, coarsely chopped
2 tablespoons grated Parmesan cheese
1/4 teaspoon garlic powder
Salt and pepper to taste

Combine zucchini, mushrooms, onion, green pepper and butter in 1-1/2–quart glass/ceramic casserole. Cover and microwave 8-9 minutes, or until vegetables are tender–crisp, stirring once during cooking. Add toma-

toes, cheese, and seasonings. Cover and microwave 2-3 minutes or until heated through.

Mrs. Olen Begly, West Salem, Ohio

CRUSTY BREAD GRATIN OF VEGETABLES

Serves 8

1 tablespoon vegetable oil
1 tablespoon olive oil
1 onion, chopped
1/2 teaspoon garlic, minced
1 pound zucchini, cut into 1/2-inch slices
2 cups cauliflower florets
3 medium-size fresh tomatoes
1 (28-ounce) can crushed tomatoes
1/4 teaspoon salt
1/4 teaspoon pepper
1/2 cup Fontina cheese, shredded
4 slices French bread, halved and buttered

Heat oils in skillet; saute onion and garlic until tender. Add zucchini and cauliflower; saute 5 minutes. Add fresh and crushed tomatoes, salt, and pepper. Cook covered, until vegetables are tender. Pour vegetable mixture into oven baking dish; place halves of buttered French bread along edge of pan; cut side down, buttered side in. Sprinkle cheese on top of vegetable mixture; return to 350-degree oven for 5 minutes to melt cheese.

Gwen Campbell, Sterling, VA

GREEN VEGGIE BAKE

Serves 6-8

2 tablespoons butter or margarine
1/2 cup chopped onion
1 teaspoon salt
1/4 teaspoon pepper
4 ounces sour cream
1 to 1-1/2 tablespoons cornstarch
1 cup broccoli
1 cup green beans
1 cup peas
1 cup American or cheddar cheese, grated
2 tablespoons butter or margarine, melted

1 cup Ritz (salad) crackers

Cook onion in 2 tablespoons butter until tender. Add cornstarch, salt, pepper, and sour cream; mix well. Stir in green vegetables. Put in casserole dish, top with grated cheese. Combine remaining 2 tablespoons butter and cracker crumbs; place on top of cheese. Bake at 350 degrees for 30 minutes. This recipe was created for those "timid" green–vegetable eaters. Also great for leftovers.

Beth Zellars, Franklin, Ind.

TWEEDLE DEE BEETS

2 teaspoons cornstarch
1 teaspoon sugar
1/4 teaspoon salt
Dash ground cloves
3/4 cup canned orange juice
1 tablespoon margarine or butter
1 (16-ounce) can slivered beets, drained

Measure cornstarch, sugar, salt, and cloves into a medium size saucepan. Stir in orange juice. Add margarine and heat to boiling, stirring constantly to keep sauce smooth. Add beets to sauce. Heat slowly 5 minutes.

Roberta Neely, Riviera, Texas

SAVORY BEETS

2 servings

1 tablespoon butter or margarine
2 teaspoons cider vinegar
1/4 teaspoon salt
1/4 cup sugar
1/8 teaspoon dry mustard
Few drops Worcestershire sauce
3 or 4 medium beets, cooked and skinned

In a small saucepan, melt butter. Add vinegar, salt, sugar, dry mustard and Worcestershire sauce. Set over low heat; mix well with rubber spatula. Slice in beets; toss to mix; cook until beets are heated through.

The remaining beets can be chilled whole and sliced when used. This is a flavorful way to serve precooked beets.

CHEESE SCALLOPED ONIONS

Serves 8

3 large onions, sliced thin
1 cup (1/2 inch cubes) Cheddar
  cheese
4 slices buttered toast, cut into cubes
1/4 cup margarine
1/4 cup flour
2 cups milk
1/2 teaspoon salt
1/4 teaspoon pepper
2 beaten eggs

Cook onions in boiling salted water until tender, about 10 minutes. Drain well; place half the onions in 2 quart casserole. Add half the cheese and half the toast. Repeat layers of onion and cheese. Melt margarine; blend in flour. Stir in milk, gradually. Cook, stirring constantly, until thick. Add salt and pepper. Add a little of hot mixture to beaten eggs; gradually stir into hot mixture. Pour sauce over layers. Top with remaining toast cubes. Bake in 350 degree oven for 30 minutes.

Margaret Hamfeldt, Louisville, KY

PICNIC ONIONS 'N CREAM

Serves 6

4 large Bermuda onions
Salt and pepper to taste
1 cup medium white sauce
1/4 cup heavy cream or sour cream
3 tablespoons bread crumbs
Paprika, optional garnish

Wash and peel onions; cover with salted, boiling water. Boil 20 minutes. Drain; cut into quarters. Place in greased, shallow (1 quart) baking dish. Season with salt and pepper. Combine white sauce with cream or sour cream; pour all, but 1/4 cup, over onions. Mix remaining 1/4 cup with crumbs and pour on top. Bake, uncovered, in 350-degree oven for 40 min-

utes or until onions are tender and top is browned.

Delicious with outdoor-cooked meat.

Agnes Ward, Erie, PA

CORN-STUFFED PEPPERS

Serves 6

1 (12-ounce) can Green Giant
  Mexicorn
4 ounces (1 cup) shredded Cheddar
  cheese
1 (2-1/4 ounce) can sliced ripe
  olives, drained
2 tablespoons chopped green
  chilies, drained
2 tablespoons chopped green
  onions
3 large green peppers, cut in half
  lengthwise

In medium bowl, combine corn, cheese, olives, chilies and green onions; mix well. Remove seeds and membranes from green pepper halves. Spoon corn mixture into each half. Place each filled pepper half on sheet of heavy-duty foil and wrap securely, if you want to barbecue outside. If using oven, heat to 350 degrees and bake for 25-35 minutes or until peppers are crisp–tender.

If barbecuing on a grill out–side, place 4-6 inches from medium–hot coals. Cook 20-25 minutes.

Sue Hibbard, Rochester, N.Y.

ZESTY ZUCCHINI BAKE

(Using zucchini you have frozen)

1 (16-ounce) bag cubed zucchini,
  peeled or unpeeled
1 pound ground beef
1/2 cup minced onion
1/4 cup diced green pepper
1 (8-ounce) can tomato sauce
1 cup dry instant rice
1 (8-ounce) carton cottage cheese
1 (4-ounce) package grated Cheddar cheese

1 can cream of mushroom soup,
  undiluted
1 teaspoon oregano
Dash of Worcestershire sauce
Salt and pepper to taste

Brown the ground beef; drain. Then add onion, green pepper, seasonings, and tomato sauce. Simmer a few minutes and add rice. Then simmer a few more minutes, so that mixture is well blended. In a 9x13-inch greased baking dish, place a layer of zucchini squash, then a layer of hamburger mixture. Next, the carton of cottage cheese. Now, repeat with another layer of zucchini, then the hamburger mixture. Spread undiluted cream of mushroom soup over hamburger and top with grated Cheddar cheese. Bake at 350 degrees for 45-50 minutes.

Jean Peterson, Port Byron, Ill.

CREAMY CAULIFLOWER SURPRISE

Serves 8

1 large head cauliflower
1 (4-ounce) can sliced mushrooms,
  drained
1/4 cup diced green pepper
1/4 cup margarine
1/3 cup flour
2 cups milk
1 teaspoon salt
1 cup shredded Swiss cheese
2 tablespoons chopped pimientos

Break cauliflower in medium size flowerettes. Cook in boiling water until crisp tender, about 10 minutes. Drain well; set aside.

In 2 quart saucepan, sauté mushrooms and green pepper in melted margarine until tender. Do not brown. Blend in flour; gradually stir in milk. Cook over medium heat, stirring constantly until mixture thickens. Stir in salt, cheese, and pimientos. Place half of cauliflower in buttered 2 quart casserole. Cover with half of sauce; add remaining cauliflower; top with sauce. Bake at 325 degrees for 15 minutes.

Jackie Baker, North Little Rock, Ark.

Home Cooking
INDEX

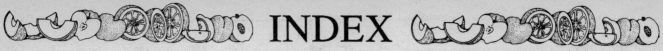

INDEX

INDEX

INDEX

specialty cookbooks

✻ BREADS ✻ SOUPS ✻ MEATS ✻ FRUITS ✻ DESSERTS ✻ SALADS ✻

Recipes From the Old South
Over 100 Recipes! ✻ Creole Cooking ✻ Louisiana Gumbo ✻ Jambalaya ✻ Creole Swiss Steak ✻ Southern Fried Chicken ✻ Sweet Potato Pone ✻ Avocado-Shrimp Salad
$1.25 (#SOUTH)

Outdoor Cooking
Barbequed Sparerib Racks ✻ Summer Salads ✻ Steak Orientale ✻ Grilled Fish ✻ Rice Stuffed Fish ✻ Stuffed Pigs ✻ Tangy Grilled Lamb Patties ✻ Texas Chile ✻ Shish Kebob ✻ Barbecue Sauces
$1.10 (#ODOR)

Easter Cakes, Cookies & Confections
Easter Bunny Cake ✻ Ice-Cream Cake ✻ Orange Sponge Cake ✻ Whipped-Cream Cake With Fresh Fruit ✻ Frostings ✻ Hot Cross Wheat Germ Ring ✻ Easter Kolacky
$1.00 (#EASTER)

Breakfast Breads
Raisin and Bran Can Bread ✻ Mixed Fruit Loaf ✻ Grape Nut Bread ✻ Fruit Breads ✻ Sweet Potato Muffins ✻ Brioches ✻ Bagels ✻ Scones ✻ Popovers ✻ Biscuits ✻ Sweet Rolls ✻ Muffins
$1.25 (#BREAD)

Sumptuous Soups
137 Soup Recipes ✻ Hearty Meat Soups ✻ Chicken Winners ✻ Chilled Soups ✻ Soups from Foreign Lands ✻ Dumplings & Toppings ✻ Cheesy Soups ✻ Potato Soup ✻ Low Cal Soups
$1.10 (#SOUP)

Dessert Special #5
Over 60 Elegant Desserts ✻ Chocolate Mousse ✻ Butter Brickle Fruit Dessert ✻ Custard ✻ Date Pudding ✻ Creme De Menthe Brownies ✻ Hummingbird Cake ✻ Frozen Lemon Custard
$1.25 (#DSRTSP)

Collection of Chowders
Vegetable Chowders ✻ Corn Chowder ✻ Carrot Delight ✻ Ministra ✻ Egg & Cheese Chowder ✻ Cheesy Salmon Chowder ✻ Poultry Chowders ✻ Maine Fish Chowder
$1.25 (#CHOWD)

Cooking with Apples
200 Great Apple Recipes ✻ Hamburger Apple Casserole ✻ Sunday's Chicken Bake ✻ Gourmet Gravy ✻ Apple Crumb Stuffed Pork Chops ✻ Grammy's Apple Blossom Cake
$1.25 (#APPLE)

Barbequing & Summer Salads #1
Over 175 Exciting Recipes ✻ Blue Cheese Burgers ✻ Steak Kabobs ✻ New Mexican Barbeque Sauce ✻ Lamb on a Stick ✻ Sausage in Foil with Vegetables ✻ Jack Frost Salad ✻ Pina Colada
$1.25 (BBQ)

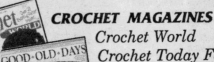